Mornings *with* Madden

My RADIO LIFE *with an* AMERICAN LEGEND

Stan Bunger

TRIUMPH
BOOKS

Library of Congress Cataloging-in-Publication Data available upon request.

This book is available in quantity at special discounts for your group or organization. For further information, contact:

Triumph Books LLC
814 North Franklin Street
Chicago, Illinois 60610
(312) 337-0747
www.triumphbooks.com

Printed in U.S.A.
ISBN: 978-1-63727-654-9
Design by Patricia Frey

All photos courtesy of the author unless otherwise indicated.

To Tharon,

my endless source of support and wise counsel,

and

To the KCBS Family:

the colleagues and listeners who made those

Mornings with Madden possible.

Contents

Foreword

Maybe you've heard me say this once or twice: I love football. I'm going to defend it. I'm going to fight for it and tell you what the NFL is trying to do to protect players and make it safer and why the game is so good.

But there was a guy who maybe loved it even more than me, someone I grew up watching on television and came to know as a friend: John Madden. John was a staunch defender of football. I think that fact and his promotion of the game certainly had an impact on me.

You could say our relationship started for real in 1999, the first time he and Pat Summerall called one of my games with the Indianapolis Colts. John didn't just show up for the broadcast and wing it. As part of his game preparation, he drilled me for about 45 minutes. He had me on the board, drawing up routes and explaining our scheme for audibles. Heck, that was even before I started yelling "Omaha!"

Here in my office in Denver I keep a great picture of John and me. It's on the field in Indianapolis. He's in his coat and tie right before the broadcast. I'm out there in my sweats and T-shirt. This is Sunday night, so we've already talked on Friday. He's already asked me absolutely every question possible. But here we are on the field. It's like, "Okay, one more thing." He never said, "Enough, I'm prepared. I got what I need."

That's the kind of guy a football nut like me can bond with. Of course, I'm not the only American who saw John Madden as somebody pretty special.

We all know the broad strokes of the Madden story: the Hall of Fame coach who became a successful advertising pitchman who became the face and voice of pro football, and along the way, launched that video game that still dominates the market.

As John took his remarkable journey through life, he became somebody we all felt we knew. He had that special ability to just be himself in a world full of folks who seem to be trying too hard. I know from my own relationship with John that he was wise, funny, and loyal. He was the kind of guy you wished you could hang out with every day.

I'm maybe a little jealous of Stan Bunger and his listeners, who *did* get to hang out with Coach Madden every day. All those chats on the radio each weekday morning, talking about whatever was on John's mind. Some of you heard those conversations and will never forget them. For the rest of us, this book is an introduction to a new side of John Madden.

You'll read about his family and life on that big bus and how he didn't like grits. Now, I grew up in New Orleans and graduated from the University of Tennessee, so I know my way around a bowl of grits. I guess on this one, Coach, we'll have to agree to disagree!

I never felt John got away from where he came from, even though he was kind of bigger than life. On his bus, traveling America, he was sort of a man among the people, very accessible, easy to approach.

When you're playing or broadcasting in the NFL, you can find yourself in this bubble where you're just around the same folks every day. It's stadium, bus, airplane (well, for John, *more* bus!), practice facility. You're not really amongst real football fans, the real people of America. So I imagine John felt the radio was a great way to be honest and talk about things that were important to him, things he's probably not going to be able to say on a national broadcast of a Cowboys-Packers game.

I think his curiosity was one of his most impressive traits. Here's a guy that coached, broadcast, and was around the game for so many years at the highest levels. Yet he was still always learning. There's a lesson there for all of us.

When John passed away, I felt a very deep sense of loss. There were a lot of things I still wanted to ask him about, a lot of stories I figured I hadn't yet heard. Just when you thought you'd heard them all, he'd have a fresh observation that would make you stop and think.

When I got word that I'd be going into the Pro Football Hall of Fame, I called a few people to share the news. John was one of them. He'd been as much a part of my football journey as anybody. He was excited for me. It was a special phone call, an emotional one, and it turned out to be the last time we talked. We had a great friendship because he was different, a very unique guy.

A few months before John died, I had my big day in Canton, joining John and all those other legends of the game. In my speech, I mentioned John's belief that the busts inside that magical room in Canton talk to each other at night after everyone's gone home. I can now confirm that they do, and I can tell you that they love to talk about the history of our great game and the people who built it.

John Madden is one of those people. He had so much to do with the NFL of today. His concern for the players, his respect for everyone associated with the sport, and his belief in football as a central part of American life all resonated with me. I feel fortunate to have known him and I'm humbled and proud to carry his legacy forward.

Stan's book adds another layer to our understanding of John Madden. You'll laugh a few times, for sure, but I also think you'll find wisdom in these pages that you'll be happy to apply to your own life, even if you never played football.

—Peyton Manning

Introduction

John Madden's lengthy career as a contributor to morning radio broadcasts in the San Francisco Bay Area began in 1982, when he joined "Emperor Gene" Nelson on KYA Radio. Nelson, one of the market's most recognizable air personalities, had switched to the station a few months earlier after leaving rival KSFO amidst a conflict over the direction of that station's programming. And because radio is radio, Nelson would find himself back on KSFO barely a year later, the result of a series of ownership transactions too complicated to detail here.

Nelson's recollection of his "Mornings with Madden" is included here as a sort of introduction, for those broadcasts were the ones that made the rest of this story possible.

—Stan Bunger

HERE'S HOW MY 12 YEARS WITH JOHN MADDEN BEGAN. JOHN WAS ALREADY on TV, doing football games on CBS. I came off the air at KYA in San Francisco one morning. We had a studio in the building where recordings were done. He was there recording a commercial and somebody said, "Have you ever met John Madden?" I said, "No." They said, "Would you like to?"

John was recovering from a broken ankle and came limping down the hallway, and I came limping down the hallway too because I had run a marathon the day before. So John turned to me and said, "The only reason a guy would limp is a broken ankle. Did you break your ankle?" I said, "No, I ran a marathon yesterday." He said, "How far is that?" I told him it was 26 miles. That's when he said, "Are you out of your fucking mind?" And then he reached out and shook my hand, saying, "John Madden."

We talked for a bit and I told him I'd had the idea of adding a sports feature to my morning show. He said, "No, I don't want to do that." It turned out part of his contract deal with CBS was that in the off-season he would do something on their morning show and he didn't like that. He didn't like reading the scores off the TelePrompTer, dealing with the scripts and the split-second timing of it. I said, "I don't want just a sports guy. I don't want the scores and who's going to win the Super Bowl. My idea for a sports feature would be two guys sitting in a bar just talking."

He said, "Well, let me think about that."

He came back in a couple of days and said, "Let's give it a try." It went well right from the start. We did it for a year and the main problem I had was this: we'd get into things and go beyond the time allotted to sports. My boss would say, "Gene, those reports are going too long." I had to ask him, "Would you really rather have us play another record, or would you like to hear John Madden talk about getting a jackhammer for a present?"

About that jackhammer: Apparently it was something he'd always wanted, and one time, he asked me, "Haven't you always wanted one?" Can't say that I had, but he was like a kid with a new bicycle. He often ended the show with, "Well, I have to go jackhammer now." I don't know if we ever established just where he was headed, but I'm glad I wasn't his neighbor.

I explained to my boss that the good stuff happens when I'd say, "Thanks for being on. Bye, John, talk to you tomorrow." That's when he'd say, "Hey, one more thing," like Peter Falk on *Columbo.* The "one more thing" was always what people would talk about. He said things that just made me laugh. We had a great rapport.

At the end of that first year, my bosses flew to New York and they said to John, "We're happy with the work. We'd like to sign you to a new contract." They said, "We're going to give you a raise." That's when John asked, "How much am I making now?" They'd also told him to pick his favorite New York restaurant so they could discuss business. He said, "Oh, my favorite, huh? Okay." And he took them to a dump of a Mexican restaurant. It was his favorite place in New York, which I always thought was funny.

That was the beginning. He and I were together for 12 years, then the station was sold in 1994 and I decided to retire. He went on to join Frank Dill at KNBR and that was the end of our relationship, but it was a good one.

Looking back on what made it work, I think it was just allowing him to be who he is. He broke barriers on TV football broadcasts. They'd say, "Oh, John, you can't do this. You can't do that," but he was his own guy. I thought that was the most basic philosophy in broadcasting: don't try to be somebody you're not. Just go on, be yourself, and hope you get enough people to like you so you could be successful. And John was phenomenally good at that.

As to why he did this for all those years, I think part of it was just being the guy from Daly City, California, whose father was an auto repairman. The Bay Area was his area and he could relate to listeners on a certain level because people knew him. I recall when we first met, I found out his mother was a fan of mine, and I think that helped. There was one time when he was on the bus. He said, "You know who's here? My mom's here." So I said, "Why don't you put her on?" I could hear her saying, "No, no, no, no!" Finally she came on. I said, "Hi Mom." All she said was, "Hi." After about 20 seconds, she says, "I gotta go now," and I hear this *thunk*. John picked up the phone and he's laughing and he says, "She just dropped the phone."

I never met his mother, but John would mention her often. We did a big event to mark my 30th anniversary on Bay Area radio. It was a live broadcast from the famous Venetian Room at the Fairmont Hotel in San Francisco, lots of guests, live music, celebrities. John didn't like that sort of stuff, so he didn't show. And the next day he said, "I want to apologize, I didn't make it to your show." I said, "No, no, John, that's fine." He answered, "Well, my mom called me and said, 'You should have been there.'"

We had a lot of requests for tapes of the show so we put them on sale with all proceeds going to a memorial fund established for my stepson, who had died in a fraternity-house fire at the University of California in Berkeley.

John called my boss, told him he would match all the money raised, and said, "Don't tell Gene." I hope he told his mom.

John would always tell me, "I wouldn't do this if it wasn't for you." I know he enjoyed the radio thing and I think the biggest reason was that he was unrestricted. He could be himself. I always said I was so lucky to have a job where I had at least one belly laugh a day. John provided more than his share.

—Gene Nelson

CHAPTER 1

An Endless Road Trip

LET'S GET SOMETHING STRAIGHT RIGHT OFF THE TOP: WHAT YOU'RE ABOUT to read is *not* a John Madden biography, authorized or otherwise. It's *not* a ghostwritten memoir either. Here's what it is: the inside story of an underreported part of the life of a remarkable man.

John spent untold hours and tallied countless thousands of miles crisscrossing America aboard his famous bus. Many of those voyages were on the big freeways that connect major cities, but there were plenty of detours onto backroads and into small towns as well. Think of what you'll find in these pages as a map, connecting the dots of John Madden's journey.

That journey included more than 30 years as a hometown radio personality. In the same way that he eased his way into American households every week during football season, he delivered a bit of himself each weekday morning to radio listeners in the San Francisco Bay Area. As big a deal as he was to football fans across our nation, to those of us in his local orbit, he was one of us, and he never failed to amuse, inform, and educate.

I originally set out to write this book for two audiences. One is the vast number of people who knew John Madden from his notable exploits as a professional football coach, television broadcaster, and the driving force behind the video game that continues to dominate its market. The other audience is already in on the secret, for these are folks who live in the Bay Area and were privy to John's many years as a morning radio personality. They'll remember the stories that fill this book, because a Madden memory tends to stick.

There's yet a third audience. Anyone who believes in The American Dream will recognize in John Madden the best version of the story that drives our country forward. Here's a guy who came from an unremarkable background, worked his ass off, caught some breaks, remained loyal to his family and friends, and built an extraordinary life which I believe can inspire others.

John proposed on one of our broadcasts that every radio station in America have someone read the Declaration of Independence on the Fourth of July. This wasn't a jingoistic "America, Love It or Leave It" approach to patriotism. It came from his deep belief in what the nation stands for, but more importantly, an abiding appreciation of the people who populate it. When John Madden dropped in on a Friday night high school football game, it wasn't to showcase his celebrity. It was because he genuinely enjoyed immersing himself in the experience.

We Americans are challenged right now. Our level of trust in each other has plummeted and our sense of collective destiny is frayed. Maybe a few stories from a guy who never pretended to be anything more than what he saw in the mirror can help. Couldn't hurt to try!

The John Madden who populates this book will be both familiar and novel to those who weren't part of the daily radio experience. His personality, wisdom, and keen observational powers were always on display during National Football League broadcasts, but his radio conversations allowed him more space to stretch out, sharing stories about his family, his adjustment to retirement, and much more.

Of the more than three decades John spent as a regular part of the Bay Area morning radio scene, I had the distinct privilege of being at the other end of the line for more than half of those years. My career as a broadcast journalist would have been more than complete without having had those "Mornings with Madden," but the experience added a very nice layer of frosting to an already scrumptious cake.

It was an unlikely pairing: John's damn-the-torpedoes meandering persona teamed with my by-the-clock, straight-arrow approach. The powerhouse all-news radio station where we connected, KCBS, was not in the habit of letting people color outside the lines. Yet somehow it worked, creating what radio programmers call "appointment listening."

I mean no disrespect to people whose creative process involves proposals, first drafts, rewrites, meetings, and more meetings, but that's not how it worked with John, me, and my morning show colleagues at KCBS. In more than 15 years together, we never held a single meeting or planned out a single broadcast. When I said, "Good morning" to John, none of us knew what would happen next, and that's how it went for thousands of episodes of "the Madden Segment." Live, unrehearsed, unscripted, often unforgettable.

Years after John's final broadcast with us in August of 2018, people would tell me—often in great detail—about a particular conversation that meant something to them. Usually, it was something funny. Often, it was a unique turn of phrase—a "Maddenism." Sometimes, it was a deeper truth revealed by Coach's agile mind.

This book relies not just upon my own memory of John Madden's radio performances, but also thousands of recordings of the actual broadcasts. Modern technology allowed me to quickly and (fairly) accurately transcribe these recordings, providing the basis for much of this book. I've chosen to present John's on-air words in *italics*. I have undertaken some light editing of his transcribed comments for the sake of clarity and continuity, but have otherwise tried to convey the sense of what Coach said and how he said it. John had a unique way with words and I've tried to carry that to the printed page.

About that word, "Coach." You'll see that I often refer to John in these pages as "Coach." No, I didn't play for his Oakland Raiders teams (nor did I ever play football), but just about anyone who spent much time with John Madden wound up calling him "Coach." It's a term of honor and I'm proud to use it. I'll generally refer to him as either "John" or "Coach." As a friend and colleague, I didn't call him by his last name while he was alive and I'd feel strange doing so now.

John used to marvel at the fact that he had three audiences and each called him by a different name. People who knew him from his days with the Oakland Raiders called him "Coach." The millions who watched him on all those NFL telecasts called him "John." And the mostly youthful crowd that played the *Madden NFL* video game called him "Madden." He answered to all of them, but the first two seem more intimate.

This book grew out of a sense of loss and also a sense of duty after John's death. The loss was felt by many people, including millions who never met him or were blessed to be in his circle of friends and colleagues. The sense of duty came from my belief that this story needed to be told, and there was really no one other than me to tell it.

I always felt that part of my connection with John came from the fact that he and his wife, Virginia, began their working lives as educators. I'm proud to be the grandson, son, and spouse of people who taught and coached in California's public schools. My wife urged me to try to tell the story of John Madden, the teacher, and I'm grateful to her for that suggestion. John left behind many lessons that I believe will reverberate for years to come.

My predecessor as the morning anchor at KCBS was a lovely man named Al Hart. After his retirement, he continued to join us once a week for "the Madden Segment," and once, from Paris, told a story that reminded all of us how important John Madden was to KCBS and to our listeners.

"We just finished a wonderful lunch," Al said over the telephone line. "And listen to this. There was a couple at the next table, and they overheard our conversation and they said, 'Do you work for a radio station?' It turns out they're from the Bay Area and they're big John Madden fans. I mean, we are everywhere. John, I can't escape you."

More than 20 years after Al Hart made that observation, I feel very much the same way. John Madden, seemingly everywhere for many years, left a unique impression on the American culture. All of us know the broad strokes of his story: remarkable success as a coach at a young age, early retirement from coaching, more remarkable success as a product pitchman and television analyst, and further remarkable success with the video game that still bears his name.

Some of us know a bit more about John. It's my distinct honor and privilege to share the story of my "Mornings with Madden" with you.

CHAPTER 2

The Making
of a Radio Star

You'd have to have missed about 40 years of American culture to *not* know who John Madden was. He exploded into the country's consciousness as the disheveled, arm-waving madman stalking the sidelines for the Oakland Raiders, sideline pass twirling from a belt loop. (Odd fact: I asked him years later if he'd kept any of those passes. "Never thought about it," he replied.)

Maybe it was John, maybe it was just coincidence, or maybe it was some larger force at play. For whatever reason, the Raiders seemed to play more than their share of epic, memorable games. Games with eternal nicknames: "Ghost to the Post," "The Holy Roller," "The Immaculate Reception." Speaking of that last one, I would learn in my years working with John that he never, *ever* accepted that playoff loss to the Steelers in Pittsburgh's Three Rivers Stadium. In fact, when the time came for the stadium to be demolished, I thought it would be funny to ask him if he wanted to push the plunger on the dynamite blast. He didn't see the humor in it.

The monkey on John Madden's back was the postseason. His Raiders won 76 percent of their regular season games, but only 56 percent of their playoff games. Lose a game in October, you lick your wounds and start getting ready for next week. Lose one in January, you bear the pain for months.

The Raiders finally broke through and won the Super Bowl in 1977, capping John's eighth year as head coach. Their hopes to repeat the following year died in the bitter cold of Denver's Mile High Stadium on New Year's Day 1978. True to form, there was controversy: Raiders fans *still* think Mike McCoy recovered Rob Lytle's fumble but that's not how the refs saw it.

Lytle, by the way, would die young. His widow would later reveal that the star running back had not only been knocked out cold on that play, but had suffered a concussion in the previous week's game as well. I find no irony in the fact that John Madden became a leading voice in the push to get football to acknowledge the brain injuries that stain the sport. (More on that in Chapter 13.)

After that unsatisfying end to the season, the Raiders returned with high expectations for the 1978–79 NFL season. They proceeded to post the worst record of John's career (though still a winning team at 9–7) and miss the play-offs. That's when he pulled the plug.

At 42, an age when many coaches are still climbing the ladder, *hoping* for a shot at a job like his, *this* coach walked away from it. "I gave it everything I have and just don't have anything left," he told reporters in January 1979. "I'm retiring from football coaching, and I'm never going to coach again in my life."

John would later joke that he figured he'd start his retirement by hanging around the house but found a house full of people who already had things to do, and even the dogs really didn't need him around. So now what?

His larger-than-life sideline persona offered immediate opportunities as an advertising pitchman. Lite Beer, Ace Hardware, Tinactin athlete's foot treatment: John Madden played himself in every one of those ad campaigns and he was Madison Avenue gold.

But on a smaller scale, John was testing the world of radio. A deal for a regular national feature on the RKO Radio Network led him to the San Francisco studios of KYA Radio. There, a young production director named

Fred Greene would record Madden's segments and be pulled into the coach's orbit.

Fred and I had been classmates in the broadcasting program at San Francisco State University—in fact, Fred had a "morning drive time" DJ slot on the campus station and I was his newsman. Nearly a half-century has gone by but I still recall an unhealthy level of jealousy on my part at the fact that Fred found a post-graduation job in San Francisco and I was slaving away in the radio boondocks—small California towns like King City and Sonora.

Once the brief recording sessions ended, John would listen to Fred's myriad entrepreneurial ideas as they did what Coach loved to do: hang out. Fred recalls those hang-out sessions often got him in hot water, since Coach had nowhere to go and nothing better to do than enjoy a good conversation, while Fred had an actual *job* with actual responsibilities.

Greene, thinking bigger than pushing buttons and turning dials in a radio production studio, had a million ideas. In his recollection, John would greet virtually every partially baked plan with enthusiasm. "Fred," he'd boom, "you gotta turn that into a business!"

In case you're not old enough to remember the telephone answering machines of the early '80s (hell, in case you're not old enough to remember *an actual telephone that needed to be answered*), these devices came equipped with two cassette tapes. One would record the incoming messages, after the other played the pre-recorded greeting.

Typically, somebody in the household would record that message, generally something clever like, "Hi, you've reached the Finkelstein residence. We're not here right now so please leave a message at the tone."

Greene's idea was to get celebrities to record these messages. After all, he had a ready supply of entertainers and athletes passing through the radio station. Maybe they'd do a 10- or 15-minute live shot with one of the DJs. Fred would snag them on the way out the studio door and get them to lay down a promo, something like, "Hi, this is Mickey Mantle, and you're listening to the radio home of the Oakland A's."

And eventually Fred, who I can attest is no shrinking violet, would go a step further and tell the celebrities that he didn't collect autographs, he collected answering machine messages. Mantle, among others, played along and, as a consequence, Fred and his wife, Joanne, had the coolest answering machine messages going.

John went beyond encouraging Fred to build a business around the idea. He contributed a few of his own, like the one where he pretends to be babysitting: "This is John Madden. Fred and Joanne are at a Pac-Man machine somewhere. Danny just made a mess out of his diaper and Ziggy's stuck under my shoe. So unless you can get over here immediately to help me out, just leave your message and the time you called. HELP!"

Of course, 40 years later, celebrities large and small would be recording personalized messages for a fee through a service called Cameo. Greene missed that boat, but he still walked away from those Madden conversations with something valuable. He says it was Coach's encouragement that led him to realize he could build his own career, and he's run his own business ever since.

It was around this time, in the spring of 1982, that morning personality "Emperor Gene" Nelson switched from KSFO to KYA. Nelson didn't just spin records. The Syracuse University graduate was witty, warm, and adventurous on the air, and he was on the lookout for program elements that would set his show apart.

That led to a hallway meeting with John Madden, both men limping to their first in-person encounter. John's limp came from an ankle injury sustained when stepping awkwardly off a curb; Gene's was earned by running a marathon the day before. Nelson suggested an on-air partnership.

In Greene's recollection, Coach's reaction was, "Ooh, I like that. Nelson's smart, he's good. And I can use what we talk about on my RKO pieces!" It might not have hurt KYA's case that John Madden's mother was a Gene Nelson fan.

And thus it began, with Madden joining Nelson as a daily fixture in the summer of 1982. It was an instant success. There's a legendary story of how KYA executives, who realized they'd captured lightning in a bottle, sought to hang on to it. As the end of Madden's first year with the station approached, they trooped to New York to meet with him. The kid from Daly City now owned an apartment at the legendary Dakota building.

The suits brought their flip charts and their spreadsheets and whatever they thought it would take to build their case for a contract renewal with the former coach, who by then was teamed with Pat Summerall to form the marquee crew for CBS Sports' NFL broadcasts.

The radio execs ran through their presentation, ending by telling Madden they'd *very* much like to have him continue his role with Gene Nelson. John paused, then said, "All sounds good. I only have one question." You can imagine what was going through the minds of the KYA team: Has Madden gotten too big for this? Can we meet his price? That's when he blurted, "How much are you paying me now?"

As John Madden's fame and fortune grew, he could easily have backed out of the daily radio commitment. After all, it required him to be available on schedule, no matter where he was. For a guy who famously traveled only by bus, the logistical challenges were significant, especially in the years before widespread cellular telephone coverage. He went so far as to have a communications package installed in the bus, offering both cellular and satellite phone links.

Yet the big guy showed up every day, easing his way into the daily routine of Bay Area morning radio. Listeners could eventually find the Nelson/Madden conversation on *both* KSFO and KYA; a series of acquisitions and spinoffs meant they were appearing on KSFO-AM and KYA-FM, both owned by King Broadcasting. But the tandem came to an end in 1994, when yet another station sale led Nelson to catch many off-guard with a decision to retire.

One of Nelson's competitors was Frank Dill, the morning host on KNBR. Dill and Nelson had both been rising radio stars in Buffalo, migrating west and for many years going head-to-head in the coveted "morning drive" daypart.

As Dill recalls, "Gene was on in the morning. I'm on in the morning on another station. So I couldn't hear Gene. He couldn't hear me. I heard that he had Madden on his program on a regular basis, but I never actually heard it."

So when KNBR management informed Dill that they'd snagged Madden, Dill wasn't exactly sure what kind of sidekick he'd just inherited.

"I really didn't know how to approach it," Dill told me. "Except I knew John a bit and I guess he knew me, or knew of me. So anyway, I said, 'John, here we are, we'll just talk every morning.'"

"Yeah, that'll be fun," Madden replied, and that was the extent of their show planning.

Dill remembers, "We started off from there and just talked about everything."

Barely three years later, Dill was ready to spend more time on the golf course and less time getting up in the wee hours of the morning. He pulled Madden aside one day when Coach had come into the KNBR studios to record something.

"I said, 'Hey John, I gotta tell you this: I've decided I'm going to retire,'" Dill remembers. He recalls Madden's response vividly. "His first reaction was, 'What do you want to do that for? That's no good. What are you going to do?' You know, the word 'retire' just revolted him."

After Dill's retirement, KNBR tried inserting a fairly well-known local TV personality into the morning slot. Steve McPartlin barely lasted a year at KNBR and he definitely missed the memo on Madden. He thought it was his show and Coach should find a way to fit in. Wrong. Within two weeks of McPartlin's arrival, John was unhappy and considering his options.

Remember, this is 1997. John Madden is at the peak of his fame as a television analyst, reportedly making more money each year than any NFL player. The *Madden NFL* video game has already been dominating the landscape for years (the 1997 edition still offered an MS-DOS version). John Madden is a Big Damned Deal, but not too big to show up every day, ready to shine on local radio.

KNBR sports reporter Kevin Radich was seeing and hearing this trainwreck unfolding in real time each weekday morning. Still, he was stunned to get a call at home on a Sunday. It was John Madden, dropping the news that he was leaving KNBR.

As Kevin recalls, John said, "Hey, I wanted to tell you personally that I'm not going to be around. I'm going to leave KNBR. And I'm going to join KCBS."

A startled Radich asked Madden why, knowing that KCBS had a reputation for being very buttoned-down—not exactly the environment where a freewheeling Madden might feel comfortable. Coach's answer points to a key fact: far from just a side gig, he saw radio as a lifetime job.

He told Radich, "You can work at KCBS 'til you die." As he tells the story, Radich laughs, and says Madden continued by saying, "Look at all the people they still have on there. They never get rid of anyone, so I'm gonna work there. I can work there until I die."

By shifting to KCBS, John was sending us all a signal. Like anyone else with a radio job that was on the rocks (or, in the industry lingo, "on the beach"—meaning you'd *lost* the job), John Madden wanted to stay on the air. He wasn't too big to do local radio at a time when he was a major national media figure; it seemed he *needed* to do it.

What happened behind the scenes? Word of Madden's unhappiness at KNBR had reached KCBS news and program director Ed Cavagnaro, who took a step outside the box at a station famed for its tightly formatted all-news programming. He recalls writing a letter directly to Madden to see if he might be interested in shifting to KCBS, which was locked in a seemingly endless ratings battle with news/talk powerhouse KGO.

In Cavagnaro's recollection, it wasn't long before he heard from Madden's agent, Sandy Montag, and it was clear right away that Madden was ready to make the move. Specifically, Montag said John was a big KCBS fan, and perhaps more importantly, it was Mary Madden's favorite station. Mom would be happy to hear her boy John on the KCBS airwaves every weekday morning.

There's one last bit of the "Madden comes to KCBS" story that I love, because it ties together two of Coach's big career decisions. Call it "the Amtrak effect," if you like. Back in 1984, when Madden's TV broadcasting career was blasting off, he met Electronic Arts founder Trip Hawkins aboard the California Zephyr to hash out plans for the video game that would become the multi-billion dollar *Madden NFL* franchise.

Thirteen years later, KCBS' Cavagnaro was also riding the California Zephyr, vacationing with his family. During a layover in Denver, he got on a call with Madden and Montag to work out the operational details of his KCBS gig. Cavagnaro remembers that call well. "I recall John surprising me by saying he wouldn't need any prep or any questions in advance."

Cavagnaro's gambit paid off. Installed at 8:15 AM weekdays with KCBS morning anchors Al Hart and Susan Leigh Taylor as well as sports anchor Steve Bitker, "the Madden Segment" was the exception to the rule at a station where news, traffic, and weather zoomed past in an endless flow of information.

Coach's connection with Hart and the KCBS team was instant. Perhaps it had something to do with their shared Minnesota heritage (John was born in Austin, Minnesota, before the family moved to the San Francisco suburb of Daly City, while Al was a Twin Cities native and University of Minnesota alumnus).

In any case, Coach's 8:15 KCBS calls became the stuff of legend. Ostensibly sports-related, they often veered far afield, depending on whatever captured John's imagination on a given day.

Listeners would talk of lingering in the parking lot to hear the end of the segment. Pure magic for a radio programmer, of course: the "lift" from Madden soon allowed KCBS to best KGO in the 8:00 AM hour and, in short order, rise to the top of the overall morning drive-time ratings.

Former KCBS senior vice president Doug Harvill (lengthy modern broadcasting industry title for "station manager") recalls the 8:15–8:30 AM quarter-hour as the single-most-listened-to quarter-hour on the station for many years. Harvill was talking about Madden's impact on radio but also much more when he said, "Everything he touches turns to gold."

Hart's 2000 retirement led to another radio shift for John Madden. That's when I joined the story.

I will never forget my first day back at KCBS in the summer of 2000. I'd spent 10 years at the station before heading off to other broadcasting ventures between 1992 and 2000.

On that first morning with Coach, I thought I knew the drill: prepare for the interview, have a couple of questions ready, listen to the answers, adjust on the fly. After all, I'd done thousands of live interviews over a quarter-century career.

A few minutes before 8:15, a producer's voice crackled in my headphones. "Madden's ready on Line 74," came the message over the intercom.

I hit the talkback button and said, "Got it," as I punched the appropriate button on the audio console to bring John Madden's voice into our broadcast mix.

And then I hit the talkback button again and asked, "What's the topic?"

There was a long silence and through several layers of studio windows, I could see into our newsroom, where a couple of staff members sported baffled expressions. Finally, the producer leaned into his intercom microphone and said, "Um, whatever you like. It's Madden."

Now that the programming statute of limitations has expired and all concerned have moved on, I can admit that we seldom kept the segment to the five minutes allotted on the program log. At one point VP/programming Mike Preston acknowledged the obvious and suggested we insert an additional traffic report before bringing John on; otherwise, commuters might wait 15 minutes between updates, a big violation on a station that repeated the mantra "traffic and weather together every 10 minutes" *ad infinitum* (or *ad nauseam*, depending on your point of view).

I used to worry that it was all too good to be true, that Coach would wake up one day and decide he didn't need the bother of a daily call from KCBS. He'd often joked that he stayed on the air so his mom would know what he was up to, but even after Mary Madden's death, well into her nineties, Coach kept showing up.

Kevin Radich, the KNBR sports reporter who would later work with me at KCBS, tried to dissect this seemingly unlikely affection for radio. "I think that it fascinated him to be able to take a topic and run with it in any direction. I think that really tickled him. I think that kept his mind going," said Radich.

There was also the notion of structure. I once jokingly asked Coach, off the air, why he bothered to get up every morning to hang out with us. He replied that if he didn't have us to get up for, he'd just "flop around and do nothing." Radich heard something similar: "He said to us once that he likes having a routine and it was definitely part of his routine. He likes having a schedule."

KNBR's Frank Dill says he's tried to analyze why John stuck with local radio all those years. "I don't know why he did this every day," Dill told me. "I don't know how much they paid him to do it, but he certainly didn't need the money. I mean, the guy was worth hundreds of millions of dollars. I can only tell you this, I had a lot of fun talking to John on the air every day, just as I'm sure you did." Amen.

On the day of our last on-air conversation, Coach paid me a massive compliment while also coming as close as I ever heard him come to explaining why he reveled in our chats.

"You're so smooth and buttoned up and all that. I listen, you go, 'Smooth, smooth, smooth.' But then I come on and it's 'Clunk, clunk, clunk' and then it goes back to 'Smooth, smooth, smooth.' It was kind of like working with Pat Summerall and Al Michaels. I could do anything and they would clear it up. And I always felt that's what made this so much fun: I could kind of do anything, go anywhere, and you'd straighten it out and smooth it out."

As I look back on the magic of Madden, I can only say that he was simply a guy who loved to hang out with people. He loved to hear a good story and really knew how to tell one. And he had a keen eye for puffery and a willingness to deflate it. It's risky to try to dissect genius, but I'll dig into some of Coach's themes later in the book.

When John was being inducted into the Bay Area Radio Hall of Fame in 2015, I sat down with him for an interview. We talked about his unlikely multiple careers. He considered himself "lucky" but quickly said a big part of his luck was having great partners. I *think* I had the decency to blush.

He shifted into nostalgia mode when he started talking about his deep love for radio. "I think everyone remembers their first radio play-by-play broadcaster," Coach told me. "Mine was Jack Macdonald."

And then the aging coach, already retired from TV work and nearing the end of his 21-year stretch on KCBS, broke into an impression of the home run call used by Macdonald as he called San Francisco Seals Pacific Coast League games in the 1940s.

"It's going…going…it's gone! Right through Aunt Maggie's window!" shouted John in a gravelly voice I can only assume approximated what he heard in his youth when Seals games were carried on San Francisco's KYA.

That might be when it truly hit me: for all his outsized success as a coach, on television, on the front of that video game box, in business…way down inside, John Madden was one of *us*: a radio guy. Radio didn't make him rich. As it turns out, it enriched him, and the rest of us too.

CHAPTER 3

"I'm Sorry For Your Loss"

It started happening immediately, as news of John Madden's death spread on December 28, 2021.

Text messages, phone calls, emails. People I knew, reaching out to tell me they were saddened by the news of Coach's passing, but more than that: they wanted me to know they were saddened for *me*.

It didn't end there. For days and weeks, people I barely knew would approach me with some version of, "I'm sorry for your loss."

"*My* loss?" I thought. John Madden left behind a wife, sons, and grand-children, not to mention a long list of other friends and associates who had to be much more involved in his life than I'd ever been. All I'd really "lost" was a former colleague, a guy with whom I swapped a few words on the radio every morning.

But the more I thought about it, the more I realized these people had it right. I'd lost someone important to me. The sadness I was feeling was not so much that John was gone, but that I'd failed to truly appreciate what he'd meant to me while he was alive.

This is the way of the world, isn't it? We speed through life, focused on whatever it is we think really matters, and often miss the subtle signals that are flashing all around us.

It's easy, of course, when someone says, "I love you." Those are heavy words, words you can take to the bank. It's not so easy to decipher the myriad ways people might show you they care. Call them the small things, if you like. I now realize that when I'd introduce John by saying, "Good morning, Coach!" and he'd reply with a hearty, "Good morning, Stan!" he was sending a little love my way, Madden-style.

A Madden insider I'd never met in person gave me a lens into this on the day of Coach's funeral mass. It was a private service, but not a small one. Attendees nearly filled Oakland's Christ the Light Cathedral, a striking modern facility on the shores of Lake Merritt that looks a bit like a football from the outside (or maybe that's just how I see it).

Matt Millen won four Super Bowls as one of the best and toughest linebackers of his generation, seemed to channel John Madden as an insightful yet uninhibited NFL analyst on TV, and was convinced, despite zero experience as an NFL coach or executive, to become the CEO of the Detroit Lions.

To say that went badly undersells the term "badly." The Lions went 31–81 during Millen's seven-year tenure. Along the way, we in the KCBS studio realized that Coach had a soft spot for Millen, who never played for Madden but was a classic "All-Madden" selectee. For the uninitiated, John's "All-Madden" team was made up of players who weren't necessarily superstars, but played the game the Madden way: tough, selfless, and maybe with a bit of personality.

It's also true that beastly NFL offensive linemen and those losing years with the Lions were nowhere near the toughest battles Matt Millen would face. He struggled for years with mysterious symptoms before doctors determined the cause: a rare disease called AL amyloidosis. It's caused by a bone-marrow disorder. The Amyloidosis Foundation figures about 4,500 Americans are diagnosed with it every year.

Millen needed a heart transplant, and as he dealt with the disease and the uncertainty, he realized time might be short. He told us that day at John Madden's funeral about his decision: it was time to make sure the people he loved *knew* he loved them.

As I recall Millen's eulogy delivered from the cathedral's lectern, he started out by approaching his own father. Apparently, Harry Millen was exactly the sort of tough, taciturn fellow you'd think a guy from Hokendauqua, Pennsylvania, would be. When Matt put his hands on his father's shoulders and said, "Pop, I love you," the old man responded immediately. He punched Matt in the gut.

John Madden was also on Millen's "I love you" list. Millen had been close to Madden for years, even as the old coach dealt with his own infirmities, including November 2015 open-heart surgery.

At the end of one of Millen's visits with Madden, he summoned up his courage and, as they were saying their goodbyes, slipped it in. "You know I love you, Coach," said Millen.

To which John replied, "Yeah."

"Not what I was hoping for," Millen told us, "but at least he didn't punch me in the gut."

Millen's delivery that day in the cathedral channeled Madden's voice and body language. We all laughed, because we could *see* and *hear* the John Madden we knew responding like that.

But the story didn't end there. Millen said he tried again the next time he stopped by the Madden house. And again, Madden's response to a declaration of love from a hard-ass former middle linebacker was less than effusive. "Yeah," Madden replied. "You told me that."

Whatever was driving Matt Millen to make sure John Madden knew he was loved wasn't satisfied with that answer. So Millen tried yet again on his next visit. "Hey, Coach, I love you," offered Millen.

To which John replied, "Yeah, Matt. Me too." That was it. No tears, no hug, no more words.

Okay, confession time here. I'm a Catholic, but not exactly an every-Sunday Catholic. In fact, years sometimes go by without me setting foot in a church. But I've always found that when I *am* sitting in a pew, I'm a little bit closer to God.

And at that moment in the soaring cathedral in Oakland, God's messenger Matt Millen hit me the way he used to hit running backs: right in the chest. He'd figured it out. People can say "I love you" without ever using those three little words. You just have to listen, watch, and maybe do a little translating.

I'd been so wrapped up in being me, in expecting people like John Madden to speak exactly my language, that I quite likely had missed many versions of "I love you" from him, and of course, from a lot of other people as well. "Men Are From Mars" and all that, right?

As the process of memorializing this larger-than-life figure played out, I struggled to explain to others (and myself) what it had meant to me to be in John Madden's orbit. Was I just starstruck, living out some teenaged sports-star fantasy? Look at me, hanging out with a mega-celebrity like John Madden! Woot!

Or was it something deeper and more profound? Did the famous old coach and the not-very-famous local radio guy actually have something more than a work relationship? And is it possible that even a work relationship (albeit one played out in front of a live audience) can have depth and emotional power?

My first pass at wrestling with the loss followed a formula I've known for more than 40 years: treat it like another news story. Round up the facts, find a lede, lay down the words, polish them until they shine.

Like the old saying goes, this story wrote itself. It was the story of John's least-recognized career: Bay Area morning radio guy. It also happened to be the lengthiest of his multiple careers.

I banged it out in a few hours and ran it by a few friends and journalism industry contacts, all of whom thought it would make a great feature piece for one or the other of our Bay Area newspapers. It turned out the newspaper editors disagreed. Despite the tragically understaffed state of daily newspapers, I was told that nobody wanted a freelance piece.

So the story, "John Madden: Radio Star," wound up in the California Historical Radio Society's quarterly journal, seen by an audience of hundreds. That should have been the end of the story. I'd done what I know how to do, without actually having to think about those more challenging emotional questions.

But the thought kept nagging at me that there was a bigger story to tell. Maybe it was those boxes of material I'd tracked down in the dusty recesses of the KCBS Radio storage closets and ferreted out on the station's computer network. I'd taken home recordings of thousands of "the Madden Segment" episodes which needed to be sorted, arranged, and revisited.

"That's it!" I figured. I'd wrestle those recordings to the ground, pry out all the memorable moments, the great bits of philosophy and humor, and make something out of it all.

I'll tell you more later about how *that* process went.

I was still ignoring the most obvious story. It was right in front of me, all around me, but I had to get out of myself to see it.

And then I got the text message from Sandy Montag, Coach's longtime agent. Accompanied by a link to the news release outlining plans for a public memorial event at the Oakland Coliseum, site of so many Madden memories, was Sandy's message: "We'd like you to have some role at the event. Let's discuss."

To say I was honored would be an understatement. Maybe a little bit of an ego massage, too, because after spending 40 years on the air, it's possible I was missing the limelight a bit, barely six months into my retirement. I've always claimed to family and friends that I didn't care about whatever celebrity comes with a radio career. My wife, who's known me for nearly 50 years, would beg to differ. Guess who's probably right?

I assumed that when Sandy said, "some role at the event," he was gently letting me know that maybe I'd sit on the stage, be introduced, stand up, wave, and generally stay out of the way. After all, NFL and broadcasting royalty would surely be on the bill and, as Kid Quill raps, "I'm just the opener/no one came to see me."

Billed as *One More Monday Night in Oakland: A Celebration of John Madden*, the Madden family saw the Valentine's Day evening event as a way to close the circle of his life in the place where the John Madden legend began: the Oakland Coliseum.

Over the years, whenever I'd slag that soulless, aging dump of a stadium, Coach would set me straight *right now*. To him, it was hallowed ground. The Raiders never lost a *Monday Night Football* game there when John Madden coached the team.

A few days after Sandy's text message, I got another one, linking me to an NFL news release. I had to read it twice to believe it, because it seemed there'd been a mistake. The speaker list included four current or former NFL head coaches (Art Shell, Steve Mariucci, Ron Rivera, and Andy Reid), plus John's eldest son, Mike, and the trailblazing sports journalist Lesley Visser, with whom Coach had worked at CBS Sports.

And me.

To borrow a phrase Coach used many times to great comic effect when describing some place he'd stumbled into, "What the hell am *I* doing here?" I thought. *Those* folks are the ones people want to hear from, not the retired radio guy.

But, in another slap upside the head, I realized that the Maddens wanted me there because I represented a significant corner of John's world. That radio segment *meant* something to him.

The night of the event was chilly. I put on my best suit and tie, gave thanks for being one of the few guys I know here in California to own a decent-looking overcoat, and headed over to the Coliseum.

Much of the world was still operating under COVID rules in February 2022. The KCBS afternoon crew was broadcasting from the press level at the Coliseum, occupying three booths, separated by many layers of glass. They asked me to sit in and share some stories. Afternoon sports anchor Kevin "The Rat" Radich was there.

Kevin first met Coach in the 1990s, during the KNBR years. Not unlike Fred Greene, the young radio production engineer Madden befriended in the 1980s, Kevin found Coach approachable and genuine. When Kevin let on that his dad, Pete, made some pretty good homemade sausage using the old Croatian family recipe, John had to check it out. You'll read more about that side of the big guy in Chapter 5, "Everyday People."

I could have gone on for hours with Kevin, swapping stories like people do when they gather to remember a loved one. But soon enough, it was time to go. A member of the production team came to escort me to the green room where friends, family and the night's speakers had gathered. My photographer friend Bob Cullinan and KCBS news manager Nic Palmer were there, pointing out the stars of the show (as if it's hard to spot Andy Reid or Ron Rivera).

Somebody said, "Hey, Lesley Visser wants to meet you." That seemed backwards; I wanted to meet Lesley Visser. This is a woman who paved the way for so many women in the sports-media business, a true legend and trailblazer.

After we'd been introduced, Lesley stopped me cold. "You know Coach really loved you," she said. "He talked about you all the time."

Lesley told me she'd had the good fortune to share many bus rides on the Madden Cruiser, rolling across the country between CBS Sports assignments. That meant she would hear John's end of our radio conversations. She later found a way to listen to the whole segment by dialing into a KCBS "listen line" from her New York home.

I can't recall what I babbled in response. Here I'd thought I was just the guy tossing the softballs to Coach each morning for the benefit of Bay Area listeners. Turns out Coach liked the way I pitched.

The master of ceremonies for the evening was Tom Rinaldi, the Fox Sports reporter who'd produced and co-directed the documentary that aired on Christmas Day 2021, just days before Coach's death. *All Madden* borrowed its name from the annual *All-Madden* team Coach cooked up in 1984 while at CBS Sports. In John's mind, an *All-Madden* selectee wasn't just a good player. He needed a certain *je ne sais quoi.* To quote Madden, "It's about a guy who's got a dirty uniform, mud on his face, and grass in the ear hole of his helmet."

Rinaldi's documentary came as a Christmas gift to John Madden's many fans. There's no way to verify what I'm about to tell you, but I strongly believe that project kept Coach alive at a time when his health was declining. I'd lived this story once before: my maternal grandmother, a French immigrant, lasted long enough to see her first grandchild married, and was gone a week after my wedding day.

The crowd in the Coliseum that night wasn't big, but it was full of love and energy. Raider Nation turned out, including some of those characters who populated the south end zone "Black Hole" for years before the Raiders decamped for Las Vegas.

A quick sidebar here: I can recall weekends during the Raiders' Los Angeles years when I'd see hardcore fans *walking* to Oakland International Airport (about two and a half miles from the Coliseum), clad in silver and black. Some wore football helmets; others had donned spiked shoulder pads and face paint. They were *flying to Los Angeles* to watch the Raiders play. I often wondered if they walked from LAX to the Los Angeles Coliseum at the other end.

Back to Valentine's Day 2022 in Oakland. Attendees paid $32.14 to be there—symbolic of the score in the Madden Raiders' Super Bowl win. The money represents another trickle in the healthy stream of philanthropy John and Virginia Madden have turned loose on the Bay Area.

One of the last charitable projects to launch during John's lifetime began in typical fashion: Coach saw something that didn't make sense to him and set out to fix it. He'd been attending his grandsons' high school football games, often getting special dispensation to watch from his pickup truck parked near the field.

One night, the game was at one of Oakland's public high schools and John, who'd shunned publicity after donating new stadium lighting to his own high school alma mater (Jefferson High in Daly City), was upset. The facilities were subpar and it didn't seem fair to him that kids should be forced to deal with the failure of adults to do right by them.

The experience led to a new scholarship pipeline, funded by the Madden family, that channels graduates of a dozen East Bay public high schools to John and Virginia Madden's alma mater, Cal Poly-San Luis Obispo. Some of them will see Coach's name live on at the John Madden Football Center, a new facility being built adjacent to Cal Poly's football stadium.

The woman John Madden met and married at Cal Poly wasn't on the dais that night in Oakland. But Tom Rinaldi knew she was the *real* star, so he carried his wireless microphone over to where Virginia sat. She brought down the house as she told the national TV audience exactly where she and her late husband stood on the issue of the NFL's departure from Oakland. "He believed in the Raiders, I believe in the Raiders," Virginia said, and then she paused for effect. "The *Oakland* Raiders. Oakland needs a football team." Cue the crowd roar.

Any nervousness I'd had about whether I belonged on stage or not had vanished by the time my turn came, possibly because when I ran into Steve Mariucci beforehand, *he* was the jumpy one. "Mooch," I said, "you do live TV on the NFL Network and you've been on pro and college sidelines with everything on the line. What's the big deal?"

"Because this is Madden," Steve replied. "It's a big deal."

Here's the talk I gave that night, accompanied by photos I'd saved of various moments with Coach:

"We're on hallowed ground here this evening, where the John Madden legend began.

Everyone in America knows John as a Hall of Fame coach, the guy who sold Lite Beer, the man who essentially INVENTED the role of the TV sports analyst and oh, by the way, just 'Madden' on the video game…but John also had an important career that only those of us lucky to call the Bay Area home knew about.

And here's the crazy part: THAT career lasted longer than any of the other ones I just mentioned.

For more than 35 years, John Madden was a part of morning radio here in the Bay Area. He started with Emperor Gene Nelson on the old KSFO…moved on to KNBR with Frank Dill…and 25 years ago, Coach came over to KCBS to join Al Hart, Steve Bitker, and Susan Leigh Taylor on the morning news.

Three years later, when Al Hart retired, I'm the guy, and the John Madden Segment became part of my life.

Not gonna lie to you here: I was nervous. I mean, John F'in MADDEN! So they set up a phone call, I get on the line and start babbling about how much I love sports and how my dad and grandpa were football coaches and how I'm just so excited to do this thing… and Coach just waits.

And finally says, 'Okay, Stan, great. Talk to you tomorrow.'

I don't remember what that first segment was about. Probably a little about football and a lot about whatever else was on John's mind.

And that's how it went for nearly 20 years. My rough math says Coach did about 5,000 live segments on KCBS. I can honestly say I don't remember a single one where we wrapped it up and turned to each other in the studio and said, 'Well, THAT sucked!'

It was usually the opposite. Steve and Susan and I were along for a ride every morning and so was our audience. You never really knew where Coach would take you but you knew it would be interesting. Listeners told us they'd be late for work, staying in their cars in the parking lot to hear the whole show.

Unlike his NFL broadcasts, where the game was the thing, on the radio, we got to do something John Madden was really, really good at…we got to hang out.

Our audience got to know John's crew. Dominic. Plisskin. Ghielmetti. Carl the Cop. John Robinson. Virginia and the boys and the grandkids and the dogs. Mrs. Crawford, the grandkids' fifth grade teacher whose little boy Brandon played football at Foothill and became THAT Brandon Crawford.

And of course, there was bocce. The Madden-Mariucci tournament provided some great material, because Coach loved to apply the needle.

I was truly blessed. It wasn't just the on-air stuff. Coach would say 'mi casa es su casa' like a joke…but he meant it. It took me a LONG time to realize that if John Madden accepted you into his circle, you were in.

Even if you pulled shit like I did at the very first Madden-Mariucci Bocce Classic I attended. Somehow…maybe NOT a coincidence… the KCBS team plays Madden's team in the first round. The match ends up tied. One ball roll off.

And of course, it's mano a mano. Me versus Coach. He hates to lose. Same here. He rolls first. Pretty good ball. Do or die for me, and as soon as it leaves my hand, I know I got it. I go all NFL wide receiver, full celebration mode.

And walk right by Coach, who had his hand out for a handshake. You think he ever let me live that down?

For many years, John would host a KCBS barbecue event at his facility in Pleasanton. We'd bring in a bunch of clients and a few listeners and eat like pigs. Virginia would bake chocolate cakes. And I think Coach really enjoyed it—because in The World of Madden, if it involved food, hanging out, and some good B.S., it was worth doing.

So many people say they remember Maddenisms. A phrase, a made-up word, a philosophy.

Our radio conversations were often funny, because John Madden was a funny guy. But they were also often deep, because John Madden was also a very serious guy when he wanted to be. And smart? Don't even go there.

I'm surrounded by NFL royalty here this evening so maybe I'm out of my lane, but I don't think it's too big a stretch to call John the conscience of the NFL. And a lot of the things he cared deeply about when it came to pro football were things we'd talk about on KCBS.

We had many conversations about head injuries, and John was very serious about changing the way people in football approached this topic. We had a lot of talks about the people who played the game and the places they played it.

He loved coaches and you could truly hear the pain when he reminded us that the firing of a coach wasn't just an item for the sports page or the talk shows—real people with real families were impacted.

And Oakland. He REALLY cared about Oakland. Really cared.

My one regret is that I could never change his mind about NFL overtime rules. He truly believed that if you lost the coin flip, you should quit griping and just win the game on defense. Once a linebacker coach, always a linebacker coach, I guess.

Here's the thing. John Madden was like all the rest of us: a regular guy. But also not a regular guy. A superstar BECAUSE he was a regular guy. And at the end of the day, a Bay Area guy. America loved him. But we owned him.

He used to say (when some local player made it big), 'Hey, that guy's from where we're from.' Exactly. And we were all lucky to be part of it. God bless you, Coach. Thanks for everything."

CHAPTER 4

Just a Doofus
From Daly City

ACTUALLY, THERE WERE *TWO* DOOFUSES FROM DALY CITY, IN COACH'S TELLING. We'll get to the other one later.

What's a "doofus"? A not-very-smart person. Various dictionaries use definitions like "simpleton," "dummy," "foolish," "incompetent," and "stupid." John Madden was definitely none of the above.

I'll tell you what he was. Coach was a very clever man who had no problem accepting a basic fact of life: we all do stupid things and we're all better off if we can laugh at them.

Just before I sat down to write these lines, I was having a bowl of cereal for breakfast. As I dug into the Cheerios, one of them hopped out of the bowl and rolled off the table. Since nobody wants to step on a Cheerio and have to get out the broom and dustpan, I eased back from the table to peer down to the floor.

No Cheerio. More careful searching under the table and chair ensued, and still no sign of it.

That's when I felt something in my slipper, and realized the errant Cheerio had managed to make its way down my leg and into my shoe. I marveled at this for a moment, then broke into laughter.

From across the room, my wife wanted to know what was so funny, and all I could tell her was that John Madden had struck again. That one-in-a-million Cheerio brought back memories of Coach talking about his eating habits.

Over the years, he told several variations of the story. In every case, he was the butt of the joke. But, honestly, as we listened, we realized he was speaking for all of us. Who hasn't come home from a dinner date or an important meeting to notice something stuck in our teeth? Or belatedly spotted a gravy stain on the lapel of a jacket and wondered how long it was there, signaling our ineptitude?

Coach's favorite rendition would involve a piece of food that escaped the table and ended up in the cuff of his pants or his shoe. Like my Cheerio, it takes a lot of luck (it's up to you to decide whether that's good luck or bad luck) for a morsel of food to stick a landing in a pants cuff. But it takes a guy very comfortable in his own skin to tell the story to others.

A classic version of the tale actually *ended* with the dropped-food trick. Coach laid it out one morning while we chatted about our mutually mediocre golf games.

"I played with a couple of guys the other day and they were so anxious to get started that they were on the tee before I got down there, so I went ahead and played, and I swear this is true. I played seven holes. I really played lousy and then on the eighth I figured out I'd never tied my shoes! My shoes were flopping around. But then I played the last two holes. I played them well. Those guys were so anxious to get going. I went out there without tying my shoes."

Our laughter had barely subsided when he took us from the course to the clubhouse.

"That is an example of a day that got off to a bad start. Then I had dinner that night and I sat away from the table. I had a beet and the beet fell into my shoe."

"What do you mean," I asked. "Come on, the beet fell in your shoe?"

"*Yeah, because I don't sit close to the table. So I finally figured that's why I have problems. Like I'll get up to go and I'll have stuff in my socks. I'll have sauce and stuff in my socks and I ended up 'beeting' my shoe. I missed my mouth and hit my shoe.*"

John's longtime friend and frequent target of on-air jibes, Jim Ghielmetti, verifies this trait, telling the story of the time he was traveling aboard Coach's bus. They stopped for a Mexican dinner.

"I looked over at him and sure enough, his shirt had part of his enchilada attached to it," Ghielmetti recalls. "I said to him, 'John, you always get food on your shirts, ever since I've met you.' He responds, 'You haven't seen the whole picture. I wake up in the morning and find it in my cuffs.'"

I think Coach knew that people would be laughing *with* him and not *at* him as he recounted these tales of sloppy dining. Like any great comedian, he knew instinctively that the human condition provides a rich vein to be mined for a laugh.

He also knew that a good story could be told more than once. Let me set this one up with a little background information.

Coach had a second home in the storybook Monterey Peninsula town of Carmel, not far from the Pebble Beach Golf Links. That scenic course is one of the venues for the annual AT&T Pebble Beach Pro-Am tournament, the stop on the pro golf tour where celebrities, captains of industry, and jocks from other sports get to show off their golf games in front of big crowds and a live TV audience.

And it's a setting where John Madden was in his element. He was enough of a celebrity that he could have the run of the place, picking and choosing his hangout spots while watching the world's greatest golfers as well as a lot of pretty-good-but-not-professional players (I once asked Coach if he'd ever been invited to play in the Pro-Am and he quickly said, "No, and there's *no way* I'd do that!")

Naturally, John Madden was a media magnet. During his years working with KNBR's morning man Frank Dill (an avid golfer) and sidekick Mike

Cleary, he would forego the usual phone call for an in-person appearance as Dill and Cleary originated their broadcast from Pebble Beach.

John never missed his airtime appointment with *The Frank and Mike Show*, but KNBR sports reporter Kevin Radich recalls it was always interesting. "Madden would appear out of nowhere," Radich remembers. "We never figured out where the fuck he came from. You know, he had these ins and outs all over that place. And he was like a magician. He would just—poof—appear and then you turn your head and he's gone. He disappeared. He'd go through a back door or something. We never figured it out, but it would freak me out. I'd turn around and say, 'Where'd John go?'"

One year, the folks at Oakland's KTVU lined Coach up to do a live shot on their *Mornings on 2* telecast. Nothing fancy, just John Madden sitting at Pebble Beach while the TV anchors back at the studio swapped some banter with him.

And that's when the story turned memorable.

In one of his many retellings of the story, Coach segued from a conversation we were having about an extended streak of rainy weather in the Bay Area and how it was wreaking havoc on golfers.

"That was like the time I was doing the interview on Channel Two. Did I ever tell you that one?" he began. Well, of course he'd told us that one before but not one of us was going to say, "Gee, Coach, I think we know that story."

So off he went.

"Well, I mean, things that can happen to one. I'm doing a live interview at Pebble Beach right out there by the putting green. Right out there in front of nothing and, you know, it's not under a tree or anything like that, and we're talking, we're on live television. I'm gonna only be on for a couple of minutes. I mean, the odds of this happening."

Now, before we hit the punch line, I want you to imagine yourself sitting down to breakfast while watching *Mornings on 2*. Or staring at a monitor in the KTVU control room.

"So I'm sitting there talking and I feel this 'pop' and I look at my left hand and a bird pooped on me. Hit me right in the hand. So now, you know, I'm on live. So

I took my right hand and I wiped the poop off. Now I got it on both hands. Then I put it on my pants and then I had it on both *hands* and *my pants."*

By now, all of us in the studio are laughing (and I can only imagine thousands of listeners are laughing as well). How many celebrities can claim to have had a bird crap on them on live TV? But of course the story isn't over.

"Then after I was done, I mean, I've never carried a handkerchief or anything and you don't have paper towels or napkins. So then after I've done the TV thing, there's people around there, people who want to shake your hand. I said, 'Well, the heck with it.' I shook their hands."

Eww.

By the way, John told another hand-shaking story more than once. This one involved the delivery of a turducken (not a six-legged turkey, another culinary oddity associated with Coach) to the broadcast booth for a game in New Orleans.

Some explanation is in order before we get to the hand-shaking part. The turducken either was or wasn't invented by the legendary Cajun chef Paul Prudhomme. It involves a lot of poultry deboning and a lot of stuffing, with the butcher cramming a chicken inside a duck inside a turkey.

The six-legged turkey sprang from the time Coach was handing out turkey drumsticks after a Thanksgiving Day broadcast in Dallas. He gave one to Cowboys running back Emmitt Smith and said he wished he'd had five more to give to the offensive linemen who'd opened all those holes for Smith. Necessity is the mother of invention, thus a roasted turkey with enough legs to go around was slapped together.

Anyway, one fine day in the Superdome, John had just finished tearing into a turducken with his bare hands. As the story goes, the turducken had been delivered by butcher shop owner Glenn Mistich, but nobody thought to line up carving tools or plates. John Madden never let a meal pass him by, so he dove in with the utensils God blessed him with.

That's about when attention-grabbing Saints owner Tom Benson (who used to prowl the sidelines twirling an umbrella...*indoors*) appeared in the broadcast booth to schmooze with John and his broadcast partner Pat Summerall.

The nattily attired Benson had missed the manual dismantling of the turducken, but he sure wasn't going to miss the chance to press the flesh with the great John Madden. So he strode over, stuck out his hand, and said hello.

Coach would recall he had little time to decide what to do, so he improvised.

"I have all this stuff on my hands and then I'm wondering, 'Do I shake his hand?'"

John's move was to lick the turducken goodness off a few of his fingers and reach right in for that handshake. It would be the last time Tom Benson and John Madden ever shook hands. In fact, Coach said they never spoke again.

But to give you a better feel for how those radio shows would often go, on the *very same morning* that Coach regaled us with the bird-poop-handshake story you read a few moments ago, he had yet another "I'm a doofus" tale to tell.

Here's how it went.

"So after the broadcast the other day, I'm speaking in San Francisco, the National Roofers Association at the Marriott Hotel. And I had a first happen to me. I don't know about you, but you can learn something every day," Coach began. We in the studio have no idea where this was going, but we were betting it would be good.

"So I'm in the bathroom and I'm going to wash my hands and all these guys are washing their hands there and I can't turn on the water. So I'm looking and I'm looking for the thing you turn it on with and I can't find it. I'm pulling one thing, I pushed the soap thing, then I figured it's probably one of those things you got to push in with your foot. So I'm pushing down there with my feet and I feel so stupid. Everyone else is washing their hands and leaving and I'm standing there. I swear this is true."

Of course it's true!

"And so I don't know how to make the water go. And there's no faucet, there's no…thing. So then finally, this is when you get to the end, when you're, you know,

in embarrassment. And I said to the guy next to me, 'How do you turn the water on?' And he goes, 'You just wave your hand underneath it.' I had never seen one of those before."

I broke in, "Really. The little electric eye?" Listening back to this exchange years later, I'm not entirely sure if I was surprised to learn that John Madden had never encountered a touchless faucet in a restroom, or if I was unwilling to admit to our listeners that I, too, had once been baffled by a faucet with no handles. Hadn't we all?

Coach replied, *"Uh, yeah. Right. I guess. And then I felt so stupid, because then here I am the luncheon speaker, this guy is introducing me saying, 'John Madden did this and did that,' and five minutes before I couldn't even wash my hands."*

Anyone who's ever worked in morning radio knows the fear of oversleeping. No matter how many years you work the morning shift, your body and brain never truly adjust to that early wake-up.

Coach got to sleep in compared to the rest of us, since his appearances were at 8:15 AM Pacific Time and he often found himself in time zones east of us, gaining an hour or two or three. I can't recall him ever missing a show by oversleeping, but he did come close once.

"I'm thinking of you guys," he said one morning, switching topics in the middle of a chat about baseball. *"How long does it take for your stuff to work after you wake up? Because I forgot to set my alarm and I overslept and I just woke up. I've been up for like three minutes."*

"So you haven't had any coffee yet?" asked my co-anchor Susan Leigh Taylor.

"No, I haven't, but I don't know how long it takes to get your stuff going, like for your brain to go to your mouth and to go to your feet…that whole wiring system that one has. My feet just hit the floor. I don't know what to do. My feet hit the floor and then the rest of me hit the chair."

Al Hart, who'd spent three years introducing Coach every morning before retiring and was now coming in once a week to join the conversation, couldn't resist a question. "Let's turn the tables here, John. What are you wearing this morning?"

"Seriously, I got up and I put on my sneakers and a baseball cap."

"That's it?" Al inquired.

"Yes. That's all I had time for."

And that's why radio doesn't have pictures.

Coach got a lot of mileage out of his own misfortunes. He also got a kick out of a good practical joke, even if he was the target.

"He was happy to be the butt of a joke," Frank Dill told me. "You knew it if you pulled one over on him. He loved it."

As an example, Dill offers a story about golf balls. Dill was an avid and excellent player, appearing for years as an amateur at the same Pebble Beach Pro-Am event that John loved to watch from the sidelines (and where the bird used Coach as a toilet).

One morning as Dill was finishing up his radio show, a representative from Titleist came by to hand him a fresh box of golf balls with his name imprinted on them.

The rep was, of course, looking for a free plug on the air from Dill. And he came loaded with a second box of balls with "JOHN MADDEN" imprinted on them.

John wasn't there. Dill had an idea. "I decided I'd play that day with John Madden's golf balls. Just in case I hit a really bad shot, it would have John's name on it. And it finally happened. I'm in a sand trap and when I blast out, the ball flies over the green, over the heads of some spectators and into a guy's backyard. And at that point I'm the only person who knows it's going to say 'John Madden' on that golf ball."

Dill reloaded, finished the round, and let the story marinate.

"And sure enough, a few days later," he recalls, "John says to me on the air, 'Hey, I got a call from so-and-so. He wanted to know why I was hitting golf balls into his backyard.' I had to explain to him and the audience what had happened. We all got a good laugh out of it. It's the kind of story that was so classically Madden."

We got a lot of mileage out of Coach's willingness to step up for pay-per-view boxing events. He was a legitimate boxing fan and could rattle off the names of long-ago fighters and describe their styles. Yet he knew the sport was in decline and acknowledged he was a promoter's best friend: an easy mark.

The day that Mike Tyson fought his next-to-last bout, I greeted Coach by asking if he was going to pay for what was being billed as "Return for Revenge," a rematch between Tyson and Danny Williams.

"*You know, it's part of an IQ test here just to see if you're still as stupid as you used to be or if you improved on your stupidity. And right now, as we speak here at 8:15 on Friday morning, I'm thinking that I'm not going to do it. But it's not over. I usually succumb. I mean, I would bet it's 50/50 right now. And then as it gets later and later, I always fall for it.*"

I needed to know how this worked. "What time does that last-minute decision normally occur, John? Within an hour of the fight? Within five minutes? I mean, when do you begin to get itchy?"

"*Within a couple of hours, because I'm not sure how to get the pay-per-view. I don't have those techniques down and it takes me time. I'm not sure if you push a button on your TV or if you have to call your cable operator or what. So it takes me two or three hours, I swear, every time to figure out how I do it. And then I'm traveling sometimes, in different places and stuff. So it's all part of your intelligence quotient. When there's a fight on, I always succumb to it. Now, what happens to me during the football season is, you can't get pay-per-view in a hotel. But I can get it on my bus. So what I do is I park my bus in front of the hotel, and then we go out on my bus and watch the fight.*"

This tickled me. "I have an image of you padding across the parking lot in your bathrobe and slippers to get out to the bus," I offered.

"*No, I don't have any bathrobe, and I've never worn slippers in my life.*"

End of story. I really didn't need to know any more than that.

Nobody ever accused John Madden of being a slave to fashion, but I didn't expect him to tell our listeners that he'd bought a pair of camouflage pants. Apparently, they'd stopped the Madden Cruiser at a Cabela's store in the Midwest one day so his buddy Dominic Mercurio could shop for some warm hunting clothing. He wasn't going hunting. He was trying to survive aboard the Madden Cruiser, where Coach kept the thermostat set somewhere between "meat locker" and "polar winter."

"I think he was trying to get to me because I keep it so cold here on the bus. That was bad. But he slept in his camo last night, he said. I bought a pair of camo pants, too."

I couldn't quite see John Madden in camo, replying, "No you didn't. Did you really? *That's* a look."

"Nah, I got 'em just because I could. I don't know what you do with them, so I'm going to just wear them like sweats on the bus. That's all I'm doing."

After the broadcast that day, I reached out to Dominic to see if he could get a photo. I mean, who *wouldn't* want to get a look at John Madden in camouflage pants? I got a cryptic email reply from Dominic, indicating there would be no photo.

When I asked Coach about it the next morning, he left no doubt about his position on the matter.

"Yeah, I told him he couldn't take a picture. I mean, what the hell are you doing?"

If there aren't any known photos of Coach wearing camouflage hunting pants, there are plenty of him wearing a baseball cap. To be honest, I don't recall ever seeing him off-duty without a ball cap on his head. One morning, I asked him for his size.

"Anything that has a number that starts with a seven doesn't fit, whether that number is a half, five-eighths, three-quarters, nine, 10, whatever number comes after seven, it does not fit."

"So you're just looking for the one that says 'one size fits all'?" I helpfully inquired.

"No, no, no. That's a lie. They have kind of like 'one size fits all,' but in small, medium, large, extra-large, that type of thing. So I need something like 'one size fits all extra-large.' I got a big, old head."

For a self-described doofus, John had a very sharp mind for business. Dominic Mercurio, who actually wore those camouflage outfits while duck hunting near the Central California town of Los Banos, got wind of a chance to buy 25 acres nearby, planted in almonds.

It was a stretch for Dominic. His duck-hunting buddies showed no interest in going in on the deal. He mentioned the opportunity to John and got an emphatic response. "He goes, 'Buy it. I'm your partner.' So we bought it. John was the controlling partner," Dominic recalls.

They were making money almost from Day 1, producing 3,000 pounds of almonds per acre, a very solid number. By the third year, JD Farms (John and Dominic) was in business, the old football coach told his buddy to start scouting for more almond acreage. They eventually owned more than 700 acres.

Not that the kid from Daly City ever did any of the dirty work. Often in spring, we'd talk about the orchards and the beehives that had to be brought in to pollinate the almond trees. The process fascinated Coach, though he admitted he was late to the pollination party.

"Somewhere in life, when they teach that in—I don't know, grammar school or high school—I missed everything about pollination and how it works. I've had to learn it in the last couple of years. I still don't know it very well. I wonder where the heck I must have been when they taught it. Sometimes if you were a big guy, not very good in class, the teacher would have you clean the erasers. I think when they were talking about pollination, I think I was cleaning the erasers."

If there's a lesson for today's anxious parents here, it's this: the kid who was always cleaning erasers wound up doing just fine, and anyone who knew him saw the gears constantly clicking.

I'll let my longtime KCBS colleague Kevin Radich, who connected with Coach in the early '90s, sum up Coach's intellect.

"I think he was born with that. I think that curiosity that he had was prevalent in his everyday life. He was present a lot, you know. It's hard to get inside his mind, but he had a lot of stuff going on up there, and he had the ability to express it. It was like a stream of consciousness. He could express these thoughts and you would just say, 'Wow, where the hell did that come from?'"

CHAPTER 5

Everyday People

LIKE JOHN MADDEN, SYLVESTER STEWART WAS BORN OUTSIDE CALIFORNIA but moved to the Bay Area as a child (and there's even a connection to the Daly City of John's childhood). He too was talented, although in Stewart's case, it was in music rather than sports.

And like John Madden, Stewart played an important role in Bay Area radio while becoming much better known for his *other* work.

I bring up Sylvester Stewart (you might know him as Sly Stone of Sly and the Family Stone) because one of his mega-hit songs, 1968's "Everyday People," reminds me of a key fact about John Madden. As wealthy and well-known as John became, he could truthfully say what Sly Stone sang: "I am everyday people."

The Stewart-Madden comparison doesn't work perfectly, of course. True, they both starred on Bay Area radio. Before his musical act hit the big time, Sly Stone was a big deal on what were then known as "Black stations." He started on KSOL and would later be heard on the heavy-hitting KDIA.

And true, just like John Madden's parents lived in Daly City, so too did Sly Stewart's. That's because the rising musical star used some of his early royalties to buy them a home in the city just south of San Francisco where John was raised and where he excelled in sports at Jefferson High School.

Where their lifelines diverged was *after* they achieved stardom and success. Sylvester Stewart was beset for years by personal and financial problems. John Madden's life still seems to read like a Hollywood script.

But let's go back to "everyday people." Coach would often drop names into our morning radio conversations. Some of them were big names, the kind you could drop if you were John Madden: Hall of Fame athletes and coaches, entertainment industry bigshots, rock stars, politicians. These were people John Madden had gotten to know because, well, he was *John Madden*.

That cast of characters included guitarist Nils Lofgren, a football fan who became a Friend of Coach when he contributed original tracks for a decade's worth of "All-Madden" telecasts. Lofgren's tender acoustic-guitar-accompanied "Miss You John" left few dry eyes when it was played on the video board at Coach's public farewell in Oakland.

But Coach also had a list of not-so-well-known people he'd bring up regularly during our conversations. Some, like Brazilian soccer stars, had only one name: Ghielmetti. Plisskin. Dominic. Others sounded vaguely Runyonesque: Carl the Cop. Adam the Pizza Guy. Floyd the Barber. Junk, Shifty, Sketch, and more.

His wife, Virginia, made for more than a few on-air mentions. I suppose it makes sense that a larger-than-life guy like John Madden would have a life partner who could match up to him. Virginia Madden was, and is, a true original.

I was among the crowd of "Madden People" who descended on Canton, Ohio, for Coach's enshrinement into the Pro Football Hall of Fame in the summer of 2006. The honor was long overdue (you'll read more about how it happened in Chapter 12, "The Hall of Fame Trail") and there was no way John Madden was going to downplay it.

He went all-in, chartering a plane to fly friends, family, and neighbors from the Bay Area to the Midwest. He also engaged his friend and on-air foil Dominic (Monterey restaurateur Dominic Mercurio) to cater an after-party at a Canton country club, complete with a barbecue crew imported from California.

With all of the Madden entourage gathered and in full celebration mode, Virginia took the microphone.

"Who would have thought when I met John at Harry's Bar there in Pismo Beach [the two attended nearby Cal Poly] that we would end up here? When he needed a job and the only job available was at the junior high school where I worked, so I had to move to the high school so he could have the P.E. job."

Talk about grounded: the John Madden Virginia knows is the guy who scraped his way through college and then thought maybe, just maybe, he could make a career out of teaching.

"Anyway, I went to the high school, and then he went to the junior college because they wouldn't hire a husband and wife in the same district. He worked there two years, then went to San Diego State. He was there for three seasons. Then he got the job as a linebacker coach with the Raiders for two years. And then Al Davis hired a man who couldn't hold a job longer than two years to be his head coach."

She brought down the house, and no one was laughing harder than John Madden. But Virginia Madden wasn't quite finished.

"Life has been so good to us. Every day is like vacation. As John says, he's never worked a day in his life and you'd better believe it. I've enjoyed every minute of it. I've enjoyed raising the kids, I've enjoyed building houses, keeping houses, doing all kinds of things, and I know better than to ask John to help. So thank God he found something he was really good at."

Virginia and John Madden marked their 62nd wedding anniversary two days before his death. But despite that long run together, somebody else eclipsed Virginia when it came to years spent in John Madden's orbit.

That would be John Robinson, a kid who arrived in Daly City at age nine and immediately became John Madden's best buddy. Like Madden, Robinson was a good athlete who became an even better coach.

He spent a year working with Madden as the Raiders' running backs coach. His next gig was as head coach at the University of Southern California, where his Trojans won the national championship in 1978. He moved on to the Los

Angeles Rams in the NFL and then back to USC. In short, John Robinson was a damned good coach, good enough to be named to the College Football Hall of Fame.

But for our story, the two Johns share something beyond accolades for their coaching success. One morning, as they prepared to work on a Super Bowl broadcast, John Madden summed up their unlikely lives.

"Just the two doofuses from Daly City. And then here we are in Detroit, getting ready for a Super Bowl. And you look back: Top of the Hill, Daly City, Our Lady of Perpetual Help, Relish Bakery, the pool hall—who would have thought? We go all the way back. All those years we were just sitting around down at Marchbank Park talking about these things. And all these years later, 60 years later, here we are in Detroit for a Super Bowl."

A couple of years later, Robinson was part of the NBC *Sunday Night Football* production crew during Madden's final year on television. Robinson was serving as a "spotter," helping Madden keep track of player substitutions. They were in Green Bay for a Cowboys-Packers game when Coach delivered these comments.

"It's great to have a guy that you grew up with alongside you. I've always said, he's more like my brother than like my friend. We grew up in Daly City, went to grammar school together, and all these years later, still being together, you know, it's pretty good. I mean, we can revert from the Dallas Cowboys defense and the Green Bay Packers offense to the Relish Bakery at the Top of the Hill in Daly City just like that."

Neither of the two Johns was ever very far from his next jibe at the other. Madden told us that he and Robinson would prepare for the NBC broadcasts by watching video and heading out to watch practice to gain insight for that week's game.

"You put it all together and see the matchups and you can kind of feel the way it's going to go. Now, having said that, half the time both of us are wrong. I always tell him, of that half, he's wrong 90 percent of the time."

Robinson had no trouble giving it right back to Madden, a tit-for-tat act that clearly went back to pickup games on "Madden's Lot" in the old neighborhood. On a number of occasions, if Madden let it be known that Robinson was nearby, we'd insist on getting the other John on the line. He never failed to slip in a friendly dig.

"I was an assistant with him at the Raiders for a year. He was diligent about everything and he hasn't changed. In fact, he's still wearing the same clothes. There's a cigar he used to have at Oakland. I think it's the same one he has now."

A cigar, by the way, that he never smoked.

The names Coach wove into our conversations were characters, all right. But they weren't fictional. At the time of John's 2006 induction into the Pro Football Hall of Fame, I'd never met most of these folks. One evening, "Madden's People" wound up in the hotel lounge, and as I introduced myself to his friends and neighbors, I started asking how they'd gotten to know John Madden.

Each story was a bit different, but the common thread was these were people who brought some normalcy into John's life. They weren't starstruck. In fact, Dominic Mercurio's "how I met Madden" story is illustrative because it's so typical.

Dominic owns a restaurant, Café Fina, on Fisherman's Wharf in Monterey. One Sunday in the 1990s, he saw a guy he recognized as John Madden amble down the wharf with a woman at his side. "He came to my menu board twice and looked at it," Dominic remembers. "And the second time, I walked up to him and said, 'Hey, what are you looking for?'"

John replied, "I'm just looking for some good clam chowder." Dominic took charge. "I said, 'Tell you what,' and I pointed to a table. 'You go sit over there. I'll bring you the soup. If you don't like it, don't pay and don't come back.'"

Dominic's a guy who figures he's been playing with house money his whole life. After all, his paternal grandfather emigrated from Sicily to Algeria to France, catching and processing sardines and anchovies. By the time the family ended up in Monterey, the men were still chasing fish. Dominic probably figured he had nothing to lose by offering John Madden a clam chowder challenge.

"When I told him that," Dominic recalls, "he sort of giggled. Virginia didn't know what to think. Anyway, he ended up coming back six or seven Sundays in a row."

It was the beginning of a friendship that led to Dominic serving as a pallbearer at Coach's funeral mass, a role he'd played earlier for John's mother, Mary. Along the way, the two invested in business ventures, ate countless meals together, and shared many an experience that wound up as fodder for our morning radio chats.

Usually, if Dominic's name came up, he was about to be the target of some Madden needling, like the morning I found a photo of Dominic with a really big watermelon. It took about a millisecond for Coach to pounce.

"He's so proud of himself. Dominic grew that, but he always wants to say he 'caught' it. I mean, he thinks he's still a fisherman. 'Dominic caught a 75-pound watermelon.' I mean, Dominic grew a 75-pound watermelon, and he's so proud of it. I mean, he's parading it around and carrying it around like it's his trophy, and with Dominic being kind of diminutive, it looks a lot bigger in his arms."

I couldn't let the topic get closed out without asking how that big watermelon tasted. And that let Coach deliver one last dig at Dominic.

"It tastes like a 75-pound watermelon."

There was the time Dominic was going to ride along as Coach headed for the Pro Football Hall of Fame's induction weekend. It was a trip that was really more of a pilgrimage for John after his own 2006 induction and he enjoyed taking others along. This particular year, Dominic had a "plus one."

"He wants to take a fish back there. We have to keep it cold the whole time. Where we're going to get the ice, I don't know. It'll be one of those things and we're going to be traveling through heat, too. So it'll be about his doggone fish. He's trying to get back to Ohio and keep it cold."

I'd seen a photo of Dominic with this big salmon he'd caught a few days earlier and I was surprised that he thought it was worth road-tripping all the way to the Midwest.

"Yeah, it's a week old, but, you know, it's a man's trophy. When a man has a trophy, he packs it around one way or another for a long time."

Dominic Mercurio may have taken a lot of good-natured grief from Coach over the years, but it was only after John's passing that I learned of a vital role he often played for John Madden.

In the years that Coach owned an apartment at the Dakota on Manhattan's Upper West Side, he liked to go out for walks. Being one of America's most recognizable celebrities, he'd often draw crowds. His way of managing that was to carry his mobile phone and place a call to Dominic Mercurio, using the call as a way to appear busy so he could fend off autograph-seekers.

"Sometimes I would be on the phone with him for a half-hour when he would walk from point A to point B," Dominic told me. "I'd hear what was going on around him, 'Hey, you're Coach Madden!' But he would keep me on the phone until he got to his home."

Steve Mariucci became another close friend and confidant. Football was the immediate connection between Coach Madden and Coach Mariucci; they first crossed paths when "Mooch" was working his way up the NFL ladder. He'd eventually settle in the Bay Area, where he was head coach at the University of California and then took the San Francisco 49ers to four playoff appearances in six years as head coach.

The Madden-Mariucci bond started with football but grew much deeper over the years, fueled by food, family, and bocce, a game they both played and would turn into a fundraising machine with an annual tournament. Mooch sometimes seemed to me like a much younger brother to Coach, though he's actually young enough to have been a son.

Many of our morning conversations involved Coach needling Mooch; Mariucci often joined us in response and he gave as good as he got. This was one that Mooch never lived down.

"Poor old Mooch. We were out there practicing bocce the other day. He's getting better and he's really taking it seriously. He says he's going to win. We were there a couple hours and then he comes out to the parking lot, he talks to me, and then he starts to walk around in circles. You know that look where someone is in a parking lot and has no idea where his car is? That's Mooch. And so he's looking around and he's walking back and forth. And it's not like he's in

an airport parking lot or that he's been away for four days. He's been away for like an hour and he can't find his car. And so he puts his keys up in the air and he starts pushing the button on his keys. But there's only like 20 cars there and he still can't find it. And he doesn't remember. He doesn't have any idea where he parked. Here's a guy who was just telling me how good he is and how he's focused and concentrating and then he loses his car in a parking lot of 20 cars. And then when he finally saw me laughing at him…I didn't help him in any way. I just laughed. I couldn't stop laughing. The last thing he said was, 'Don't tell anyone.' I said, 'Okay.'"

There are probably people out there with a story about John Madden big-timing someone; I imagine it's impossible to spend that many years in the spotlight without pissing someone off or disappointing someone who expected a different interaction.

But I was always amazed by the joy Coach expressed after the sorts of experiences that you might think would become ordinary for a man of his fame and fortune. In a way, he never outgrew the big kid from Daly City. This exchange in 2007, when the New York Yankees were in full dynasty mode, stuck with me for years.

"I had a great experience last night, and not to talk too much about it, but I'm leaving Yankee Stadium. I get to the top of the stairs, where you go out, and someone says, 'The Yankees want you to hold here.' I thought, 'What the heck is this all about?' And they said, 'Someone wants to talk to you.' I didn't know who it was. So I wait a few minutes and the security guy comes and gets me and says, 'Roger Clemens wants to see you.'"

We in the KCBS studio are pretty impressed by this but we're a bit surprised that John Madden seems to be turning into a fanboy.

"So I go back down through the bowels of the stadium into the Yankee clubhouse, which is pretty much a sanctuary. And then I'm kind of standing outside. I thought Roger Clemens was at his locker, but he wasn't there. So I'm standing outside and Derek Jeter is inside and he waves at me and says, 'Come on in, sir.' And I thought, 'Here's the greatest guy in baseball, and he's calling me 'Sir,' and inviting me into the training room.'"

"I mean, it was only Mariano Rivera in there, Clemens in there, Jeter in there, and Jorge Posada in there."

For the uninitiated, that's Yankee royalty we're talking about, gathered in a place that's off-access even to the news media. And this is where John Madden becomes a bit more like you and me and bit less like the mega-celebrity he has every right to be.

"And Madden was in there. Which one doesn't belong? Just meeting those guys and talking to them in the training room and seeing what they go through. I mean, you can be in this thing forever and ever. I've been in a lot of locker rooms and big games, Super Bowls and all that stuff. And, you know, it's still big. I mean, it's not something you ever take for granted and think, 'Oh, heck, I belong here.' I mean, I don't feel I belong there. And it's just kinda humbling and it kind of gives you chills when you're in there. I was thinking about it last night when I got back from Yankee Stadium and I said, 'If I ever get to a point where I don't get excited and thrilled by something like that, I don't want to do it anymore.'"

It wasn't just modern-day superstars that could fire him up. Coach was almost old enough to qualify for Medicare when he launched our conversation one morning with this story.

"Hey, guess who I met. I'm in Saint Louis the other night, and we're out to dinner on Friday night. And guess who I met?"

I took a swing at the question. "Stan Musial?" I asked, referencing the Cardinals baseball legend.

"Good guess. No kidding. That was a real thrill. Our whole production group goes out to dinner at an Italian restaurant on Friday night, and up walked Stan Musial. He really looks good. I mean, he's 80 years old. He's just had a knee replacement. He says it had to be replaced because he hit too many triples."

I'm getting goosebumps because Stan Musial is in my baseball pantheon, and not just because we share a first name. If you're of a certain age (and if you're not, you can Google it), you can *see* "Stan the Man" coiled up in that unique left-handed batting stance.

"You know, we were talking about how as a kid, everyone, *sometime in their life, they got into that Stan Musial stance. So he got in the stance and he said,*

'When I first came up, they said, You can't hit that way.' And of course the rest is history."

The audience, I imagine, is trying to wrap its head around the image of two sports legends chatting it up at Café Napoli in St. Louis on a Friday night. We'll never know what Stan Musial thought about meeting John Madden, but we certainly know it was a big deal to John.

"I mean, that was a real thrill, because when you grow up, there's Joe DiMaggio and there's Ted Williams and there's Stan Musial and then Willie Mays, I mean, those are the guys. And then when one comes up to you, you think, 'Holy moly, this is Stan Musial!'"

Coach wrapped up that conversation by admitting he might have been too star-struck to get either an autograph or a photo with Stan Musial. Nor did he ask for another baseball legend's signature when they crossed paths, but he again sounded like a little kid telling the story.

"You know who I met yesterday? It was great. The first time I've ever met him. The ex-Chicago Cub baseball player. Mr. Cub. Ernie Banks. Nicest guy in the world and really interested in football. Wanted to know what my ex-Raider players were doing. You know, 'Where's Ken Stabler? What's he doing? Where's Willie Brown?' Knew all the players and loves to play golf. He says he plays golf every day. Wanted to know if I had a tournament, wanted to come and play in my golf tournament."

Coach had to disappoint the great Ernie Banks by admitting he didn't have a golf tournament to which he could invite him.

At the other end of the spectrum from Stan the Man and Mr. Cub would have to be one of Coach's favorite whipping boys, his buddy Plisskin. To use one of John's favorite phrases, "I swear this is true." For several years, I didn't know Plisskin had a first name. It turns out it's Larry, but I never heard anyone use it.

Plisskin was an easy target because he was a diehard Cleveland Browns fan, and the Browns had a special way of failing even *before* owner Art Modell hauled them off to Baltimore, causing the NFL to plant a new franchise in Cleveland. The updated version wasn't any better.

For reasons that remain unclear to me, my colleague Steve Bitker declared himself a Browns fan, often wearing a ratty Browns T-shirt to work. One morning, Steve volunteered that he'd been invited to join a club of Bay Area Browns fans. Coach pounced.

"This is good, Steve. They invited you to join the club? At no charge? And they didn't invite Plisskin."

Now Coach had us piling on. I said, "Plisskin is not even a member of a club that charges nothing to be a member. Oh, this is good."

"Yeah, well, he'll say, 'Good.' You know, he didn't want to be in it anyway."

Two of my KCBS colleagues could claim a much longer relationship with Coach than mine. Kim Wonderley and Kevin Radich first met Coach in the 1990s, during his years at KNBR. Both had grown up in the East Bay, and both gravitated toward the big everyman who had become a superstar.

Kevin first met John Madden in person when Coach stepped off an elevator to visit the radio station so he could record some network feature segments. Like Fred Greene tasked with the same job years earlier, the younger broadcaster simply clicked with Coach. "I noticed his shoes were untied. I said, 'What's up with the shoes?' He goes, 'I don't like tying my shoes and I don't like being in an elevator, to tell you the truth.'"

It was the first of many conversations Kevin would have with Coach. "I don't know how it got around to my dad, but Madden loved food, so I told the story about how my dad started this whole thing called SPEDS, the Society of Professional Eaters and Drinkers. After he retired, he'd open up his garage door and all his buddies would come over at lunchtime, including the mailman, and the mailman would spend three hours there and then nobody got their mail on time. They'd eat food and get shitfaced, like three times a week. This became a thing and they made T-shirts that said 'SPEDS' on them. Madden loved the story. He goes, 'How do I become a SPED?' I go, 'Well, you got to get initiated, man. You got to come over for lunch.'"

Coach didn't need a Michelin-starred restaurant or A-list dining companions. He was happiest when he was hanging out with regular folks like "Prosciutto Pete" Radich. "My dad had this wine cellar built into the side of a hill," Kevin remembers. "It was a beautiful wine cellar, and he hung prosciutto in it. He'd cure the hams. He made his own wine and brandy. Madden was fascinated with all of this, the whole story behind my dad making this shit and then having friends over and the whole SPEDS thing."

"He was a curious guy, you know. He was curious about the background, the stories. He'd ask, 'How did you start doing this?' And it fascinated him. I think he just liked hearing about Americana, the everyday people, and he liked the fact that my dad had tradition with this stuff."

Another great American media figure, Will Rogers, died the year before John Madden was born. Rogers famously said, "I never met a man that I didn't like." I can't say whether Coach agreed with that sentiment, but I do know this: I doubt he ever met a person of whom he didn't want to ask a few questions. Quite a few of those people wound up in his orbit.

CHAPTER 6

A Good Fork Man

In one of those statements that probably didn't actually have to be made, John Madden once told us, "You know, I don't miss too many meals."

Coach loved to eat, loved to think about eating, loved to *talk* about eating. Heck, he even *wrote* about food (his 1998 cookbook *John Madden's Ultimate Tailgating* paid homage to the sort of grub that could really get Coach on a conversational roll).

Anyone who saw a meal as more than just something you had to do to sustain life was part of John's crowd. For those who showed a little extra love for dining (fine or otherwise), Coach had a special honorific: "a good fork man."

It wasn't like Coach ate *everything*. He definitely had his likes and dislikes. He was on a Southern swing one morning, having just crossed the line from Georgia into Florida when he phoned in for our conversation.

The topic of breakfast came up and I asked if he'd ordered grits with his eggs and bacon.

"I've never gotten grits," he started. *"I mean I know it's something you should try and I'll try anything and I'll try everything. But sometimes you try it and you think, 'Okay, there has to be something here,' but there's nothing there."*

By now, everyone from south of the Mason-Dixon line is ready to rise in protest, but Coach isn't finished.

"I mean, grits doesn't taste like anything. I remember when I was a kid, I used to have something that wasn't oatmeal, but it was called mush. And I think, 'That thing called mush, I think that's grits.' And grits is like mush, and mush was nothing. Two things as a kid I didn't like: I didn't like liver and I didn't like mush. And then I was an adult. I still don't like liver and I still don't like mush."

A Madden topic was never really closed. I was never quite sure if he went back to review our conversations or if ideas just popped into his head. In any case, "mush" made a comeback a few days later.

"You know, the other day we were talking about, 'What happened to mush?' You used to get up and say, 'Give me a bowl of mush.' And that was your break-fast, and then you'd go on with your day. Now we got these cafés or lattés or mocha things. So I'm thinking, 'Well, we got that straightened out.' Maybe we'll get some mush back, your basic hot cereal, a basic sinker that would stick to your ribs. That's the other thing. They'd say, 'You gotta eat something that'll stick to your ribs.' I ate a lot that stuck to my ribs. That's the doggone problem!"

In February of 2001, Coach was on cloud nine because his buddy Davis Love III had just won the AT&T Pebble Beach National Pro Am, the golf tournament played in John's Carmel backyard.

But as thrilled as he was to see "DL3" win the golf tournament and cash the $720,000 first place check, Coach might have been more excited to tell us something *else* about Love.

"He's one of the best fork men that I ever knew," Coach began. From there, he slid into an explanation of the Madden way to approach the act of ordering at a restaurant.

"I always thought that if you see some entrees when you go to order and you don't know what you want—do you want this or do want that?—well, you order one and then you order the other one for the middle, and I thought I was the only guy that did that. But Davis, we had lunch the other day and he ordered one thing for him and three *things for the middle."*

Full disclosure here: there were times when my attention drifted from the conversation we were having with Coach. There was often a lot going on in Studio A, what with the flow of news, worrying about the clock, et cetera.

Thus I felt the need to clarify what I'd just heard, since this whole concept of "one for the middle" was new to me.

"Let me get this straight," I asked. "Three for him and one for the middle?"

"No no, no no, one for him and three for the middle. You know some people just do it with desserts. But if you don't really *know what you want, instead of taking nothing you take everything. You order one of what you want and then you order the other ones 'for the middle' and just put them in the middle of the table."*

Some readers may think Coach was talking about the "small plates" concept that's been in vogue in recent years. They would be wrong. Coach never went small when it came to food. After all, this was the guy who once summed up his take on the healthy-eating movement quite succinctly.

"You hear people say, 'Your body is your temple; be careful what you put in it.' I like to say, 'Your body's a garage; put anything you want in it.'"

His transcontinental bus routes gave him a chance to pull off the interstate in many places. His celebrity certainly could have gotten him the best table in whatever house he chose. But that wasn't the way he rolled, as he explained a few years after retiring from television broadcasting. Coach was about to load the bus for his annual August run to the Pro Football Hall of Fame induction ceremonies in Canton, Ohio.

"I used to be able to go into the small towns and stop someone like a policeman or roll by the firehouse or something like that, and ask, 'Where's the best local place in town?' And then over the years, there started to be fewer and fewer local places. It was all fast food and chains and stuff like that, so I did a lot of stopping there. Then I met Guy Fieri and he does the TV show Diners, Drive-Ins and Dives. *I love that show. I watch that show all the time. He was going to give me a list and it was too late. It was after I had already retired, but he was going to give me a list of all the places across the country. If I were going to be someplace for lunch or dinner, I would tell him and then he'd give me the list of places in that area to go."*

It was clear that when it came to breaking bread with real Americans, John Madden was seeing the end of an era play out before his traveling eyes.

"The only way you really see anything is you have to get off the interstate. And, you know, that's what we try to do; go into the smaller towns. But the smaller towns are really being faded out. There are fewer and fewer of them. I mean, the towns are still there, but there's not much in them anymore. Years ago, we'd always stop at the mom and pop restaurant, the local restaurant. And there are fewer and fewer of those."

He's right, but there's still a roadside American food scene worth chasing. Partially in tribute to Coach, when I retired from KCBS in 2021, I set out with my wife on what turned into an 11,000-mile road trip around America. Our rule: whenever possible, eat local.

I'm pretty sure Coach's karma guided us into a few places on that trip. I only wish he'd had the chance to scarf up the food Chef Seymour dishes out at the Birch Run Deli in Michigan, an unlikely spot for a Black guy from Louisiana to be rolling out gumbo and po' boys. Stan says, "Check it out!"

My predecessor, Al Hart, continued to be part of the Madden conversations after his retirement from daily anchor duties. Al would come in once a week, and Coach always brightened at hearing Al's voice. One morning, they got to talking about the sort of stuff that folks without much money ate in their youth (Al was nine years older than John).

"The kids brought lard sandwiches to school," Al said. "Nobody had any money back then so they'd bring a lard sandwich, and the teacher would keep all the lard sandwiches in her desk. And then if a kid smarted off or acted up in class, they wouldn't get to eat the lard sandwich and they'd have to go hungry for a long time."

Coach was right there.

"I had those, too. I mean, I've had some stuff. I've had an onion sandwich. I've had a tomato sandwich. Just sugar sandwiches."

I needed some clarification. "And did you go for the brown sugar on that, John, or just the straight white stuff?"

"I've had both. I've had just the straight white stuff, with butter or with lard."

I'm feeling a lot better now about all those peanut butter and jam sandwiches Mom used to pack in my lunchbox. My mom also came out ahead one year when my birthday rolled around. Somebody in the newsroom told Coach, so he started our conversation by wishing me a happy birthday.

"Thank you," I replied. "Susan did something really sweet. I mentioned a long time ago that when I was a little shaver, my mom used to always make strawberry shortcake for my birthday. And Susan brought strawberry shortcake in this morning."

Coach jumped right in.

"A real one or a phony one? Did she make a real homemade strawberry shortcake, or the shortcut kind of phony deal?"

Well, *that* put me on the spot. Here I am, sitting in Studio A with my on-air partner Susan, who's been thoughtful enough to remember my childhood birthday treat. I waffled for a moment, saying, "That's not the kind of question I'm going to answer."

"She must have done a phony shortcut one. Susan, you didn't do that old 'pound cake and throw some strawberries on it,' did you?"

I confirmed it. That's exactly what she'd done. In her defense, Susan said, "Hey! The strawberries were real!" John then amped up to the tone of voice he must have used when a referee missed a pass interference call back in his coaching days.

"Oh no! You didn't!"

Susan got called for another 15-yard food penalty on a different occasion. It was the morning of the annual KCBS Madden Barbecue, and she'd suggested she planned to dress her bratwurst with ketchup.

"Did you say 'put ketchup on the brats?' No, unh-unh. No, no, no. All the people in Green Bay and the whole state of Wisconsin or every place that brats are from would just…I mean, you just can't do that."

It wasn't that Coach was anti-ketchup. He was simply following the laws of bratwurst eating as he knew them.

"I don't think anyone in the history of brat eating ever put ketchup on—but you can put ketchup on a lot of stuff. I mean, you can put ketchup on the lamb or you can put ketchup on the pork or the chicken or the tri-tips or anything else."

With Coach, a food conversation could break out just about any time. One year, on the eve of the NFL Draft, I innocently asked if he was all set to settle in for two days of draft-watching (not my cup of tea, but then I didn't live and breathe pro football like John Madden did).

"Well, I'm not sure. I have a decision to make. You know what's going on in Stockton this weekend? The Asparagus Festival. It's hard. It's the old deal, 'Where do I go? Do I watch the draft or do I go to the Asparagus Festival?'"

In the studio, I can see my co-anchor Susan Leigh Taylor lighting up. "Susan says that's not a tough call," I venture.

"Easy call," she says. "Asparagus Festival." And that's when this "Madden Segment" took off.

"But you know, some things don't deserve festivals. You think asparagus really deserves a festival?"

Quick answer from Susan: "Okay, maybe not as much as Brussels sprouts...."

"I don't know. Someone says, 'I love asparagus.' I say, you can eat asparagus, you can have it on your plate, but how can you like asparagus?"

Susan is going to stand her ground in defense of one of California's spring delicacies. "I just had some asparagus tempura the other day, dipped in ranch dressing. It was to die for," she said. Coach wasn't having it.

"But then it's about the tempura and it's about the dip. You ever see that salad? Yeah, I know. We're off the subject. Well, we haven't gotten on a subject."

Stating the obvious, I urged him on. "We don't need a subject."

"Arugula. When I was a kid, I swear that was weeds. I used to have to pick that stuff that they call arugula. I used to have to pick it out of the grass. Did you ever have to pick arugula? I mean, did you ever have to pick weeds?"

This literally hits me right where I live. "Did I *ever* have to? John, come over to my house any Saturday or Sunday. I'm still picking 'em."

"Yeah, but the stuff that you call weeds is arugula. Stuff that just doesn't look like lettuce. It looks like weeds. How can you like that? How can someone say, 'I like arugula?' I just like saying the word 'arugula.' And asparagus. How can you like asparagus?"

If Coach *did* like something, he'd stick with it—and not just the food, but the place that served it. It didn't have to be fancy. It *did* have to fit his traveling schedule. This is not a guy who was going to wait hours to get into the buzzy new joint everyone was talking about.

"The whole thing with eating is, when do you get there? Sometimes there'll be a real good place to eat but you go through at two in the morning. It kind of has to measure up, but there's no place that I've ever gone to that is worth setting my schedule for when I leave or when I get there just for a restaurant."

I personally tracked down a few of his go-to joints, like Chili John's in Green Bay, Skyline Chili in Cincinnati, and Chuy's, the family-run Mexican joint in Van Horn, Texas, that was a regular Madden fuel stop for years.

I often wondered how much of a bump Coach's constant mentions of his favorite places gave to their business. One day, I got some mail. I introduced Coach that morning and started right in.

"John, I got a letter. So I open it up and inside is a scrawled note from a guy named Mike, and there are three photos from Chuy's Restaurant in Van Horn, Texas. One of them is of the big chair that says 'John Madden' on the back, and one of what looks like a half-eaten plate of food in front of that chair."

Now, I've been to Chuy's and seen that chair. My on-air partner Susan has never had the pleasure. She asks, "Are other people allowed to sit in the chair that clearly has your name on it, or are you the only one who sits in that chair?"

"I'm the only one that sits in that chair when I'm there and when I'm not there, it's open season. That's a good table. It's in the back. It's right in front of the television set. That's a prime location at Chuy's, so I know they wouldn't save that."

Susan has a follow-up question. "Because there was some chow left on that plate, I thought, 'If John had really been sitting there, there wouldn't be that much food left on the plate.'"

"There wouldn't be any."

Now I try to describe these photos sent in by our listener. "It's kind of weird, though. I'm looking at the chow, John. You know what it looks like? It looks like french fries. Who goes to Chuy's and orders french fries?"

"No, that's not right. You know, the same guy that orders a hamburger? Yeah. 'Let's go down to Chuy's and get a hamburger and fries!'"

That just didn't work for Coach. Dining didn't have to be elegant, but certain rules had to be followed.

"Last night. I go to a restaurant. I order osso buco. I'm an osso buco eater from way back. Any time I see osso buco on the menu, I order it. So the guy says to me, 'How do you want that cooked?' So I say to the guy, 'That's not a question that goes with osso buco.' I said, 'It's not a rare or medium or well.' I mean, osso buco is slow cooked and it's the same all the time. If you order osso buco and a guy says, 'How do you want it done?' you should probably change your order."

Coach may have known the true way to prepare a lamb or veal shank, but he wasn't stuck on tradition when it came to *when* certain dishes could or should be eaten. Amid a discussion about Thanksgiving menus one morning, he laid out his philosophy.

"One of my favorite things is leftovers, eating the turkey sandwich later or the next day or whatever. I mean, that just seemed to be as good as the main event. But what I can't understand is why turkey, which is so good at this time of year on Thanksgiving, but then the rest of the year, you never have that same meal again. Hey, why don't you have that meal in March?"

Coach was cool with the concept of "fusion cuisine" long before anybody ever started writing about it in the food section. I still remember how fired up he was one March morning.

"I got a new one for Saint Patrick's Day coming up this weekend. I probably shouldn't be giving out recipes, but listen to this. My daughter-in-law made this and I had it last night. And I'll tell you, it was great. It was a corned beef and cabbage pasty. You know, you chop up corned beef, cabbage, potatoes, and carrots and put it in a pasty. I'll tell you, it was really good."

The Cornish pasty had been a frequent topic of conversation on our broadcasts. That's because Coach's longtime friend Steve Mariucci once brought a sack of them aboard the Madden Cruiser in Green Bay. "Mooch" may be of Italian heritage, but he grew up in Iron Mountain, on Michigan's Upper Peninsula. Cornish miners brought their pasties with them in the 1800s and the culinary tradition stuck. Perhaps John's omnivorous ways had something to do with his own upbringing.

"Being Irish, you know, we're lousy at food. We just take anything you find and you put it in a pot and boil it, and that's Irish. But this is a way to hide it. I mean we're all thinking of corned beef and cabbage, Saint Patrick's Day. But that's not a good deal. Boiled corned beef, boiled cabbage, and boiled potatoes aren't very good. But if you chop them all up and put them in a pasty, that is really good. I hope Mariucci is listening to this."

He was, and later told us he thought Coach might be on to something.

You could get John pretty excited by bringing up the topic of chili. He knew exactly where to track it down while traveling. Now, while some chili-heads have very strict rules about what does or doesn't belong in chili, Coach didn't much care, although he might have drawn a line the day he told us about an event at his hometown fair.

"They had a tug-of-war at the county fair between the Alameda County firemen and the sheriffs. It was over 150 pounds of chili. So instead of going into the water, you go into chili. I think two things about that. I think, 'Yeah, that's pretty cool.' But then, I mean, I love chili. Chili is one of my favorite foods and to have 150 pounds of it with some sweaty old guys flopping in it is kind of a waste of chili. But then I think if I were there and I were part of it, it wouldn't have been wasted. These guys are going in there with their boots and stuff. Maybe you take a bite of chili that a boot just got pulled out of."

Coach definitely had the "consumption" side of food and drink down but he got into "production" too. A conversation one morning about former NFL executive Carmen Policy's plans to get into the winemaking business led Coach to break some news about his own foray into viniculture.

"I have petite sirah now. Petite. You know when they mentioned this, I said, 'Hey look, I don't do anything petite. I've never ordered half a sandwich in my life. If I go where they have salad and they ask, 'Do you want a full salad or a half salad?' I say, 'I never ordered half of anything.' Give me the full, what are you talking about, 'a half'? It's the same thing when they said, 'Petite Sirah.'"

He's clearly getting a kick out of saying the word "petite" and he's on a roll.

"I've never had anything petite in my life. That word has never gone with me in my life. I tell them I don't want petite. And then they had to tell me, 'Look, no, no, you're wrong. The only thing petite about sirah is the grape.' The wine is a bold, strong wine. So if anyone is looking for some petite sirah out there, heck, I got some."

It always seemed to me that Coach got just about as much joy out of talking about food as he did actually eating it, and trust me, he did like to eat. He also liked to give a healthy plate full of grief to his buddy Dominic Mercurio whenever possible. One morning, Coach was looking forward to that night's dinner.

"I'm going to have an eating festival tonight, I think. Dominic and my son Joe went on a fishing trip last week to Alaska and they got some salmon. So tonight Dominic is going to cook the catch. I talked to him last night and he said he's going to cook it five ways, you know, 'Salmon Five Ways.' He must have just made up the number because he said, 'I don't know how I'm going to do it.' So I said, 'Well, how are you going to do it five ways if you don't know what the five ways are?' He's going to have to cook salmon five ways, and between last night and tonight he better figure it out. I mean, he probably has, like, two ways."

Our archive doesn't reveal how Dominic pulled it off, but we do know this: there was no sashimi.

"What's sashimi? They don't cook it, right? I mean, this is probably good enough that you wouldn't have to cook it. But I don't like raw fish. I'm not into that."

We've already established Coach's bona fides as an eater. He also claimed to know his way around a kitchen.

"When I'm on the road, I cook one night a week. I'm the only one that can cook, and the stuff ends up on the wall."

While trying to process the image of big John Madden slamming pots and pans around, we asked what he cooked.

"I made pasta, and I remember last year when I did that, I put in pork and beans and everyone laughed at me. I didn't put in pork and beans this time just because I didn't want everyone laughing. But I made the thing and I just make a

mess that goes with it. I think a lot of good chefs are that way. They cook and then someone else cleans up their mess. I made spaghetti and I looked after I was done and there was a mess all over the stove, all over the table, all over the sink. And it was up and down the wall. And then I looked and it was up and down my shirt. I had it all over my shirt and I didn't know it. And I wore the shirt all day."

Coach had no trouble identifying a good fork man, nor did he ever fail to spot those who didn't make the grade. Our super-slender colleague Al Hart was definitely in the latter category. After one of the annual KCBS barbecues at John's production facility, he blew the whistle on Al.

"I saw Al's trick. Everyone is going to look at his plate, see? And he knew that. So he put stuff on his plate. But I think he just pushed it around the plate. I think he used a piece of fruit and a couple of pieces of lettuce, then he put some meat and some other stuff and kind of filled the plate up, but it was the same fill all the way through, if you know what I mean. I think he threw it under the table. I found some under the table. There's probably still some stuff there."

Bon appetit.

CHAPTER 7

Being "Coach"

Long before I met John Madden, I had a pretty good feeling for what it meant to be "Coach." I don't just mean a coach. I mean "Coach," an honorific borne by those who have coached.

I recognize that may seem a bit confusing. It may also seem a bit silly to anyone who's never played a team sport. But trust me: if you were a player, the person who coached you will forever be "Coach."

My dad and his dad were both high school coaches and my father, now in his nineties, is still called "Coach" by men who are well into their retirement years. I can recall feeling a thrill as a young adult when veteran NFL quarterback Craig Morton, who'd played for my dad at Campbell High School before starring at the University of California, saw Dad at a Cal game and said, "Hi, Coach."

Being "Coach" is a lifetime deal, not unlike "Judge" or "Senator" or "Governor."

Like my father and grandfather, John Madden was a credentialed teacher, too. We live in an era that sees fewer and fewer teachers doing the coaching at American high schools. Coach Madden and my dad and I agreed: it's not a healthy trend.

As head coach, Madden famously led a diverse, raucous bunch of Oakland Raiders to success. He didn't worry too much about how they wore their hair or what music they favored.

"I only had three rules: 'Be on time, pay attention, and play like hell when I tell you to.' That's all I had. Because these other teams said you have to wear a suit and tie on the road, you can't have any facial hair, your hair has to be cut, you have to have short hair, all these things. And to me, that didn't have one doggone thing to do with winning or losing."

The sports world being what it is, many of our morning radio conversations would veer toward one controversy or another. Coaches were being hired and fired, players were in hot water, owners were saying or doing dumb things.

One morning in 2003, after the Oakland Raiders had finished a dispiriting 4–12 season, the headline was that head coach Bill Callahan was about to be fired amidst general player discontent. For many, the last straw was Callahan's decision to suspend two players, including future Hall of Famer Charles Woodson, for missing curfew.

John didn't blast Callahan nor did he directly condone the breaking of rules; after all, one might argue that Woodson had broken Madden Rule Number One: "Be on time." What he did was explain how *he* viewed the task of managing wealthy star athletes.

"There's certain players that you hold the bus for. That's the old coaching thing, you know: 'I tell you this player's so good he's one player I'd hold the bus for.' You know, the bus is leaving at 10:00, but it gets to be 10:10. You tell the driver, 'Hey, you check that timing chain yet? How about, before we leave, I want you to check those tires.' You kind of wait until the guy gets there. And then you play the guy and then *you fine him."*

One of my favorite Coach Madden stories is one he told about a training camp incident. It featured a young defensive back who would go on to a stellar career with the Raiders.

"Lester Hayes is in his rookie year. We're playing in a scrimmage with the Dallas Cowboys down in Thousand Oaks and Tom Landry is out there. He's a

real gentleman as a coach and I'm…not so much. So Lester Hayes intercepts the ball. He's running down the sidelines, holds it up in the air, gets hit, and fumbles. Now since this is a scrimmage we're out on the field. It's about 110 degrees. And for some reason I'm wearing a sweat jacket. So I start running across the field. I'm so upset. I'm going to get him. And by the time I get there, Lester's saying, 'I know, I know, I'm sorry, I'm sorry.' But I'm so tired and hot and overheated, I can't say anything. So I don't say a word to him. I waddle all the way out there and I just turn around and go back."

It's a funny story already, but then Coach dials it up a bit.

"So at lunch, Tom Landry says, 'John, I was really impressed with you. I mean, that kid did a stupid thing and you really held your composure.' My composure? I'd damn near passed out."

It reminded me of a story from my dad's high school coaching days. One of his players recovered a fumble and started toward the end zone with 50 yards of clear sailing ahead of him. But then he fumbled, giving the ball right back to the other team.

The hapless defensive player jogged slowly to the sidelines, head down, and went straight to the bench. That's where Dad caught up with him, sitting next to the player and throwing an arm over his shoulder as he leaned in for a quiet conversation.

Later that evening, a fellow faculty member told Dad, "Coach, I was really impressed with the compassion you showed that kid after the fumble." To which Dad replied, "It might have been different if we hadn't been leading by three touchdowns."

I would describe my own athletic career as "extremely modest," and even that may oversell the reality of it. For a while, I thought my first name had been changed because a high school basketball coach habitually referred to me as "Fucking Bunger!"

It wasn't until one morning with Madden that I realized having an unusual name might simply be a way of feeding a coach's muse. We were in the midst of a discussion about the colorful New England Patriots tight end Rob Gronkowski.

"You know, that's good name to yell, isn't it? Like there's some names that just bring about yelling. If you were coaching Gronkowski, you'd always put 'Hey' in front of it: 'HEY GRONKOWSKI!'"

Long after he'd coached his last game, John remained keenly aware of how to succeed on the sidelines. As reports surfaced that veteran NBA star Jason Kidd was going to leave the floor and move to the bench as head coach of the Brooklyn Nets, Coach told us that Kidd would be fine when it came to the "X's and O's." But he had some advice.

"You always have to know what you don't know and then admit you don't know it and then get someone that does know it and then let them be responsible for it."

John Madden resisted the easy "hot take" when it came to coaches. He saw coaches first and foremost as human beings, trying to perform amidst intense pressure and endless scrutiny. By the time we connected on the radio, John had spent many years as a "recovering coach."

One morning, yet another job change for basketball-coaching legend Larry Brown was in the news. Coach Madden dug in.

"I was thinking, I just saw Bill Parcells at the NFL owners meeting. He took that Dallas job we were talking about. The old 'can't live with it, can't live without it.' You know, once you're a coach, you have that passion. It stays there and you always come back. I think Larry Brown is that same guy. I think that he's a heck of a coach. And when he's coaching, he has a tough time living with it, and then he gets out of it and he can't live without it. So he gets back in it."

I asked, "Is that a disease, John? They simply have to keep coming back like a moth to a flame?"

"Yeah, that's it. And you know, that's what you are. That's what they are. And the thing gets very, very big while they're doing it, to a point where it gets overwhelming. And the big thing is, the longer you coach, the more you win. You really don't get the satisfaction from winning that you used to. And the low of losing is so much lower than it ever was because your expectations are so high. You know you're supposed to win. So when you win, it's just, 'Okay, I did what I'm supposed

to.' And then because you're supposed to win, when you lose, that takes so much out of you that it's tough to take. And the longer you coach, the more the losses are tougher to take. And the wins don't mean as much."

A bell is going off in my head, because this sounds like the John Madden who walked away from coaching at age 42. "So the answer is to pull a John Madden and get out while you can?" I asked.

"Well, yeah, but I stayed in it. I mean, I stayed in for 10 years as a head coach. It got a pretty good hunk of me. But the thing is, had I not gotten into TV, I would have gone back to it."

Listening back to this segment, I'm a bit embarrassed to note that I didn't do the interviewer thing and jump in with the obvious follow-up question. Didn't John Madden just admit that he *would* have gone back to coaching after telling everyone long ago that he'd never coach again? We'll never know, of course.

"It just worked for me that when I went into TV, that took the place of it. I mean, I went from playing to the next year I was coaching and then from coaching, the next year to broadcasting and that worked and that was normal. But some other guys have tried that and the broadcasting doesn't do it for them. So they go back to coaching. They can do something else too. But it doesn't satisfy them. I mean, it doesn't satisfy them to not have wins and losses, and then it's the winning and losing that eats you up."

It's a theme he'd come back to often. He understood the desire to coach but also understood the reality, and was clear-eyed about the commitment it required.

"Coaching is so tough today that the only way that anyone should do it is if they can't live without it. And if you can live without it, then you shouldn't do it because there's no way you can just stick your toe in the water in this deal."

I suspect that in many, if not most, coaches, there rests the soul of a player with some unfinished business. John Madden's own pro football career ended before it really started when he suffered a serious knee injury during the 1959 Philadelphia Eagles training camp.

The Eagles were led by the fiery veteran quarterback Norm Van Brocklin, who would become a pivotal figure in John's life before going on to his own coaching career.

"I started hanging out with Norm Van Brocklin and watching film with him. And then I started getting interested in football as a coach. It's funny how when you're a player and before you get hurt, school, class, education is not very important. And after I got my injury, school became important again. I mean, I just want to be honest, I just went to school to play football and I figured I'd play all my life. At some point, I was in the hospital for a long time; I had infections and so on. So I kind of knew then and my next thought was, 'What am I going to do the rest of my life?' And I went from a guy that really didn't care about school to become pretty interested in school."

He earned both a bachelor's degree and a master's degree in education at Cal Poly and even began coursework toward a PhD. His playing days were behind him, but he told us that the player was always inside him.

"When I first started coaching, that was a tough thing, going from being a player to where you can't play anymore and the finality of it. So when you first start coaching, you think you're still a player. I used to wear regular football shoes in those days at practice and I used to wear arm pads and I used to get out there and I used to scrimmage with them. I mean, I used to have the guys hit me. I didn't have a helmet on, but they did."

I always got the sense that John Madden could have been handed the syllabus on the first day of school and handled any subject. He certainly had the classroom management skills, and there was never any doubt about the smarts. Heck, he even taught a social dance course at Allan Hancock College.

"I was on the curriculum committee. In those days, everyone had to take a P.E. class. So I was making the point that just because they're in college, that doesn't mean that everyone wants to take P.E. and go out and play basketball or soccer or softball or one of those things. I said we ought to have something a little more passive. So I said, 'We ought to have a class in social dance, for those that really don't want to get out and do the physical stuff.' And I was assuming that

the women's department would teach it. So anyway, lo and behold, they said they wouldn't teach it. I said, 'Well, who's going to teach it? We got it in the curriculum now.' And they said, 'The guy that put it in—you.' So I had to teach it and I didn't know anything about it. I bluffed. I got those record albums and I'd look at the steps on the back and I would step through the steps and have them do it, and I'd have them watch each other. It was a complete bluff."

My takeaway: if a former defensive lineman can teach rumba, tango, and mambo steps to college kids, there's probably not much he *can't* pull off.

As big a competitor as he was—and make no mistake, John Madden did *not* like to lose at anything—he often made it clear that it was the teaching that made coaching worthwhile. He truly enjoyed the long, sweaty days of pro football preseason camp.

"I loved training camp because it was a time that you could coach and you could teach and you could do all those things without the pressure of having to get ready for a game. In pro football, and probably in any football, during the season once you start playing games your week is just game preparation so you don't get to do a lot of teaching and coaching. When you're in training camp, before you have games, you can just teach and coach. Even when you have preseason games, we would teach and coach on Monday, Tuesday, Wednesday, and Thursday, and then maybe work on the other team on Friday and then play them on Saturdays. That was always fun. I think basically what I really was in life was a teacher and I enjoyed the teaching part second most. I mean the part that I obviously enjoyed the most was the coaching in the games, playing the games."

He was the kind of teacher who was always looking for the unseen side of his students.

"I always had a rule: before I cut someone or gave up on someone, I'd give them a chance at another position. If I had a guy and he was maybe the fourth tight end and I was only going to keep three, I would, a day or two before I cut him, I'd move him over to linebacker or something like that. If you can see a guy who's not going to make it at one position, before you make any big decision on him, you want to look at him someplace else. I did a lot of that."

John often reminded me that he and Virginia had started their careers as schoolteachers. Their time in the educational trenches taught him plenty about the process of imparting knowledge.

"I've always believed that the best teachers were the 'C' students because if you're a 'C' student, you can understand 'C' students, you can understand average kids, you can teach them. Kind of anyone can teach an 'A' student. If you've been an 'A' student, you can't understand: 'How can someone not get it?' And I think the people that were 'A' students, and this is just a generality, I think they tend to become frustrated with people that can't learn quite as quickly as they did."

Coach may have left the sidelines behind at an early age but he was still drawn to the sights, sounds, and smells of football.

"I used to love the line. You know, one of my favorite things, and I still have one at my place, is that seven-man sled. You've seen it there. [True. It was in the parking lot behind his office, seemingly awaiting a bunch of guys in full pads.] *A seven-man sled was one of the great things. And I'd start with it every day. I don't even know if teams use the old seven-man sled anymore, but you have seven pads on a machine and then you have seven guys. So that would be your five offensive linemen plus you have two tight ends, you have a quarterback who gives a snap count and then BOOM, you hit the seven man sled. It's for takeoff and everyone getting off together. And if it's a good takeoff, you can hear it. I used to stand on it. So they had to not only hit the seven-man sled and push it, but they had to push me."*

More than 20 years after he'd walked away from coaching, John was plenty fired up talking about the sensation of having close to a ton of professional football players slam into the pads on that blocking sled while he stood on it.

"I would say, 'Blue Go!' And then I'd go, 'DRIVE, DRIVE, DRIVE, DRIVE, DRIVE!' I could do that all day and they had to do it. I'd keep doing it because I loved it. I mean, I loved that, right? You know, that BOOM, it kind of lifts you up. That first hit with seven guys kind of lifts you up. Then you just tell them to 'DRIVE, DRIVE, DRIVE, DRIVE, DRIVE!' Sometimes I'd get carried away."

He proceeded to get carried away that morning on the radio, directing everyone in the studio to get into a "set" position so they could hit an imaginary sled. From his end of the phone line, he decided that some of his "players" weren't where they should be, so he coached them up. And then he called the snap count and shouted, *"DRIVE, DRIVE, DRIVE, DRIVE, DRIVE!"* for about 30 seconds, stopping only long enough to take a few breaths. Laughter ensued. This became a classic segment that found its way into the "Best of Madden" replay rotation for many years.

It made me think that if someone would have let John Madden just show up and do the fun parts of coaching, he might have stayed with it. One guy who *did* stay with it was his boyhood buddy John Robinson, who'd won a college national championship and four Rose Bowls at USC, spent nine seasons coaching the Rams in the NFL, and raised some eyebrows at age 64 when he took over a University of Nevada, Las Vegas team that had gone 0–11 the year before. Five years after that gig ended, Coach Madden expected even more.

"I'll tell you something about John Robinson. He's a coach and that's what he is and that's what he does. And it doesn't make any difference who he's coaching. I mean, he would go out and coach his grandkids. His son is a junior college coach. He goes and helps him. I guarantee you this: if someone were to offer him a job today, coaching someplace, any place, he'd go take that job because that's what he is and who he is, and he's one of the best that's ever done it."

Robinson was standing by that morning, and he had a reply.

"Well, what I'm trying to do now is get John to buy a team. I want John to buy a team and then make me a special teams coach. I don't want a big job, just special teams or something like that. But seriously, I think all of us would still be coaching if it wasn't for age or health or whatever."

One morning, for reasons I no longer recall, I asked Coach if he still felt any of the spark that continued to animate his buddy John Robinson. I asked, "Would you ever want to go back to coaching at a place different from every place else, maybe a place like one of the military academies?"

"You know, it's funny you bring that up. I haven't wanted to go back into coaching in a long time. But when the Army job came up, I said, 'If I ever did— and it's just a fantasy—I would like to coach at Army.' I mean, seeing them being

0 and 12, losing to Navy, was just an embarrassment. The program ought to be better, the football ought to be better. The U.S. Military Academy, West Point, ought to be playing top teams and have top guys. I mean, I was watching the Army-Navy game and one of the announcers said they don't get the biggest or the fastest players. And I thought, 'Why not?' I mean, do you have to be slow to go to Army? You could recruit all over the whole country. If there was a challenge out there that you were looking for and you really wanted *to do something, that could have been a little entertaining."*

It was an "exclusive." John had never said anything publicly about considering un-retiring to coach at Army. By the next day, I had a follow-up question. "I did some further research, John. It turns out that the head coach at Army is expected to lead the team in calisthenics and in some training runs. Were you prepared to go that far?"

"Well, you know, every tradition is made to be broken."

We never knew when an item in the news would trigger a story from John's coaching days. There was the time the Dallas Cowboys' new stadium had opened, complete with a massive set of video screens that hung over the playing field. One of those screens had been hit by a punt during a Cowboys-Titans game in 2009 (it's happened several other times since), and Coach was ready with a memory.

"It happened with [Raiders punter] Ray Guy when I was coaching. We were in the Superdome in New Orleans and they had the gondola there. We were there for the Pro Bowl. In practice, Ray Guy hit it and then he said, 'I can hit that thing.' So now we're in the game, and he starts to go in to punt and he said, 'Is it okay if I punt it and hit the gondola?' And I go, 'No, no, it's a football game, doggone it. You can't do that, blah, blah, blah.' But then I started to think, 'What the heck, It's a Pro Bowl.' So I called him back and I said, 'Go ahead, hit the doggone thing.' And he goes, BOOM! And he hits the thing. After that, they had to move the gondola up in the Superdome."

John was not shy about telling others the proper way to do something, but he also knew his limits. He was friends with longtime baseball man Tony La Russa, who would occasionally join us on the air to swap barbs and tall tales with Coach. One time, La Russa gave John an opportunity: he could show up while the St. Louis Cardinals took infield practice and hit some grounders with the skinny version of a baseball bat known as a fungo bat.

"I swear this is true: the first thing you do when you get a fungo in your hand is you hit your shoe, like to knock the dirt out of your spikes. Now the only thing that La Russa does with his fungo is, he hits grounders to Mark McGwire. So he offered me the chance to hit fungoes to the first baseman."

I'm thinking we have a heck of a story unfolding. The legendary football coach and broadcaster crosses sports lines and helps one of baseball's biggest stars get ready for a game? Priceless. But that's not how it played out.

"Had I known he was going to offer that, then I would have gotten a fungo. If you're going to hit some fungoes to Mark McGwire, you have to at least have a fungo. And I've never had a fungo in my life. You got to hit some fungoes before you go to the game to hit the fungoes."

By now, he's just having fun saying the word "fungo" because, well, it's a good word to say, right? The suspense is killing sports anchor Steve Bitker, who asks, "So did you hit fungoes to McGwire?"

"No, no, no. I wouldn't do it because I hadn't done it before. I'd never hit a fungo in my life. I played a heck of a lot of baseball. But the only guys that ever hit fungoes were coaches. There's not much wood on a fungo. I don't know where you're supposed to hit it or how. And I could have seen myself: swing and miss and then have to pick it up and swing and miss again. Pick it up. Swing and miss again. Pick it up. Swing and miss again. Then FWAP! And crack the fungo bat."

Postscript: La Russa later gave Coach his very own fungo bat. It stood for years in a corner of his office, just in case he ever decided to show up to coach infield practice.

John was a catcher when he played baseball at Jefferson High School and Cal Poly. By tradition, a catcher's gear is known as "the tools of ignorance." Yet the catcher is the one player who can see every other player on the field, and a disproportionate number of Major League Baseball managers have been former catchers.

I suspect that if John's passions had led him toward baseball rather than football, he'd have wound up a manager. Baseball managers are often referred to as "Skipper," or "Skip" for short. Who knows, we could have been calling him "Skip" instead of "Coach."

CHAPTER 8

Bus Life

IT'S ENTIRELY POSSIBLE THAT JOHN MADDEN WAS AMERICA'S ALL-TIME BEST-known non-flier.

Coach was claustrophobic, and once he realized he didn't actually *have* to white-knuckle his way through confinement in an airborne aluminum tube, he stopped doing it.

For a while, he rode Amtrak. Then, starting with a weeklong journey on a tour bus borrowed from Dolly Parton, John Madden traveled America on a bus.

He started his regular morning radio appearances in 1982, a year before the enormous Motorola DynaTAC 8000X cellular phone hit the market, so making that daily connection with the radio station often took some planning.

Former KNBR morning man Frank Dill recalls John as "Mr. Reliable," despite the obvious logistical and technological challenges of connecting to the studio in pre cellular times. "Even if he was traveling in the bus, we'd talk to him from his Madden Cruiser, no matter where he was, no matter what else was happening," Dill remembers. "It was very rare that John took a day off from the radio." Many years and many miles later, I can confirm that.

For the majority of my years with Coach, his travel schedule would stretch from NFL training camps in July to playoff games in January, often with a February Super Bowl tossed in. Sometimes he'd get a few days at home if his TV broadcast schedule worked out that way. Often, he'd be hundreds or thousands of miles away.

I'd often try to guess where he was, and there was a simple answer.

"Wyoming is always a good guess. If you don't know, just say Wyoming or Nebraska, and you'll be right 90 percent of the time."

One December morning, Coach spoke to us just hours after arriving home at the end of a very long road trip.

"Three in the morning, that's a tough time. You like to get home either late at night or in the morning some time. And that 3:00 AM is kind of betwixt and between."

Sports anchor Steve Bitker inquired, "Can we assume that Virginia was not up waiting for you?"

"As a matter of fact, she was. I don't even know how to get into the house. I've been gone so long, I actually had to call her to let me in. And then I looked and she was sitting outside on a chair. How long have I been gone? When I left here, the trees had leaves on them."

I told you earlier that I regret not fully appreciating the nature of my relationship with Coach until he was gone. I can almost hear him responding to that sentence by saying, "that's a heavy one." But I have one more regret regarding John Madden: I never rode with him on the bus.

Those who took that ride have told me it's an experience they'll never forget, and I'm pretty sure I know why: they got to have uninterrupted "hang time" with a guy who knew how to hang out and who reveled in the joy of discovering roadside America.

Sometimes, his fascination was with the weather he'd see outside the windows of the Madden Cruiser. Remember, a lot of those bus miles were during the fall and winter months when the weather can get a bit nasty.

"Well, I'm in Indiana and it's seven degrees. If you're wondering if seven degrees is cold, I can tell you it is cold because we stopped for fuel. I got off the bus and took like five steps and turned around and walked right back in."

Here in the Bay Area, that's not the sort of weather with which we have any experience, so I tried to put it in perspective. "One of those deals where it feels like somebody actually has a dagger in your lungs when you try to breathe?" I asked.

"Yeah, I think so. I mean, I wasn't out there long enough to test daggers and stuff, but I guarantee it's cold and it's bright. I mean, the sun is out. It's funny. It's one of those things. It's just too cold to snow or anything else."

One morning, as he was headed home from Indianapolis during yet another winter cold snap, I asked him if they'd managed to avoid a sleet storm that was making news around Dallas.

"Yes, we did. And we came down that way, too. You know, we came across Interstate 40, which is the old Route 66. And the weather was really pretty good. I mean, it was cold, but it was clear. And you talk about cold: in Indianapolis, you know, they had no degrees."

I plugged into Coach's way of saying "the temperature dropped to zero" and piped up, "It was less than no degrees at one point, right?"

"Yeah, less than no. But when you get less than no, it doesn't make any difference what less is like. So it's six degrees below zero. Somebody will say, 'No, I think it's eight below.' What's the difference? When it's below zero, I'll tell you, it's cold."

At that point, the veteran traveler confessed to a rookie mistake.

"You know, I always brag about this, 'No, I don't pack. I just take an hour just before I leave and put some stuff in,' and I always forget stuff. You know what I forgot?"

Time for me to play along. "What? Did you forget your socks?"

"No, no, no. I wish it was socks. I forgot a jacket. I thought, 'The weather's nice here.' I've had all my years of experience traveling. I've always made that mistake. I dress the way the weather is where I'm leaving from rather than where I'm going to."

He was always going *somewhere*, and the odds were pretty good that he'd been there before. He wasn't above showing off his geographical knowledge, as he did one morning when I was tipped off to his location by my producer Ted Goldberg.

"And how is Tennessee at this hour?" I asked as I introduced Coach.

"It's fine. Do you know your Nashvilles and your Knoxvilles?"

Busted, on live radio. "Man, I get confused. Which is at which end of the state? I think Knoxville is west and Nashville's east. Am I right?" Somewhere, one or more of the fine people who taught me in Bay Area public schools is cringing at this point. And John couldn't wait to pounce.

"Nope. Backwards. That was a good try. You know, you got two shots at it. The other way around. Nashville's first, and then Knoxville. So right now we're between Nashville, which is where the Tennessee Titans are, and Knoxville, where the University of Tennessee is."

The geography lesson hasn't ended yet. From her position on the other side of the studio, my co-anchor Susan Leigh Taylor chimes in, "Where's Chattanooga in this mess?"

"Chattanooga. What'd you throw me that one for? I know my Nashvilles and my Knoxvilles. Not that sure of my Chattanoogas."

Heck, we didn't even get to Pulaski or Murfreesboro.

As I said, a ride with John was something special. But there was one passenger whose story stands above the rest.

It happened in September 2001, a few days after the terrorist attacks. The nation was still reeling and tens of thousands of travelers were stranded after an unprecedented closure of U.S. airspace.

Closed airspace meant nothing to John Madden and his bus. He'd been in New York City on 9/11, awaiting the weekend NFL broadcast. He'd delivered a memorable account to our listeners that morning. Unfortunately, all we have of that broadcast is our memories because I've never been able to find a recording. He was still stunned on September 12th—and that broadcast *is* in the archive.

"Everyone that you see or talk to was either around the Twin Towers or has a good friend that was in the buildings and they still haven't heard from. This thing here in New York isn't going to go away. I've never experienced anything like this before. And I sure as hell don't want to ever again. Don't want anyone else to either."

By September 14, he was on the road.

"I got out as soon as we heard that they weren't going to play the NFL games. I had someone pick me up and take me out. The bus was in New Jersey and so I went over where the bus was and took off and got out of town. The whole week was surreal. The farther you get away from it, it kind of becomes a blank. Just seeing everything and knowing that you'd been there when this happened and that you were leaving was a surreal feeling. And then when I got out, I was just happy to get farther and farther away."

The Madden Cruiser was near Omaha that morning when Coach broke the news that he'd picked up a rider.

"In Wilkes-Barre, Pennsylvania. Peggy Fleming was stuck there. To make a long story short, we've picked Peggy Fleming up. You know she lives out there in the Bay Area. So I have a rider."

The 1968 Olympic gold medal-winning figure skater aboard the Madden Cruiser? Of course I asked John to hand her the phone, and she gave us the details.

"I was stranded there. I was doing a speech in Wilkes-Barre for breast cancer survivors. And then this whole thing came down and I was supposed to go to Washington, D.C., and give two more speeches, and I was supposed to be staying in a hotel in Arlington right down the street from the Pentagon and giving my speech right down the street from the White House. So I thought maybe it wasn't a good idea to go near that place."

Fleming went on to speak with emotion about what they were seeing at ground level as the bus rolled toward home.

"It's a beautiful, beautiful thing. We see a lot of flags at half staff along the way at farms and rest stops. It's really incredible. I feel so safe in this little bus. And John is my hero forever. This is such a nice guy."

For us, the beauty of having John on the bus was the unpredictability. You couldn't script stuff like this if you tried.

"We just got stopped. There's a cop here that wants to talk to us. The Indiana State Police are stopping us. Go ahead, open the door."

The great TV analyst went into play-by-play mode.

"We're going to get arrested right here, right now on the radio."

Talk about a "turn up your radio" moment! Next, we heard Coach talking to the law enforcement officer who'd just climbed aboard.

"We're heading to Chicago. I'm just doing a radio show here."

And with that, Coach handed the phone over to the cop, who quickly and cheerfully identified himself as Trooper Chris Barr of the Indiana State Police. Steve Bitker posed the question, "We want to know why you stopped Mr. Madden?"

"Oh, well, I tell you, he's pulled off on the side of the ramp with his Outback cruiser, the big coach here. So I was just checking to make sure everything was all right."

And to get an autograph from Coach, Trooper Barr readily admitted. With that, he bade us farewell and is, no doubt, still telling the story of the day he climbed onto John Madden's bus.

Another great "on the road" story took place in Nebraska. This one involved not only Coach, but a couple of his regular foils, Jim Ghielmetti and Dominic Mercurio (the former always referred to by his last name and the latter by his first name). Those two had flown from Green Bay to Lincoln, Nebraska, following a Packers game while the Madden Cruiser rolled across the heart of the country. The plan was to meet up for lunch. Coach filled us in on the plan on our 9:15 AM segment (we had Coach on at both 8:15 AM and 9:15 AM Mondays and Fridays during the NFL season).

"We're just outside of Lincoln. And we just got a call. They're already there. They're waiting for us. And they've already chosen a restaurant."

I jumped in, "Oh, they're at the restaurant? See, because I had something set up for you here."

"What'd you have set up?"

"Well, I hooked up with my friend Bob the Cornhusker. And Bob the Cornhusker says you've got to go to a place called Misty's. It's a Nebraska tradition. And in fact, to encourage you to do so, we've contacted Jay, the bartender at Misty's. Jay, are you there?"

Jay was there. This could have gone sideways in a hundred ways. Who knows what will happen when you stick a Nebraska bartender on the air with

John Madden? I continued, "John Madden's on the other line. You want to give him a pitch, see if you can get him to re-vector for lunch there?"

Jay piped up, "John, how you doing?" already on a first-name basis with Coach.

"Yeah, yeah, I'm doing well. But the guys went to Perkins."

At the time, Perkins had about 450 restaurants spread across more than two dozen states, meaning this would not be a unique dining experience. You could hear the disappointment in Jay the Bartender's voice as he replied, "The guys went to Perkins, huh?" John's reply began with one of his trademarks: rapidly repeating "yes" or "no."

"Yeah, yeah, yeah, yeah. They landed, got there before us, and then they went to Perkins. We're going to meet them now. How far are you from Perkins?"

"Oh, we're probably three miles away. You've been downtown here?"

"Yeah, yeah, yeah, I've been to downtown Lincoln. What do you have at Misty's?"

Now Jay the Bartender senses an opportunity, and he may have an idea that John Madden likes to eat and eat big. "We got steaks, a brewery, great prime rib." This might be working.

"You're open now?"

"Yes, we are."

I rejoined the conversation saying, "You know, John, you could double dip," thinking maybe he could meet Ghielmetti and Dominic at Perkins and then roll into downtown Lincoln for some of that Misty's prime rib.

"Well, I've been known to do that. Known to go one place for breakfast and then a half-hour later go to another place for lunch."

And this is the moment when Steve Bitker, who'd been silent through all of this, asked a question none of us ever forgot. "Jay," Steve inquired, "can you recommend Perkins in all good conscience?"

Jay delivered an equally memorable answer, after a perfectly timed pause. "No, I cannot." Laughter all around, as Coach explained the situation.

"Well, that's what they picked out. You know, we usually go through the whole, 'I don't know, what do you want to do? Where are you going?' thing. We didn't even

go through that this time. We just got word that—what's the word?—unilaterally, they went and chose Perkins, and they're sitting there waiting for us now."

Jay the Bartender is not going to let this one get away. "Well, you just pull your bus on up another three miles and stop in here at Misty's downtown."

I have a chance to pile onto Coach's buddies. "Yeah, I think that's a good plan. Because you know, it looks like Ghielmetti and Dominic went off half-cocked on you."

"Yeah, I know they did. It just has to do with patience. They lack patience. They wouldn't just sit there until we got there. They have to go someplace. Both of them are that way. You know that. 'Okay, where are we going now? Let's go.' So they had to go someplace. But how in the heck do they end up at Perkins? I don't know. You know, what would be a better move would be for me to just drive right by, don't stop at all in Lincoln, and let those two jablonies sit in Perkins."

Co-anchor Susan Leigh Taylor now needs to know, "What are jablonies?"

"I don't know. It's where you just put letters together and it comes out as 'jablonies.'"

A memorable Madden conversation, to be sure. But there was a post-script, delivered the very next day.

"Yesterday we were in Nebraska, and those guys were at Perkins. So then we were going to go to Misty's and we had three options. We could just drive by and leave them sitting there at Perkins. We could go pick them up at Perkins and take them over to Misty's. Or we could just eat at Perkins. Then I came up with a fourth option: we could go to Misty's, leave them at Perkins and then call them when we're done."

"Good idea. Is that what you did?" I asked.

"I didn't do that because here's what happened. Danny from Los Banos is listening [Danny runs the barbecue crew that's been part of many a Madden event]. *So he calls Dominic and tells him we're going to Misty's and even gives him the address. Those guys have a car. So those guys started to go to Misty's, and then they called me and said, 'We heard about it from California. We're on our way to Misty's.' We met at Misty's and Stan, by the way, that was a good call. It was really good."*

I tell him my friend Bob the Cornhusker will be happy to hear this and Coach wraps the whole thing up by bringing Jay the Bartender back into the story.

"I asked him how he thought he did on the radio. Old Jay, he said he thought he did pretty good. He said he'd done worse. He'd been on other shows and he got too nervous. Thought he did okay, so that's how he critiqued himself."

I offered, "We thought maybe he was a little nervous until Steve asked him that probing question, 'Can you in all good conscience recommend Perkins?' At which point he said, 'No!'" That got a laugh out of Coach.

"That's what made me decide. His answer was just, 'NO!'"

For Coach, the episode checked off a few boxes: a great meal, fodder for a good story, and the kind of human interaction that made his day.

Misty's was already a Lincoln institution the day the Madden Cruiser rolled down North 11th Street, but that day was a big enough deal that a photo of Coach's visit still hangs just inside the front door.

That's not the only place where a Madden visit is memorialized. In the dusty town of Van Horn, Texas, there's a Mexican restaurant that went to the trouble of putting a sign up on a tall pole out front, trumpeting itself as part of the Madden "Haul of Fame."

Van Horn sits on Interstate 10, at the base of the Guadalupe Mountains. Fort Stockton is 120 miles in one direction and El Paso is the same distance the other way. I want to say this delicately, but Van Horn is not exactly a garden spot. I'll let Coach describe it.

"It looks like one of those deserted towns, the kind you see in an old Western or something, the street going out of town with no people on it. A place that used to be something but is not so much anymore."

So how in the world did John Madden and Chuy's Restaurant become a thing?

"Here's how I first hit it. It was a Monday night in 1987, and this was before I had TV on the bus. I wanted to watch the Monday night game, and I hit a bonanza. I found a Mexican restaurant with a TV. That's perfect!"

It was so perfect that the Madden Cruiser became a regular sight in the parking lot for years and years. The owners installed a big chair with John's name on it, smack dab in front of the big-screen TV. We often heard Coach talk about a dinner he'd had there the night before, but one morning, he was changing things up.

"We're in Van Horn, Texas, where we go for lunch and dinner. And this is the first time we're going to try ol' Papa Chuy for breakfast. Papa Chuy opens at nine, so he has a breakfast. But every other time we've gone through here, it's either been lunch time or dinner time. Here, we're hitting them at breakfast, so we'll see."

My co-anchor Susan wanted to know what a typical Madden meal at Chuy's was like.

"Well, Papa Chuy owns the place and Mama Chuy actually has some special thing, some kind of chicken thing that they make. And then she makes tortillas and stuff. It's a special thing that we've been getting for years and years and years. We'd call ahead and Mama Chuy would make it. Now we get down here and it's breakfast time, and I don't want the Mama Chuy special. I had to call Papa Chuy. And he says, 'Yeah, yeah, I have huevos,' so I think we're good."

John Madden tallied up hundreds of thousands of miles aboard his buses (he went through several of them over the years, each fancier than the one before it). It took 50 hours, more or less, to cross America, though most of the trips zigged and zagged depending on John's TV assignments. I never really could keep track of his comings and goings.

"A week from today, I will probably be talking to you from Salt Lake City, Utah, because I'm going to be leaving a week from last night. So Wednesday, I'll be in Utah someplace. Thursday I'll be in Chicago. I'm going to the Bears practice on Thursday night, and then I'll be on my way to Canton, Ohio. And that's the Hall of Fame game, which will be on that Monday night."

Got all that?

The Madden Cruiser was John's *sanctum sanctorum*, a 45-foot-long rolling private space where he could be himself with those with whom he chose to share the privilege. His boyhood buddy John Robinson was a frequent passenger, allowing the Two Doofuses From Daly City to slip back into their old roles together.

In Coach's telling, Robinson would start the "When are we gonna get there?" refrain familiar to all road-tripping parents within hours of leaving the Bay Area. One time, Robinson made a last-minute decision to join a run to the Midwest and floated the idea of flying back to California.

"Once you make a commitment to the bus, you make it to go and to come back. You know, it's not just a half-commitment. He honored the whole commitment and he's still here. And then on top of it, the frosting on the cake is he bought breakfast. Last time he bought me something was at the Relish Bakery, Top of the Hill, Daly City. An ice cream cone."

I floated the idea of nicknaming Coach's passenger "Round Trip Robinson," but that seemed too formal for the Master of the Bus, so "Round Trip Robby" it was.

Lest you think John Madden's vagabond life was all freedom and frivolity, he let us know that he felt as though he'd failed to fully exploit the possibilities offered him.

"I always feel guilty. I mean, for so many years, I've gone to great cities like New York, Philadelphia, Washington, D.C. And I haven't seen anything. I haven't done anything. And, you know, when I think about it or if I say it, I really get embarrassed by it. When you're on the road, life is just a hotel or a stadium and back and that's it. You go a lot of places, but you don't see a lot of things."

One thing we never saw or heard of, in all John's years on the road, was a crash or a breakdown. They *did* hit a deer one night in Kentucky, but considering they were clocking between 50,000 and 100,000 miles a year, the Madden Cruiser was a very safe place to be.

Nobody goes anywhere on a bus without a bus driver. For most of my years on the air with Coach, he had two of them, Willie Yarbrough and Joe Mitchell. Willie had come over from Greyhound in 1987, when the bus line provided the first Madden Cruiser. Joe was the "young guy," having joined the Madden Cruiser crew in 1997.

Aside from expertly piloting their famous passenger, Willie and Joe served multiple additional roles aboard the bus. Depending on the day and the situation, one or the other might be a bodyguard, a tour guide, or a concierge.

Maybe because he was the senior guy, Willie seemed to be the one who most often wound up a part of our morning conversations, like the time Coach told us about a stop at a rattlesnake roundup in Texas.

"People would do things with rattlesnakes. They were in a ring, I mean, like a boxing ring. People would get in there and they'd throw the rattlesnakes on them and stuff."

I'm a bit queasy already, so about all I can say is, "Yikes!" But Coach has more details.

"Willie Yarbrough was right there. They would come out and bring the rattlesnake up and say, 'Who wants to hold it?' And I'm like, 'I'm going to have to do this.' But Willie did it. Willie grabs the rattlesnake like they tell him. They put this big rattlesnake in his hand, and the guy said, 'Don't move your thumb. If you move your thumb, they think that's something to eat.' Anyway, Willie started to shake. He took one for the team."

It wasn't just rattlesnakes. Another long-running wildlife topic involved Willie and the creatures seen from Interstate 80 in Wyoming, a regular Madden Cruiser route. Somewhere along the way, Coach told us that Willie was convinced he was seeing gazelles in the grasslands beside the freeway.

Naturally, just about every time we spoke with John while they were rolling through Wyoming, we'd ask about the gazelles. Now, you need to understand that Willie Yarbrough was a serious kind of guy, and apparently, this gazelle fixation was no lark.

"Willie, I swear, he stopped. This is true. He stopped the bus and got out. And he started looking with binoculars and with a camera. There were some big antelope and some little antelope, and some kind that had different horns. And he's taking pictures and looking through the binoculars and swearing that there's some gazelles there."

Steve Bitker suggests, "Probably prairie dogs."

"I don't know what the heck they are, but I mean, he's the only one that got out. He got out and went up to a fence and started with my binoculars. Then he had a camera and he took some shots. So, I don't know. He's building a case for something against someone. And I have no idea what it is he wants. I tell him you guys laugh at him all the time."

That last part is true. One morning, Willie got a chance to defend himself. Coach launched our conversation with another jab at Willie's wildlife search.

"Joe's at the wheel and Willie is in the other seat looking for gazelles."

I pounced. "Can you put Willie on for a second?"

"Hold on a minute. I sure can. Here, Willie."

Willie came on the line, we exchanged greetings, and I asked, "Are you sure those were gazelles?"

Willie replied, *"They were part of the antelope family."*

This is not exactly the version of the story Coach has been telling us, so I toss Willie a life preserver. "Oh, okay. See, John may have misrepresented your position slightly."

Willie answered, *"Well, I think a lot of people did. I've been hearing about this a lot this morning."*

Coach told a lot of people over the years that John Steinbeck's *Travels With Charley* inspired his see-America lifestyle. Instead of a pickup camper and a poodle, John traveled with a big bus and two drivers, but he had the same eye for what was just *off* the road.

"If I'm traveling, if I see lights on at the stadium, I have to stop and watch. One night I stopped in Omaha and watched a minor league baseball game. And in the seventh inning, they had this big raffle for a case of pork and beans. And I swear you would've thought they were giving away a Porsche. It was a case of pork and beans and the guy won and he got so excited and the crowd went crazy and he got his pork and beans. And I said, 'It doesn't make any difference whether it's a car or pork and beans.'"

It's hard to hide a full-sized bus, but Coach usually got preferential parking. Once, in Canton for the Hall of Fame game a few years after his own enshrinement, they wound up right in the middle of the action.

"*They put the goalposts pretty close to the road up on top, and we parked right behind the goalposts. The kicker kicked one and it went right through the goalposts, perfect kick, and FWAP! It whacked the bus. I think that's the first time that we've ever had that.*"

The bus became such a central part of John Madden's persona that the occasional upgrade cycle provided an opportunity to take stock of things. Not long after his 2006 Pro Football Hall of Fame induction, Coach arrived back in the Bay Area, marking his last trip on the current bus. I asked him if he'd thought about what he'd do with it.

"*I don't know. I haven't gotten to that. You know that old thing, 'You take it one game at a time, one day at a time?' I really am taking this one day at a time. You know, the bus is 'The Bus' until the other one gets here and proves that it's ready to run and go. So you don't just jump off and say, 'Hey, we're done with you,' because I don't want to have to go back to it and say, 'Hey, I was just kidding,' because you can hurt the feelings of a bus. I wanted the bus to have all the respect that it normally gets until this new one comes in and proves that it can handle the job, until it gets here and proves it deserves to unseat the other one, to be the starter.*"

My co-anchor Susan wanted to know where old Madden Cruisers go when they're replaced in the starting lineup.

"*I think I'm going to build up buses. I'm going to keep it. I think I'll probably paint it another color and that'll be the 'B' bus. My grandson Jesse calls them 'Grandpa's bus' and 'Grandma's bus' so it'll become a Grandma bus. Then you have the problem: Where are you going to park them? If you build a place to park them, the place that you build costs more than the buses themselves cost. I mean I got a whole bunch of things racing through my mind that I'm not ready to deal with. So I'm just going to let them keep racing.*"

It's a great way to remember John Madden: a guy with a constantly racing mind on a forever-rolling bus.

CHAPTER 9

Tall Tales and Off-Center Observations

Each morning on the radio with John Madden was a one-off. No script, no outline. Often, our conversations were dictated by the news of the day: a big game, a big contract deal, a big-name coach being fired.

But just as often, it was a game of "anything goes," and on many memorable occasions, it was time for John Madden, Master Storyteller, to emerge.

Most of Coach's stories were true, the product of a curious mind spending a lot of time out and about in America. But there were also the Maddenesque flights of fancy. I was startled to realize that some of our listeners took John at his word, unable to sense that his tongue was firmly in his cheek as he spun these yarns. For example, he often spoke of his time on the Iditarod Trail in the annual 1,100-mile mile sled dog race (more about that in Chapter 15, "Man's Best Friend").

Let's go back to a fine April day, when the world's greatest distance runners were lining up to run the Boston Marathon. We jokingly asked Coach if he'd be among them.

"No, I'm gonna skip this year. I found that in 'The Boston'—we don't call it 'marathon,' we just call it 'The Boston'—I found that in 'The Boston,' you can't run back-to-back-to-back-to-back. You run one, then you take a few years off and kind of collect yourself and let your muscles and your tissues and your bones kinda get back to where they want to be and then you go, 'BOOM' and you go run another one."

Cleverly, Coach hasn't actually *said* that he's ever run *any* marathon, let alone "The Boston." He's just imparting insider wisdom.

"It's what we call 'layering' in marathon running. I'm just kind of layering, and in the process of layering, 'The Boston' has been eliminated this year.

It's possible that John Madden, Mythical Marathoner, had just gotten bored.

"It always looks the same. It's slow going at the beginning. You know, we always have a slow start because you kind of have to wait for everyone to get going. And then finally, after about mile six, seven, eight, you finally get a little spread in the deal. The slower runners jam everything up, and you have to wait for all the faster runners to get started and then all the middle runners to get started. And then you finally get to go. And by then, everything's bunched up."

As to why nobody can seem to find a photo of John Madden wearing his Boston Marathon race bib, there's a ready answer.

"I haven't really done those things on the day that everyone else does because they're too crowded. You always do it when there's no one there. That's why a lot of people don't know it, because you run the Boston Marathon later. Like people run it now in April but why not go and run it like I did in October?"

Let's shift our mental image now from a lithe marathon runner to a burly construction worker. One morning, with my morning anchor predecessor Al Hart in the studio for a visit, Coach latched onto a conversation about hobbies.

"You know, guys have different hobbies and they do different things and one of my things has always been a jackhammer."

Of course that demands some explanation, so Al asks, "So you just dig holes with it or what?"

And now John is off and running.

"No, a jackhammer is not to dig holes. A jackhammer is to tear up cement. You dig a hole maybe after *you jackhammer, or something is covered by cement that you don't want covered and you have to get to it. You know, you look at cement or stuff and you know there's something underneath that cement that you have to get to? So you use a jackhammer to get there and then you have to know the style to do it, because weight is important."*

I was once thrilled to be described in print as "lanky." Al Hart could have gained 50 pounds and still qualified for that description. John, at the other end of the body-shape spectrum, seldom missed a chance to make note of that fact.

"Al, you'd have a tough time being a jackhammerer, because the jackhammer would throw you all over the place. You got to get into it. You get it started, then you got to give it that lean and that's why most jackhammer guys have a little something hanging over their belt, 'cause then you hang that over the top and then that gets the jackhammer going. And then usually the back of your pants will fall down to a certain level. You've never seen a jackhammerer that doesn't have the back of his pants down a little."

Now that's a mental picture you can't forget. But we're on a roll, so Al asks Coach if he's available, in case anyone needs a driveway torn up.

"I have my own jackhammer and I travel it. I mean, it's something that not everyone can do and not everyone is interested in. I even got the boots because, see, you have to have steel-toed boots because sometimes the hammer gets away from you. Sometimes it'll bounce up on your foot so you can't wear sneakers."

"That would smart, wouldn't it?" I suggested.

"Well, yeah. I mean that's the thing. You don't know Two-Toe Tony? That's what happened to Tony."

Coach's excursions into fantasy could come out of nowhere. Occasionally, he'd pick up on something that we'd just said on the air, like the morning when sports anchor Steve Bitker wrapped up the pre-Madden sports segment saying, "and in college basketball, Cal beat the University of Albany 95 to 61. The Bears over the Great Danes. Of course. What do you expect? They played like dogs."

My cue to bring in Coach. "Let's move on. John Madden's on the line. Good morning, John." Right out of the gate, Coach was on top of that item.

"It's always great when Cal beats Albany. I've been watching that game for 32 years. Every year we have a tailgate party. Everyone comes over for the Cal-Albany game. You get those Great Dane fans that woofed it up before the game. I know they don't have any fans, but we just bash Albany. Everyone hates Albany. We're all Cal fans, you know, 'Go Bears' and 'Kill Albany' and all that. Nothing I look forward to like this…well, I look forward to Santa Claus. But this is right up there."

A casual sports fan is probably smiling a bit. After all, Cal's rivals are schools like Stanford, USC, and UCLA. The real depth to the gag is this: Cal had *never played a basketball game against the University of Albany before* (and hasn't since). Yet John's delivery was entirely straight-faced.

It seems to me that a really good bullshit artist can deliver the goods even when everyone knows the tale is too good to be true. Longtime Bay Area radio personality Mike Cleary, who spent a few years with Coach as Frank Dill's partner on KNBR's "Frank and Mike Show," knows "funny" when he hears it. Cleary spent years writing "bits" for the morning show, complete with fictional characters and place names.

Cleary's take on John's tall tales: "He was a funny guy. I think he liked doing that kind of thing. He liked that shtick. And he couldn't do it on TV."

That's an important point. For as funny and seemingly off-the-cuff as he could be as an analyst on those NFL broadcasts, television's John Madden was always hemmed in by the game itself. The broadcast rolled along at a predictable pace: action (called by Pat Summerall or Al Michaels), analysis by John, repeat, repeat, repeat.

Only on his morning Bay Area radio appearances could Coach go anywhere he wanted, like a jazz soloist improvising within a given key and time signature. I'm a little shocked that I just compared John Madden to a jazz musician, but I think it works. He knew the rules of morning radio and understood that pushing their limits was where the magic happened.

The same impish instinct that led Coach to concoct these journeys into alternate reality sometimes led him to stick a sharp needle into any nearby object. In this case, it was the relentless hyping of "Doppler radar" by every TV station weather department in the country.

"Is it one Doppler? Do we all use the same Doppler or do we all have our own Doppler?"

I've again been dragged to the edge of Smarty-Pants Land. I can launch into a windy explanation of what Doppler radar is, how it works, where Doppler went to college, and so on…but John Madden will keep up the attack anyway.

"Does KCBS have a Doppler?" he demands.

"Oh yeah, we got Doppler," I reply.

"We've got our own Doppler?" Coach persists.

At this point, my head is whirling with the thought that the radio station's vaunted credibility is on the line. Can I possibly admit that we don't *really* have our very own Doppler weather radar (and would it matter if we didn't)?

Traffic anchor Ron Lyons, himself a veteran Bay Area radio personality, tries to float his own line of B.S. "We have our own personally autographed Doppler," he suggests.

John is having none of this.

"I don't know. I don't know. This is what I always wonder. You hear, 'The Doppler says,' but I don't know if there's just one Doppler that everyone uses or if there's a lot of different Dopplers that a lot of different people use, or if everyone that uses a Doppler has their own Doppler."

Well, we *could* have been talking about the ins and outs of the NFL salary cap. It might have been easier to explain.

Many of my favorite chats with Coach involved his ability to look at the world and see the weird in it. One November morning found him in New York City the day after the New York Marathon. He told us he was familiar with the post-marathon scene in the Big Apple.

"For about two days you'll see people wearing bags around, because you know when they finish, they give them those garbage bags. There's that, and then I want

to know, 'How do you pick up someone?' Someone says, 'I'm going to run 26 miles,' so they start 26 miles away. They end up in Central Park. And then where do you park to pick them up? And then they get lost. Oh, yeah. You'll find people flopping around, sleeping on the benches."

He has me giggling at the thought, so I jump in. "So there's some woman who ran 26 miles and her husband was supposed to meet her in that neighborhood. And he's still driving around and she's walking around who-knows-where?"

"Right, and so they can't find her. They forget or whatever. But I mean, that's happened every year. Imagine in New York City trying to say, 'Yeah, yeah, you go run 26 miles. I'll pick you up in a few hours.' Doesn't work."

This probably should have been enough about the aftermath of the New York Marathon but Coach always had more stories to tell.

"I remember years ago, Bobby Beathard was the general manager of the Washington Redskins. Bobby and I played in college together and Bobby ran in the marathon in the morning. It was a 4:00 PM game in New York. He ran in the marathon in the morning, and he didn't bring any money with him, so he couldn't get from the end of the marathon to the stadium."

Probably not something that would happen in today's NFL, but John's stories could reach well into the past. We've already established that Coach is familiar with marathon training, so I ask, "That wasn't the year you ran the marathon, was it?"

"No, no, no, no. I didn't run it that year because I had to work. Sometimes I would run it like two weeks before. Kind of get loosened up a little."

The image of John Madden on a racing bicycle is hard to conjure up, but he knew that I'm an avid cyclist. Furthermore, the way the time zones work, each day's stage of the Tour de France would often end just before John joined us at 8:15 AM Pacific time. One July morning, Steve Bitker updated the Tour de France results ahead of John's segment. Coach got right into it.

"I was just thinking about that Tour de France. Over all the years that they've been racing bikes, why can't they make the seats more comfortable? Maybe you're

not supposed to sit. Is that what the deal is with those bikes? I mean, in furniture in years gone by, seats were hard. And we've gotten past that. We had hard, narrow seats in cars, we went from horses and buggies to cars and all that. Why can't they do something for bicycle seats?"

At this point, I did way too much explaining of why racing bicycle seats are the way they are and how you get used to them and on and on. Thankfully, Steve rescued me, saying, "You know, John should do the Tour de France. He's done the Iditarod. He's done marathons. Why don't you do the Tour someday, John?"

For once, John was bowing out of a chance to tell a tall tale about an athletic event. He was emphatic.

"No, no, no, no, no, no. The seats are too hard and the tires are too thin."

So, no bike racing for Coach, and not much interest in winter sports either.

"I'll be honest. I don't get a lot about this Winter Olympics. I don't understand them. I don't know what they're doing. I don't know how they judge them. They do something and throw numbers at you and you're supposed to nod knowingly and heck, you can't have any 'knowingly.'"

I took the bait and rose in defense of curling, which had captivated me. No sale.

"Enough of the curling. It's crazy. And it just sounds funny. I mean, when you say 'curling,' you know that there's a joke coming later. If you say, 'the men's downhill,' you know that's the men's downhill, everyone gets it. But if you say, 'curling,' ha, ha, ha, are you kidding me? Is that a sport?"

That conversation led to an invitation from a local curling club to come give it a try. I showed up for a "Learn to Curl" event, found it to be a lot harder than it looks on TV, and reported this back to John. He remained unconvinced.

Coach loved to play with words and he had a keen ear for how others used them. Here's a short example. Maybe you've tossed out the standard "How's it going?" and had someone reply, "I'm well, thank you." Not sure about you, but I always feel a little inadequate in that moment because *my* response to the same question is always, "I'm good," or on a really fine day, "I'm great, thanks!" Grammarians are cringing, I suspect.

So here's how John dealt with the uncertainty one fine morning. I rattled off my usual introduction, "All right, John Madden here now, sponsored by BMW/San Francisco. How are you this morning, Coach?"

"I'm very good. Very good. Doing well. Actually, I'm not sure if it's 'good' or 'well.' So I threw both of them in."

Covered all the bases, didn't he?

Wordplay could spin wildly out of control once Coach got on a roll. We were discussing the future Pro Football Hall of Fame offensive lineman Larry Allen one day when I brought up his college days at Sonoma State University, whose athletic teams were then known as the Cossacks. John immediately replied.

"What'd you say they are? The 'hassocks'? What's a 'hassock'?"

I tried to set the record straight, saying, "No, no it's the Cossacks."

"Well, a Cossack's like a hassock, right? I mean, what is *a Cossack? Is it an animal? Vegetable? Mineral?"*

A game of "20 Questions" has just broken out, and John is running away with it. I try to tell him that a hassock is a piece of furniture, but he's not having it.

"No, no, no, no. A hassock, I think, is something you wear."

Before I can explain that I think he's now referring to a "cassock," Steve Bitker further muddies the waters. "No," Steve says, "Hasek's a hockey goalie. Dominic Hasek." Coach is undeterred.

"No, I think a hassock is something that religious men wear, that looks like a dress. I think that's a hassock…or a cassock."

There'll be a test on this material later.

Football is the sport that made John Madden famous, but he'd been a pretty good baseball player as well, solid enough to star in high school and play at the college level too. So maybe it makes sense that some of his memorable moments came out of deep left field.

"One of my things in life, I always wanted to be a sumo wrestler. You know, one of those things where, if you could be anything? Because then you could eat as much as you want. I've never had anyone say, 'You got to get your weight up.' You know what I mean? But if you were a sumo wrestler, you'd have to get your weight up. So someone would say, 'Hey, Madden, you got to get your weight up!' I'll tell you, I know how to get my weight up. I know how to get my weight up better than anyone in this universe."

A guy who could convince people (well, at least *some* people) that he'd mushed the Iditarod Trail or run the Boston Marathon had to be equipped with a pretty vivid imagination. One of my favorite Madden flights of fancy was his notion of what happened at the Pro Football Hall of Fame in Canton, Ohio, after everyone went home at night.

"I was thinking what would be really cool, and you don't know if it doesn't happen, but I was wondering if at the end of the day in the Hall of Fame, with all the busts in there and then, you know, there's the visitors and people going through the museum and stuff. Then they all go home, then all the workers go home. And after the last guy walks through, I wonder if the busts talk to each other. Wouldn't that be cool? Just think of all those guys. George Halas or Vince Lombardi. Reggie White. All of them just having conversations."

This chat happened before John's own Hall of Fame induction, so I asked, "What if they put you near Hank Stram?" Stram was the longtime coach of the Kansas City Chiefs, a guy with a sideline persona every bit as big as John Madden's and a fierce rival. But while John rambled around in an often-untucked shirt and eschewed a sport coat, Stram usually looked like he'd just stepped out of an upscale men's clothing store.

Maybe Coach was mellowing as his days coaching in the midst of the bitter Raiders-Chiefs rivalry slipped farther into the past, but the idea of his bronze bust and Stram's chatting it up after dark didn't faze him.

"No, I'd have conversations with Hank. I'd be like, 'Hey, remember when they had rats in your locker room?' It would be great. No one really knows if the busts do that. So, you can't say that they don't do it, can you? That excites me."

It is true that our daily conversation happened at an hour when a few people might still have been eating breakfast. It is equally true that Coach didn't care about grossing people out.

This story happened after he'd taken a rare trip to a National Hockey League game. I can't tell from the available records, but it might have been to see the *other* John Madden play. That John Madden was a hard-working forward who got to hoist the Stanley Cup three times during his career and whose jersey had a place of pride aboard the Madden Cruiser.

Our John Madden couldn't remember a lot about the hockey game he saw, but he did deliver some memorable reporting.

"I was right by the penalty box, so I got involved in watching the guys in the penalty box because they have a bucket in there. Now, here's what I was watching because it was right in front of me. I don't know if anyone knows this. They got a bucket in there where they keep the pucks, because they've got to keep those pucks cold, so they keep the pucks in the bucket. Now, when the official comes by and he needs a new puck, he gives the guy the old puck and there's this official guy who's the official guy of the pucks and the bucket and also the official of the penalty box. You see what I'm saying?"

It's starting to sound like a bit of a shaggy dog story, but Coach is really energized as he's telling it.

"So this guy takes the puck out of the bucket and gives it to the official. So then a guy gets a penalty. Now he comes in there, he's sweating and stuff, right? Now that's the only bucket in the penalty box. And I swear this is true. I'm not making this up. He thinks it's a spit bucket. So the official is looking out toward the ice, then the guy who's in the penalty box is spitting in the puck bucket. But the guy, the official, doesn't know it. Then he reaches his hand in there to get a puck and he gives it to the other official. But the guy that's in the penalty box was just spitting in the puck bucket."

Coach was a keen observer of the human condition and seldom missed a chance to spot the little fibs and social conventions with which we surround ourselves.

"You know how everyone says, 'If you didn't know how old you were, how old would you feel?' And everyone says that they would feel younger than their real age. You know the one I'm talking about. I mean, they're 40 years old. Ask them how they feel today. Everyone feels 25."

Most "Mornings with Madden" produced a laugh or two, but there was often a healthy dose of insight. All those hours and miles crisscrossing America on his bus gave him the opportunity to do some thinking. He was somewhere in Wyoming one morning, taken by all the open space.

"I think that's what makes this whole country work. You know, the people who live in the big cities, they couldn't live out here. And you get the people that live out in the middle of nowhere on farms and ranches and stuff, if they would go to the big city, they couldn't live there. So because of that, it makes the whole thing work. I mean, big city people would be scared to death out here. And farmers and ranchers and people that live in these areas would be scared to death in the big city."

Every now and again, I'd bumble my way into something good with Coach. This exchange happened on a Friday when I'd lost track of the day of the week, thinking it was only Thursday. Coach had some advice.

"Always get ready for things before they become the thing. You know, like people say, 'Hey, man, don't live in the past.' So that's a bad thing. Living in the past is a bad thing. So then you know, your alternative, if you're not going to live in the past, is you can live in the here and now. Which is a way to do it."

"Live in the moment," I offered.

"See, that's easy because you have *to do that. I mean, you have no alternative there. Or you can be thinking all the time of the future, living in the future, going ahead like, 'Live today like it's tomorrow.'"*

Yes, I know the standard admonition is "Live today like there's no tomorrow," but John Madden didn't live a standard life, and he didn't give standard advice. That said, 20 years after he delivered that line, I'm still trying to figure how to live today like it's tomorrow!

CHAPTER 10

Golf, Madden Style

OVER THE MANY YEARS I WORKED WITH COACH, I NEVER MANAGED TO GET out on the golf course with him. I wish I'd had the chance, and here's why: by all accounts, John Madden is among the few people ever to play golf without letting the game frustrate him.

Sports reporter Kevin Radich is a solid player. He's a great partner on the course. And he's never played with anyone quite like John Madden.

"Madden was Madden," recalls Radich. "He didn't give a shit about golf. I mean, he'd hit a ball in the weeds and his thing was FIDO: 'Forget it and drive on.' He wouldn't spend two minutes looking for the ball."

John Madden was not the golfer who'd have a good front nine and fall apart on the back nine. Radich says, "He'd play eight holes or nine holes and then leave. That was it. You'd never finish a round of golf."

Radich's candid description of Madden's game: "It was bad. But you know, once in a while, he did hit a shot. And he'd say, 'Blind squirrel finds an acorn' or something like that. I learned to appreciate his attitude. 'I'm not good. I don't care. I'm just going to have fun and just rip it.'"

Coach's "grip it and rip it" attitude didn't dull his curiosity for the minutiae of the sport. One spring day, he veered away from a conversation we were having about how video games are produced (a Madden veer didn't need any logic or pretext behind it; it just happened).

"I got some golf clubs for my birthday and I just opened them up and here is my dilemma. I haven't played with these irons yet—they're new irons. But I got a 10 iron," said Coach.

Right on top of my game, I replied, "a 10?"

"Right. I have no idea what a 10 iron is. So I have a 10 iron and a W, which is a wedge, and an SW, which is a sand wedge. So does it go 9, 10, wedge, sand wedge?"

Made sense to me, so I tossed in, "That's what I think."

"That's what I would think too. But then I was talking to Sam at the bakery and he said it goes 9, wedge, 10, sand wedge."

Part of me is starting to calculate how many of our listeners truly want to know where a 10 iron fits in a new set of clubs. But the curious know-it-all part of me thinks maybe he can help. "Do they have the degrees of loft marked on the clubs?" I asked, while sports anchor Steve Bitker, perhaps seeing a way out of this, offered, "John, I think for golfers like us, it really doesn't make much difference."

We've already established that John Madden isn't much of a golfer. But he doesn't like unfinished business or mysteries.

"I mean, when do you use a 10 iron? When do you use something that there hasn't been one of before? I mean, when do *you pull out your 10 iron? 'Okay, here's a shot I'm going to pull out my 10 iron for.' What's that shot?"*

Never having come across a 10 iron at that point in my life and loath to sound like any kind of golf expert, I tried to wrap the bit up and move on. Nothing doing.

"I don't mean to go on too long here," Coach continued (of course he didn't really mean that), *"but if you never had a 10 iron and now you finally get a 10 iron, you have no history. You know, you can't say, 'Well, yeah, every time I play golf, I use a 10 iron when I get in this situation.'"*

The historical record does not indicate whether John Madden ever worked that new 10 iron into his game. The record *does* suggest that if he did, it didn't help much.

The Bay Area, blessed with some world-class golf courses, has produced many terrific golfers. Coach was not among them, but that didn't stop him from entering the hallowed grounds of places like San Francisco's Olympic Club. His day-after report went like this.

"It was kind of foggy over there and it was just like growing up in Daly City. It was just like I went back to my childhood. It was great, except I can't play. I mean, I'm the worst player and now I have the data to prove it."

In a typically Maddenesque twist, he intentionally mispronounced the word "data." He said "dater," and then went on to say it over and over again.

"I got data. Data! If you put all the data together, you have to come up with this: I'm just a loser. Because what we did is, we had a foursome. Right? So we changed teams every six holes. So the first six holes I play with Mike Hannah, we lose. The second six holes, I play with Dr. Hannah, we lose. The third six holes, I play with Mike Madden, we lose. So the only constant in this data that we put into the computer was that among the four players, there was only one guy that lost all the time. And that was me."

"Big John, the loser," I offered.

"Yeah, I'm just terrible. And you get to a point, if you're terrible and you care, then that equals frustration. So the key is you have to not *care, because if you're terrible and then you don't care, then you don't get frustrated. So I just took all my money out 'cause I didn't win anything. I lost everything. I mean, they got greenies, side bets, all that stuff. I just put my money on the table. I said, 'Here, have at it.'"*

In the midst of one of our many golf conversations, we learned that Coach's philosophy about lost balls went a little deeper than simple expedience. He saw that errant ball as an enemy.

"I don't like to look for golf balls, you know, so I have one trick that helps if I hit one that I don't like. If it goes bad in some place, I get mad at the ball, so I won't go and get the ball and I don't want anyone else looking for it either. I just call it a FIDO. Forget it. Drive on."

Coach distilled golf to its essence one morning, uttering a phrase that those of us afflicted by the game should probably have stitched onto our golf bags: *"In golf, anytime you think you got it, you don't."*

But as bad of a golfer as he professed to be, John embraced the inherent weirdness in the sport.

"There are things you do on a golf course, like talking to a golf ball, and things you wear to play golf you would never do anyplace else."

I think we've already established that Coach didn't exactly take the stuffy country club approach to the game. He also didn't have much patience for the banalities you often hear out on the course. His son Joe tells me that his dad's version of the hackneyed "Hit 'em straight" was to tell someone about to tee off, "Hit a house!"

And phony cheerleading didn't work too well for him either.

"You ever play golf with the kind of guy, someone that'll have either a good hole or a bad hole on like the first or second hole. There will always be someone to say something like, 'Well, there's a lot of golf left to be played.' Of course there is. We just played two and there are 16 more!"

One morning, Steve Bitker had a story about Victor Schwamkrug, a professional golfer who could crush it off the tee but apparently didn't have much more to his game. The story said the guy used a low-lofted driver with which he could carry the ball 330 yards in the air. Coach was underwhelmed.

"Yeah. I mean, you know, then what? That's the whole thing with the long drive. Like Dominic, that's the way he plays. He thinks that golf is a driving contest and if he out-drives everyone, he thinks he won the hole. He'll be lying one with his drive and then, you know, six shots later, he gets it in the hole. So he gets a seven but he out-drove everyone."

Once Coach got started on his buddy and long-time target Dominic Mercurio, he often kept on rolling.

"And then there's the way he takes the tee out of the ground. When he hits a long drive, he bends over and kind of snaps the tee out like, 'Take that. Your turn.'"

From his perspective, Dominic recalls rounds with Coach would involve some low-level wagering, a fair amount of woofing, and even a few practical jokes, like the time Dominic found some novelty stink capsules and deployed them in John's golf cart.

One morning, I got an email from Dominic, alerting me to a big moment that had occurred while he and Coach were playing a few days earlier. They'd gone out to get in a quick nine holes when it happened. I prompted John for the details.

"So we play the first. Nothing happens. We're not bothering anyone. We play the second hole, nothing happens. Go up to the third hole. And Dominic says, 'You know, if you're ever going to get a hole in one, you're going to get it on this hole.'"

Which Dominic proceeded to do.

"I've been around golf. I'm not any good. But I was a caddie and all my life I've played and obviously I've never had a hole in one, but also I've never seen one. That was the first one that I've ever seen."

There was more to the story. It turns out Dominic had broken out one of the commemorative balls bearing the Pro Football Hall of Fame logo that the Madden family had given out at John's Hall of Fame induction. I still have my sleeve of those balls and would never consider actually playing one.

"I couldn't believe when he pulled it out. It was that Hall of Fame Callaway ball. So he hit that ball into the hole when he shouldn't have even been using it."

We're not finished with this story, because now John and Dominic think they need to play a full 18-hole round in order for Dominic's ace to be legitimate. As best I can tell, a 9-hole round would have sufficed, but I wasn't there that day to make the case.

"So now we're out there scrambling. Now we've got to get through. You know, we were just playing a little leisurely golf. And now we got to go get the score card. We got to fill in the whole thing. And we have to make it an official round, which we did. I'm the witness. I have to attest. He had to do the paperwork and then I told him he had to go to the bar and say, 'Okay, drinks for everyone!' But they don't do that anymore. They put you in a computer, they register you, and then everyone in the club gets one free drink that month or some doggone thing."

As we've established, the hidebound traditions of golf didn't mean much to John Madden. He wasn't the only golfer who thought it was time to shake things up. I thought maybe we were telling John something he didn't know when I brought up the Alternative Golf Association. It was the brainchild of a group of Bay Area movers and shakers who thought golf needed some goosing.

Turned out Coach was already inside the ropes on this one.

"Scott McNealy has something that he was working on. He's part of this. I was at a dinner with him and he was explaining it to me. He has a little money."

Coach was referring to the Silicon Valley billionaire whose son Maverick is now a journeyman on the PGA Tour. Of course, being "a journeyman on the PGA Tour" can pay pretty well; Maverick McNealy is approaching $8,000,000 in career earnings.

John may not have been as good a golfer as Maverick McNealy (or Scott McNealy, who's carried a low-single-digit handicap at times). But he had a clear view of the boom-and-bust cycles that seemed to plague the game.

"You know, there was a time when everyone was taking up golf, especially younger people. And so there were more golfers than there were golf courses or opportunities to play. So then they started building all these golf courses. Then it went the other way. Now there's more golf courses than there are golfers. And so they have to do something with this excess golf capacity."

That got the economics lesson out of the way. I was curious as to what Coach thought about some of the ideas being proposed by the Alternative Golf Association in the name of making golf more fun for duffers.

I started in, "John, we've spoken before about your game. Of the following things, which would you be willing to do or have you done in the past? Let's start with spraying Pam, the cooking spray, on the head of your driver [this would supposedly lead to longer, straighter drives]?"

"No, I haven't done it, but if I knew that it would have done something that would help me, I would have done it."

I continued, "All right. Number two, tee one up in the fairway?"

"No, I've never done that."

"Would you do it in the future?"

"Oh, probably."

Now, nobody who plays with me would mistake me for a member of the Rules Committee, but this seemed a bit much. "I have trouble with that. It doesn't seem right, you know?" I replied. At this point, Coach reconsidered, but not because he was concerned about the sanctity of the sport.

"Yeah, there's a problem. What you do is you count your bend-overs and you try to eliminate bend-overs. So teeing up just adds bend-overs. I mean, the next thing would be to just eliminate all bend-overs."

We agreed that the idea of replacing the sand wedge with a "hand wedge," allowing renegade golfers to toss their shots from bunkers on to putting greens, seemed excessive. Then I brought up the "mulligan," the outside-the-rules custom of allowing a golfer to re-do one shot every nine holes or 18 holes (in my family foursome, we call this a "breakfast ball," though we generally tee off after noon).

"I don't like that. I mean if you really can't do it, a mulligan is not going to help you. If you really could play, you wouldn't need a mulligan. And if you can't play, a mulligan is not going to help you. What are you going to do, take that lousy swing that you have and groove it?"

Coach might not have had much of a golf game himself, but he loved to watch the sport on TV and in person. Many of our conversations centered around golf's "majors," the four tournaments that golfers focus on as the pinnacle of their sport.

One morning, we were joined by Tom Watson, the golf legend who won three of the four majors during his career, including five British Open victories. Watson was promoting a charity appearance in the Bay Area and the conversation quickly turned into a Watson-Madden Mutual Admiration Society meeting.

Coach noted how well Watson was playing, and the veteran pro replied, "I've had a good year. I can't complain. I've driven the ball particularly well, and that always sets up the rest of the hole. It's like a kickoff runback. If you can run it back to the 40 or 45 yard line, boy, that sets up your offense."

The ol' football coach jumped right on that.

"It's a lot easier to do everything. I mean, if you can drive and get yourself in a good position, that's like being able to run the ball so then you can play-action pass

and you can set up your whole other game. It's the same type of deal: if you can do one thing, then that makes it so you can do a lot of other things well."

John may not have had Tom Watson's silky swing, but he also didn't go to the other extreme. One July morning, his segment was preceded by a commercial for the American Century Championship, the annual celebrity tournament at Lake Tahoe.

"I'm just thinking about that celebrity golf championship. To be interesting, I think you either have to be real, real good in golf or real, real bad. And what would that tournament do without Charles Barkley? I mean, you wonder how a guy who has to be a good athlete, he was a great professional basketball player for years, how he can have—and you know, I'm not a guy to talk about a golf swing— but Charles Barkley's golf swing is ugly. He starts out, then he has something else, then he has something that kind of goes crazy in the middle of it and then he has something else and then he goes back and then a little more crazy and then he hits the ball."

Anyone who's ever taken a golf lesson has just had their mind blown. Are we talking about the stance, the grip, the takeaway, the follow-through, or what?

"You know, we really never look in the mirror at our golf swings either, although we can get them on video, I guess. But sometimes we think, 'Boy, that's really an ugly swing.' And then you think, 'What do you think you do?'"

Coach wants to make it clear. He's not really mocking Barkley. In fact, there's a sort of morbid respect.

"That's my point. If you're not real, real, real good, then be real bad if you want to be interesting. If you're mediocre or you're right there in the middle, you're not interesting and no one pays any attention to you. But if you're really good or really bad, then they love you one way or another."

Barkley's golf game came up on another occasion, when I asked Coach to imagine a mythical match between him and Sir Charles. "If you and Charles Barkley teed off," I asked, "who'd have to spot whom how many strokes?"

"He would have to give me strokes. I don't play with anyone that doesn't give me strokes. There's no one in the whole world that is a worse golfer than me. It

would be a thrill for me to have to give strokes, but I'm just thinking about it right now. I don't think I ever have or I ever would, even with Charles."

John had great respect for great golfers and admitted he thought he might be able to pick up a few tips. During the 2012 U.S. Open, played at the same Olympic Club course where Coach had managed to lose three matches in one 18-hole round, he shared his game plan.

"The thing that's a pretty good trick is to go to the practice tees and then you can watch a bunch of golfers at one time and then kind of follow them after that. They usually go from the practice tees to the putting green to the first tee. That's an interesting little loop there. What you're trying to do is copy. And that's what I did. One time I went out there and I figured, 'I'm going to find out what a golf swing is. I'm going to find out where they get their distance because, you know, I'm a coach and that's what I do.' So I went out there…and I didn't learn a thing. I remember I went out specifically to watch Fred Couples. I was going to study Fred Couples, who I think has the greatest-looking swing ever. But I mean, me trying to be like Fred Couples, when you really think of it, is stupid. Just dumb."

Because the coach in him wouldn't let him stop trying to figure it out, John made it an annual habit to hang around the driving range during the AT&T Pebble Beach Pro-Am, the tournament contested within a few miles of his waterfront home-away-from-home in Carmel. He always figured he'd spot the secret to better golf.

"Those guys have such nice swings. A friend of mine, [PGA pro] Mike Hulbert, was hitting some balls and someone handed him a driver and said, 'Try to hit it to the wall.' So he said, 'Okay, I will.' And he hit it to the wall. And I was thinking, 'Okay, now he's really going to come out of his shoes.' But they don't swing any differently. When they swing hard, it's their normal swing. They have a swing that is grooved and it's the same swing all the time. I try to analyze where it is that they get their power, and I can't find any single spot. So therefore I realize that's what the answer is: it's just a total swing. It has nothing to do with any one thing, you know, like takeaway, or how you come up or when you come down, point of impact, follow-through, any of those things. It's none of those things."

True. Because they're not playing the same game we hackers are playing.

"In golf, any time you think you got it, you don't. And then you always play a little better the first time back when you haven't played. But then you'll make up for it for the next time that you play."

I'm thinking the coach in John Madden will be able to explain this, even if he's not much of a golfer himself. I ask, "Now, why is that? Is it because I'm thinking too much?"

"Probably you groove your bad habits, and then thoughts jump into your head. You know, bad thoughts jump in your head. You remember the last time you did this or you start doing something and then you try to compensate for it, and then you don't know how to compensate for it because you're not experienced enough. So then the thing just gets worse. And then now you're playing with a compensated thing that's worse and worse. And it just goes on and on. I mean, it's the most frustrating game there is. But if you're no good and you're never going to be any good, then the only thing you can do is get to a point where you don't care. Because if you're no good and you care, I'll guarantee you that equals complete frustration."

Coach *did* think there might be a key to the golf kingdom. Of course, so do a lot of other golfers, else the golf-equipment industry wouldn't be the multi-billion dollar behemoth that it is.

"All these reps are here, the TaylorMades, the Nikes, the Callaways, the whole thing. The reps are bringing all these clubs to try and I swear, there'll be 10, 15, 20 yards difference in a club. They'll go, 'Here, try this driver.' I mean I saw a guy try a driver with some sort of yellow shaft on it and that thing went 10 or 15 extra yards. So equipment? There's something to that. And there's something to the golf balls, too."

Most of those who catch the golf bug try to shake it at some point, only to learn that the darned game just won't leave your system. Do we ever really become ex-golfers?

"I mean, all you have to do is put the club on the ball and I just can't do it. I've been playing so little golf right now that I don't know if I actually play anymore. You know, like someone says, 'Are you playing?' and I don't know if I'm a golfer. Well, I never really was a golfer, but I don't know if I'm playing anymore."

And here we reach the crux of the matter. Is a guy with a set of golf clubs "a golfer," or is he "a guy who plays golf?" I think Coach saw himself as a guy who could find some fun on a golf course, but never wanted to let the game consume him. That's not to say that he was totally at peace with golf, a game that seems to have been designed from the start to drive its participants crazy.

"There's so many things that don't make sense. 'You got to swing easy, you got to keep your head down.' Football players always keep their heads up and hit hard. So it's always the opposite of everything you know. And why do you have to play 18 holes? I mean, why can't you play 11 holes and that's it? But you have to play 18. And that takes four or five hours. Take tennis. If you're bad in tennis, it's over quickly. If you're bad in golf, it takes a long, long time to play bad."

I'll close the chapter with a memorable bit of Madden golf philosophy. One morning, former Raiders tight end Raymond Chester joined us on the air. Chester's post-football career saw him running the Lake Chabot public golf course in Oakland for many years. John was happy to chat with his former player, but made it clear that one part of their long relationship was out of bounds.

"Ray is a guy that you never want to play with because he has his own golf course. That's one of my rules. My dad told me that a long time ago. 'Never, never play golf with a guy that has his own course.'"

CHAPTER 11

Players and Coaches Are People, Too

OCCASIONALLY, OVER THE YEARS, I'D MEET SOMEONE FROM OUTSIDE THE Bay Area who didn't have the good fortune to hear our John Madden conversations on KCBS. At some point, John's name would come up, I'd confess that I worked with him, and the response would be something on the lines of, "Oh, so you do a sports talk show!"

That's definitely *not* what we did. I'm defining "sports talk" as that show where one or two guys (almost always guys) deliver "hot takes," provocative comments, and within any given two-hour period it's almost certain that either one of the hosts or a caller will demand the firing of the local head coach and/or the trading away of whichever player has fallen out of immediate favor.

Coach didn't dig that. His affinity for people who coached and played prevented him from objectifying them. They might have been famous multimillionaires, but John still saw star athletes for what they were before they got rich.

"It's funny how because someone is an athlete, people think that gives them the right to tell them what to do with their life and career. And I know that they're public people, but the key word is that they're people.*"*

His empathy grew even deeper when the person in question was a coach. John knew full well that coaching could be a highly transitory gig, but he knew what it was like when a head coach got let go.

"People sometimes just talk about coaches like they're pawns or something. 'Oh, you know, just fire the coach, get rid of that coach.' And they don't realize that they're people and they have families and they have assistant coaches. It affects a lot of people. You have to move and heal and uproot and all those things, and that's the life of a coach. It's a very difficult deal."

Think back to the last story you saw about a player being traded. Did the story say anything about the player's family? It's something John thought about and expressed often.

"With players, sometimes we tend to think that they're pawns, that you just pick up a guy and, like playing Monopoly, you put them over here and pick up someone else and put them over there. You know, checkers, you jump a guy and take his thing. We have to remember that they're people and they have the same things that all of us do. I mean, they have families and kids and kids in school and things like that."

In the summer of 2001, aging Tampa Bay Devil Rays (the franchise didn't drop the "Devil" from its name for another seven years) first baseman Fred McGriff was traded to the Chicago Cubs. McGriff resisted. Coach sympathized.

"Tampa is where he's from and he got a no-trade clause in his contract for a reason and they gave it to him and now he's exercising that option that they gave him. Maybe he just doesn't want to go live in Chicago and maybe his wife doesn't want to go or maybe the kids don't want to go. And just because Chicago has a better stadium, when you look at the whole thing and a person's life, that's not always a reason. I mean, if some place in Tampa had a better radio setup than KCBS, you probably wouldn't go there."

With no disrespect to the fine people of Tampa, St. Petersburg, and in fact all of Hillsborough County and Pinellas County, he was right about that.

There's a description often heard in the world of sports: "a players' coach." It can be a rather squishy term, but it's generally understood that there's a spectrum from "stern disciplinarian" to "players' coach." I'm sure there were guys who played for John Madden who didn't think much of him, but I never met one of them. John respected his players and treated them as grownups. His Three Commandments (be on time, pay attention, play like hell when I tell you to) pretty much made up his rulebook.

It's not as though Coach was Mr. Warm and Fuzzy, but he genuinely cared for his players. Long after his coaching days were over, our radio conversations would often veer toward a hard truth of competitive sports: fans, owners, and, yes, broadcasters are often pretty harsh in their assessment of an athlete's performance.

Even fan favorites can find themselves on the outs. All it takes is a bad game or two. In San Francisco, we had a front row seat to the Tim Lincecum phenomenon. The slightly built pitcher with the unique delivery was a fan favorite from the time he made the Giants Major League roster after only a year in the minor leagues. But in 2010, he had a couple of rough outings, and some San Francisco fans booed him.

"You know, the word 'fan' means that you're a fanatic and you really become a fanatic, the good and bad of that. And Lincecum is a guy—I mean, he's a Cy Young Award winner, he's the face of the Giants. Everyone says, instead of 'Let's go to the Giants game,' it's, 'Let's go to the Lincecum game.' And then when things don't go well for him and he gets knocked out and he has two bad outings in a row, they get a little frustrated and usually with frustration, they start to boo."

Never having stood on a baseball mound in front of 42,000 fans and tried to hit the outside corner with a slider, it seemed reasonable to ask if pro athletes were aware of the boos.

"Oh yeah. They say they don't hear it. They hear everything. Everything. And then you know one of the deals about a real pro is he's able to shut it out. But no,

they hear everything. I mean, if you were to ask Tim Lincecum right now, today, he knows he was booed. A guy like him would probably say, 'Yeah, I heard them booing and I was with them. I was booing myself.'"

If Coach had a soft spot for players, he had an especially soft spot for the ones he figured didn't get enough respect. Not coincidentally, these would be the guys who played the positions he played: offensive line in football and catcher in baseball. A mid-February conversation focused on the start of baseball spring training, which traditionally began with the pitchers and catchers reporting before the rest of the squad.

"I'm an old catcher, you know. So as an old catcher, you got to stand up for them. Like offensive linemen, they never get a lot of credit. Catchers were the only guys that used to be able to wear their cap backwards. That was kind of your badge of honor. I mean, they call the stuff you wore, the equipment, they call it 'the tools of ignorance.' And then your badge of honor was that you could wear your cap backwards because you were a catcher. Now everyone wears a cap backwards."

The ol' catcher was on a roll. Next target: position players who showed up early for spring training.

"It used to be pitchers and catchers first. A catcher'd go down there and maybe someone would talk to them for a newspaper article, maybe they'd put them on television. And now the other guys show up. I think Jason Giambi's down there, isn't he? What the heck? He's not a catcher. He's not a pitcher. These guys. They're going to show everyone that they're really excited about getting started. They can't wait. So they go down there a day early. It's, 'Whoa, oh boy, this guy's ready this year!' Catchers get no respect. It's like bad bodies. That's why I started that group, the Brotherhood of United Bad Bodies of America, BUBBA. It's the same type of thing. You got to start a group for catchers so they get more respect."

While we're on the subject of respect, let's head in a different direction. There was the time a well-paid baseball star served notice that he felt disrespected and wanted to be traded, presumably to a place where he'd get the respect he felt he deserved.

"I don't know where that thing comes from. I mean, there are so many things in sports and words that come up that I really hate. 'MY team' is one of them. 'MY

game' is another one. And 'respect' and 'disrespect' is another one. I mean, how much money—I think they're paying him $10 million, aren't they? I think that's showing $10 million worth of respect. That's heavy respect."

Otis Redding wrote the '60's hit song "Respect" and Aretha Franklin turned it into her signature tune. The word meant plenty to them, but maybe not so much to Coach.

"That's a word that doesn't mean anything. You just throw it around, like, 'They don't show me respect.' We get the same thing in football. All these teams, you know, the Giants were saying, 'We don't get any respect.' The Ravens said, 'We don't get any respect.' Where does the respect come from? Do you pour respect? Do you show it? Do you throw it? How do you put respect on?"

Another thing that really bothered Coach was the tendency of fans and pundits to focus on who lost a game or series rather than on who won.

"I think that we don't seem to want to praise the winners or talk about how well the winners played or what the winners did. But we want to say, 'Who do we blame? We have a game here and it was a big game. Who do we blame?'"

He'd been out of coaching for many, many years, but John couldn't shake one of the aspects of the coaching life that really bothered him.

"I've always thought that everyone ought to have a record. You know how in sports, if you're a coach, everyone knows how you're doing. I mean, they don't have to come up and say, 'How're you doing?' Read the paper, the paper tells how you're doing, because they always print your record. Every coach, they put his name, comma, record, comma, and then go on. And so you always know where he stands and what he's doing. And that's baseball, basketball, all the sports. I've always thought that should apply to everyone. In other words, if you go to a lawyer, you ought to know what his record is. You know, like, 'What's your record?' You go to a doctor, you ought to have his record. You know, just like coaches, they oughta have their records up there. You go to an insurance guy, any guy ought to have his record up there. How he's doing?"

It seemed a bit of a stretch to me, but it also didn't seem like Coach was joking.

"You know, you go to a dentist. I mean, what's his record on root canals? Or a plumber. You call a plumber, what's his record? I mean, the guy may have gone to 50 jobs and only 48 of them ever worked again."

I should point out that Yelp wasn't founded until three years after that conversation.

The modern media environment practically demands that sports people be show people as well. It's not enough to score touchdowns, block shots, or rip line drives. You need a TikTok feed and a big Instagram following and your postgame soundbites had better be snappy and Tweetable (I can't bring myself to write "X-able").

Despite his obvious comfort in front of cameras and microphones, Coach understood the fact that public speaking isn't easy for everyone who makes a living in sports. My co-anchor Susan Leigh Taylor once asked Coach about giving speeches.

"Everyone gets, whether the word is butterflies, anxious, nervous, scared to death, or whatever. Everyone gets that and everyone gets it at that moment. You know everything that it means and you have everyone there. I mean all your friends, your family, you know, it's very emotional. So it's a difficult thing to do, no matter how much you do it. So I had some of that, whatever word you want to put on it, I have it."

None of this professed stage fright slowed him down back in his coaching days. Nobody ever accused John Madden of stuffing his emotions. His sideline histrionics were notorious, though he always reminded me that he was only assessed one 15-yard penalty for unsportsmanlike conduct during his coaching career. It came against the Denver Broncos when Raiders safety Jack Tatum had been flagged for an out-of-bounds hit. Coach Madden disagreed with the official.

"So I called him a name. Then the guy comes back and he said, 'Who did you call that name?' And I said, 'You. There's only one blankety-blank out here, and that's you. You're blankety-blank.' So he throws a penalty on me. He asked me the question! The next day I called the league office and I said, 'You know, it was honesty.' I mean, he asked me and I said, 'Yeah, it was you.'"

Yet the arm-waving coach had little use for the sort of me-first showman-ship that pervades modern sports. One morning, we stumbled onto the topic of Bill Mazeroski, the legendary Pittsburgh Pirates second baseman whose ninth-inning, Game 7 home run ended the 1960 World Series.

"You know what I liked about that Mazeroski thing was that, as you know, he was a great player and a great glove man and all those other things. And they show that famous home run because that World Series was not only against the Yankees, but it was Game 7. But I like the way that he hit the home run and ran around the bases. You know, now they got these things where they hit a ball and then they have to stare at it like they're so proud of it. And then they get into some stupid jog or run and then they make a sign. I mean, he just ran. I remember seeing pictures of Joe DiMaggio, the same way. He just kind of put his head down and ran around the bases, and he gathered speed as he went around."

Not that he was always Mr. Crankypants when it came to on-field cele-brations. Coach drew a line between passion and premeditation.

"I kind of like celebrations but I'm a purist and I love sports and I love sports for the passion. I don't mind the celebration. I don't go all goofy when someone cele-brates. But I think the thing they're trying to outlaw in the NFL is those ones where someone wants to not only choreograph it, but choreograph it for a group to do it."

At the time of this conversation, I'd just watched the great distance runner Meb Keflezighi celebrate an Olympic Trials win in the 10,000-meter event by dropping to the track to do a push-up before springing to his feet to run a joyous victory lap. Coach, who was the absolute physical opposite of Meb, was of the same mind on this one.

"I think if one guy decided, 'If I win this, I'm going to do a push-up and then I'm going to take a victory lap,' I think that's pretty cool! I think it's the one where you have the whole thing with three or four or five guys or you're out there hiding cell phones in the goal post wrapper or a Sharpie in your socks. Those are the kind of things that are so premeditated. That's what we're trying to do away with in football."

Coach could get a bit bent out of shape when he started talking about the cult of personality that has grown up around college coaches. This conversation started during March Madness one year, when John felt the telecast was spending too much time focusing on the coaches.

"I think they show the coaches too much in this. I mean, the coaches are just guys. In grammar school, their best course was recess. And then they played basketball or some sport in high school and then they majored in P.E. in college."

Having basically just described himself, he went on to decry modern college basketball courtside decorum.

"They never used to get out of their chair. They used to sit those guys, those basketball coaches, in a chair. And now they're standing up all the time. I don't know where the rule changed on that. And then they started paying them a heck of a lot of money. Coaches at one time, you know, we were underpaid and then they went to being paid fairly. And now, to be honest with you, the coaches are overpaid."

It would have been interesting if Coach had lived long enough to absorb today's world of college sports, with the Name, Image, and Likeness (NIL) deals and the relaxed transfer rules. My guess is he'd have been happier with a system that gave more power to the players than one that made coaches into peripatetic multimillionaires.

John spent a lifetime around football and had true empathy for the people who played the game and suffered physically as a result. That's something you don't feel while clutching a cold beverage in your family room while the game unfolds on your TV screen.

"You hear people say, 'Oh, that guy really likes to hit.' I haven't seen many people who really like to hit and I haven't seen anyone that really likes to get hit, you know, get their clock cleaned. I think that sometimes we look and say, 'Oh, these guys are spoiled. They pay them all that money.' The fact is, they really get hurt. Sometimes I think fans think that it doesn't hurt them, but they're human beings. They do have nerve endings and they do have gray matter and you know, gray matter goes to the nerve endings and tells you that's pain. And the other thing I think is that because it's someone else that's getting hit or hitting, you don't think it hurts, but I'll guarantee it hurts."

Since fans, journalists, and the people who set gambling odds don't feel the athletes' pain, they seem to have no trouble talking about injuries as if they're something abstract. A typical question would be, "Will you be ready to play on Sunday?"

"I don't mean to use the word 'dumb,' like, 'they're really dumb,' but those are dumb questions because no one knows how they're going to feel. And that's what people don't understand. You know, you ask a guy on Tuesday how he's going to feel on Sunday, and if you've ever had an injury, you have no idea. I mean, you know how your ankle feels today and you don't know how it's going to feel when you wake up the next day, nor do you have any idea how it's going to feel in five days. And they keep wanting that question answered, and no one can answer that. I mean, just think of any injury or illness or whatever you've ever had. If someone said, 'How are you going to feel in six days?' you have no idea how you're going to feel."

Coach never saw the people who play the games we love as machines. He saw them as flesh-and-blood humans just like us, but also superhuman in one key respect: they showed up ready to play.

"If it were easy, everyone would do it. And it's not easy. You have to be able to psych yourself up to get ready to do whatever it is. You have to get ready to play because you have so many games and you don't always feel like it, but you have to make yourself feel like it. There's no other way you can get through it. If you don't, you're going to fail and you're going to get hurt. You know, they say 'He's a real pro.' He's a real pro because no matter how he feels, he can play his best."

You can probably sum up Coach's wisdom regarding the gulf between players and spectators with this line he delivered after my colleague Steve Bitker played table tennis against some Olympic hopefuls for a feature report.

"You always think you can do something until you watch someone who can really do it. Then you realize you can't do it."

Words to live by.

CHAPTER 12

The Hall of Fame Trail

IT WASN'T UNTIL 2006, THE YEAR JOHN MADDEN TURNED 70, THAT THOSE who select inductees to the Pro Football Hall of Fame finally got around to enshrining him. It was way, way overdue, but still a pinnacle of Coach's life, and our radio audience had front-row seats.

Long after Coach and quite a few of his backers had abandoned hope, an ember flared to life in the summer of 2005. I was on a Maddenesque journey of my own when the news broke that Coach would be on the ballot for the Hall of Fame Class of 2006.

I was driving across America with my daughter Brenley as she headed back to college in New Jersey. Colleague Jeff Bell was filling in for me that August morning as he welcomed Coach, saying, "We all want to pass along our congratulations. And we have a surprise guest on the line who also wants to weigh in. Good morning, Stan."

My cue, so from the passenger seat of our aging Volvo with my daughter doing the driving, I chimed in, "Hey, good morning, everyone. John, I'm thrilled about Rayfield Wright's nomination to the Pro Football Hall of Fame," name-checking the *other* finalist in the "Senior" category, reserved for those who'd been passed over for many years after the end of their playing or coaching career.

"That's good. I'm also very happy for Rayfield Wright. He was a heck of a tackle."

Coach had been graceful enough to bypass my lame attempt to be funny by ignoring his big news, so I continued. "In all honesty, I just want to tell you how exciting it was to get the news. I got off the road last night and I walked into a restaurant and the TV was on in the bar and I saw the ESPN guys talking about your nomination. And at this point, I want to offer my help in any way I can, John. I will ring doorbells. I'll work the phone bank and we'll even put a front lawn sign out, if that'll help."

"Well, you know, we really don't need that. But I appreciate it, and it's nice after the long trip you've had that you can still call in like this. That's great. It's really exciting. I got the call from the Hall of Fame after the radio show yesterday. It has to be one of the most exciting days of my life and all it means is I'm a finalist. There's still one more vote. There are going to be 15 people on the ballot and so Rayfield Wright and myself will be two of the 15. The afternoon before the Super Bowl, so that'll be in February, they'll vote. They can vote for as few as three or as many as six out of the 15. So that's where we stand right now."

Back at the KCBS studios, Susan Leigh Taylor spoke for many, saying, "We actually assumed that John was *already* in the Hall of Fame. John, did you have an inkling that this was coming or did this catch you by surprise?"

"No, no, it caught me by surprise because it's been so long and so many years where they would have this vote and you're passed over. So then, when it comes and goes, it's been coming and going for so many years. It's not a thing that you really look forward to or even put on your calendar or even know about. There was a story in the Chronicle *on Sunday, so I knew that the vote was coming up Wednesday. And then yesterday morning, you know, about 11 o'clock here, I got a call and I was one of the two finalists. But no, I didn't have any inclination at all. There are people that assume that I am or have been in the Hall of Fame. I was a finalist like 20 years ago or something. You drop off the 'Modern Day' list which goes five years after you stop playing or coaching. And then the next thing is at 20 years when you become a 'Senior.' So there's a period of about 15 years in there where you're kind of in no man's land."*

Back to Susan, who said, "Well, all I can say is it's about time. I mean, if ever there was an ambassador for a sport. Good grief."

"Thank you, Susan. I appreciate that."

From somewhere on Interstate 80, I wrapped things up. "And all I would do is urge those who have votes to follow the dictum of the old Cook County Democrats: 'vote early and vote often.'"

Reaching the list of finalists for the Pro Football Hall of Fame was a big step, but the journey to Canton was nowhere near over. Here's how the Hall describes what happens next (there have been some slight modifications since John's journey in 2005–2006):

In advance of the Hall of Fame selection meeting, the selectors are provided detailed biographies on each of the Finalists. At the annual meeting, each Finalist is thoroughly discussed by the committee before a series of reduction votes are taken. First, the Coach/Contributor and Seniors Finalists are discussed and voted on for election. They must receive the same 80 percent affirmative vote as the Modern-Era Player Finalists. Next, there is a vote that reduces the Modern-Era Player Finalists list from 15 to 10. Following that, a vote is taken to reduce the list from 10 to 5 names. The five remaining Modern-Era Player Finalists for Hall of Fame election are voted on individually (yes or no) for membership.

In order to be elected, a Finalist must receive a minimum of 80 percent of the vote. All ballots are collected and counted by an accounting firm. No vote totals are announced—only the winners of the various reduction ballots are revealed to the Selectors and the Hall's representatives.

The Annual Meeting of those Hall of Fame Selectors takes place shortly before the Super Bowl every year. Because candidates in the "Senior" category may have careers that current selectors know little about, the Hall of Fame brings in consultants to tell the stories of those candidates. It's important to remember here that although John Madden was, at the time of his nomination, still seen by much of America as the voice and face of the NFL, the Hall of Fame selectors were weighing his impact as a coach. He'd left that occupation more than a quarter of a century earlier.

For the next six months, we carried on with our daily radio chats, but surely, the Hall of Fame question was never far from Coach's mind. The big announcement came the day before Super Bowl XL. John was in Detroit, preparing to cover the Sunday game, when he learned he was going to be enshrined in Canton.

Because he's John Madden, the story had a few wrinkles. The Monday morning after the Super Bowl, we didn't have much interest in rehashing the Steelers' win over the Seahawks (sorry about that, Yinzers, but priorities are priorities).

I launched our conversation saying, "He's on the bus somewhere in the middle of America. John Madden, sponsored this morning by the Bank of Walnut Creek. And John, may we be among the first million people to congratulate you on your election to the Pro Football Hall of Fame?"

"Well, thank you very much. I'll tell you, this was an exciting weekend for us when you get elected into the Hall of Fame on Saturday and do a Super Bowl on Sunday. And it's just great. I mean, everything about it was great, such a great feeling. And we're just leaving Detroit now. We're just pulling out of Detroit."

I replied, pulling in a surprise guest, "Hey, John, I know there will be many more of these kinds of conversations in the months to come, but we wanted to take the opportunity to bring in a guy you spent some time with over the years, and he beat you to the Hall of Fame by 26 years. Jim Otto, good morning."

Otto is generally acknowledged as one of the best centers ever to play pro football, anchoring the Raiders offensive line throughout the Madden coaching years.

Jim Otto: *"Good morning. Congratulations, John."*

John: *"Jim, thanks a lot. Thank you very much."*

Jim: *"I was sitting here watching that program on Saturday morning and I said, 'Come on, baby.' And all of a sudden they were talking to you and I was just very, very excited. I saw the excitement in your face and it made me feel great."*

John: *"Well, it was amazing. And I thank you for it, and the guys you played with because like I said, I've never* not *realized that it was the players, because the*

John Madden with KYA Radio production director Fred Greene, 1984.

John Madden with "Emperor" Gene Nelson at KYA studios.

Outdoor advertising deployed during John Madden's tenure with Gene Nelson.

KNBR morning personality Frank Dill with John Madden, 1994.

John Madden with longtime KCBS Radio news and program director Ed Cavagnaro, 2010. *(Courtesy of Ed Jay Photography)*

KCBS Radio morning anchor Al Hart with John Madden at the 2009 Madden BBQ. *(Courtesy of Ed Jay Photography)*

Commissioner Roger Goodell shares a laugh with John Madden in the Madden Cruiser, 2010.
(AP Images/Rob Carr)

KCBS Radio promotions director Shannon Disney-Durko-Krey with John Madden, 2001.

The author with John Madden and John Robinson at Lambeau Field, Green Bay, 2008.

John Madden speaks to the audience at a KCBS/Madden BBQ, 2013. *(Courtesy of Ed Jay Photography)*

Virginia Madden shows off her chocolate cake at a KCBS/Madden BBQ, 2009.

(Courtesy of Ed Jay Photography)

John Madden poses at a KCBS/Madden BBQ with guests George and Martha Barron, 2006.

Peyton Manning and John Madden talk before a 2007 Colts-Chargers game at Qualcomm Stadium. *(AP Images/Paul Spinelli)*

John Madden rolls during annual the Madden/Mariucci Charity Bocce Tournament, 2013. *(Courtesy of Bob Cullinan)*

John Madden with Raiders owner Al Davis after his Pro Football Hall of Fame induction ceremony, 2006.

John Madden surrounded by former players at his Hall of Fame "afterparty," with sons, Mike and Joe, in the foreground.

John Madden speaks at an event honoring former Raiders punter Ray Guy, 2014.
(Courtesy of Ed Jay Photography)

The author speaks at
the public memorial
service for John
Madden, 2022.

(Courtesy of Bob Cullinan)

players win games and they should always get the credit. And if you didn't have good players, great players like you were, then none of that would be possible. I'm thankful as heck to you."

Jim: *"Well, it takes a great coach to lead a team. And we went through those years with a lot of victories, had a lot of fun, and it's something that I'll always have in my heart. And the years that we were together with all the guys, the group that's part of the Hall of Fame, you've got quite a few of us guys in there [13 Raiders who played under John Madden are in the Pro Football Hall of Fame] and you know, once you're in there, you're in there forever. You're in."*

The fact that Coach wasn't already in the Hall of Fame by 2006 was a constant source of surprise to many sports fans and deep irritation to Raiders fans. My recollection is that there had been numerous stories in the weeks ahead of the 2006 announcement suggesting that at long last, it was John Madden's time.

I continued our conversation that morning, "You knew this was coming, right, so you were prepared for this?"

"No, I wasn't. I didn't know it was coming. I wasn't ready."

Steve Bitker jumped in from the sports desk, "If you saw John's reaction, you'd know he was not prepared." That gave Coach a chance to give our listeners an inside look at how one of the biggest days in his life went down.

"Here's the whole deal. I was told they're going to have a press conference at two o'clock to announce it. But between one and two, they will call you to tell you that you made it so you can get over there to be at the press conference. So one o'clock comes, nothing. One thirty comes, nothing. Quarter to two comes, nothing. Two o'clock comes, nothing. So I'm like, 'Well, I didn't make it.' And then we turn on the NFL Network and Rich Eisen is up there saying that they're ready to announce the Hall of Fame class. Still no call. And so I thought, 'Well, I didn't get in.' And then Fred Gaudelli, who was our [Super Bowl broadcast] producer, said, 'You want to turn this off or turn the sound down?' I said, 'No, let's watch and see who made it,' thinking, 'Well, I didn't make it.' So I kind of decided that was over; let's just see who was in. It's alphabetical order. The first name that comes out is Troy

Aikman. The second one, Harry Carson. And third was John Madden. And I was just in shock."

"And you had your lifelong friend John Robinson right near you. And your son Mike was there. I guess you had a lot of your peeps there," I said.

"Mike took a picture for some reason. He took a picture at that moment."

I replied, "I love that picture. The *Chronicle* ran it yesterday. It's a little blurry, but everybody looked pretty excited."

"It was *blurry, Mike said he doesn't know how he was even able to take the picture. It was exciting as heck. And then, just everything since and, I mean, even this morning, having Jim Otto call in, I mean, these are all gorgeous special moments that have to be captured and remembered."*

It was becoming an emotional experience for all of us. I tried to capture some of that in what I said next. "The thing that occurs to a lot of us who have special moments in our lives is that most of ours happen rather privately. Yours is being played out on the big stage of the whole world. The Bay Area has been watching and waiting for all this, and you've handled it all with such grace. But like a regular guy, which I guess is what endears you to so many people. Here's this big guy from Daly City at a loss for words at a time of something exciting. It's kind of neat to watch. I had to tell you that."

"It was something that I didn't prepare. I wasn't even sure how it worked. I've never understood what happens to all those acceptance speeches at the Oscars and the Emmys when they don't win. You have to feel stupid if you're there. You got a speech in your pocket, all ready to thank everyone and then someone else gets the award. What do you do with that speech? So I always thought, since I was stupid, I would never do that. So I was totally, totally, totally unprepared. Anything I said didn't come from my mind. It came from my heart."

Six months later, John Madden officially entered the Pro Football Hall of Fame along with Troy Aikman, Warren Moon, Harry Carson, Rayfield Wright, and Reggie White, whose honor was posthumous.

He'd waited a long time for the honor. He wasn't going to miss a moment of the experience. It was such a big deal that John even boarded an airplane. No, he didn't fly, but he did charter a flight for 150 friends and family members and went to the Canton airport so he could climb aboard and say a few words of welcome.

I was honored to be among the invitees but because of work commitments, I missed that charter flight and made my own way to Canton. I stood along the parade route, sat in the hot sun to watch Coach and the other inductees give their speeches, and made my way backstage after the ceremony to pull John aside for an interview that would air on KCBS the following day.

Just before we talked, I spotted Coach and Al Davis, the Raiders owner whose willingness to turn a young linebackers coach into an NFL head coach opened so many doors for John. I snapped a photo of the two of them sharing a private moment next to the bronze bust that's now inside the Hall of Fame. John was sporting his new gold Hall of Fame blazer.

Here's the interview in its entirety.

Me: *Nice jacket.*

John: *Yeah, it's really something. You know, they have a ceremony where they give out the jacket the night before, and they gave it out at dinner last night. And Al Davis, who was my presenter, wasn't at the dinner. So my two sons, Mike and Joe, were able to present it. And that was one of the highlights of the weekend, getting the jacket and then knowing it's your Hall of Fame jacket and having your two sons there with you, giving it to you.*

Me: *I saw the photo in the paper of you slapping a hug on Joe. It looked good.*

John: *I think that was Mike. We both hugged, and then all three of us hugged.*

Me: *Madden group hug.*

John: *Yeah, it was good. It was good.*

Me: *So you got up there today and talked without any notes, as it turned out. "Wow," was, I think, the first word out of your mouth. And I guess "wow" is probably still on your mind.*

John: *Yeah. That was the thing. People would say, "Well, you know, what are you going to say when you go to the party? What are you going to think when you're going in?" And I thought that myself. What am I going to say when I get up there and I said, "I don't know, because I'm not up there." You know, you have to wait until you get up there. And I thought whatever comes out is going to come out. And* it was just, "Wow," you know, that was all. It wasn't written. It wasn't, you know, pre-thought-of. It wasn't anything. It was just that I wanted to say what my first thought was when I got up there and it was just, "Wow."

Me: *You've had maybe five minutes now, all told, to process this and you've been going like a madman for about four days here. At some point you're going to sleep for six days.*

John: *I haven't slept worth a darn. I mean, even when I got a few minutes to rest or take a nap, I couldn't do it. Last night, we were up late and then I knew the parade was coming. I had to get up at 5:00 in the morning. And I think back in California, that's 2:00 in the morning. And then, you get into that whole thing where you really just foul yourself up, you know, "Should I go over anything before I go to sleep?" So you start to go over something, then you decide, "No, I should go to sleep." And anyway, you don't sleep. So I haven't had a normal night's sleep in well over a week.*

Me: *They do a parade pretty well here, don't they?*

John: *They know how to do a parade. They have over 100,000 people there at that parade.*

Me: *They told me one of those high school bands had 330 kids in it. There are whole Bay Area high schools that don't have that many kids.*

John: *They say that it's the biggest non-holiday parade in the country, and I believe that. I mean, it's the Midwest and this thing has grown and this is a tradition and this is what it is. And those are all highlights. All those people you see in the parade, all the people you see at the induction, all the people at the dinner. It's just amazing that a small town like Canton, Ohio, puts on something as big as this.*

Me: *Now they're tearing the whole place down even as we talk, because they're going to play the football game. I guess they're going to have it torn down in like five minutes, right?*

John: *Well, we have to play the football game here tomorrow night. And, you know, you talk about a weekend! I mean, I got this whole Hall of Fame weekend and then the next day, which is still the same weekend, I'm doing my first game* with NBC. And I told Al Michaels the other day on the phone, I said, "Man, you're going to have to do a heck of a cleanup job on this one."

Me: *I was going to say, in your whole career, you probably never said, "I don't feel like I'm wanting to go to work." This might be the day.*

John: *No, no, no, no. I want to go to work now. I wanted it this way. I mean, I said, "If we're going to do it, let's do everything." Someone said, "Maybe you'd rather not do the game." No, I'd rather do the Hall of Fame game. Do the game, first game with NBC, you know, really make a memory. I'm going to remember this 2006 August in Canton, Ohio, forever.*

Me: *You are great at picking snapshots out of scenes. You know, the thing you see, the guy you meet. What snapshots are in your mind from today, what are the moments that stick in your mind?*

John: *Just being there with my class…the class of 2006, I will always be identified with them forever. Troy Aikman and Harry Carson and Reggie White and Rayfield Wright, we're going to be together forever. And Warren Moon. Having those guys there, we kind of have developed a camaraderie. And then behind you, all the history and the great players. We had a luncheon yesterday where all the players [prior inductees] talked to us and we couldn't talk. And then, my players that were here, guys that played for me, some that are in the Hall of Fame. But the other players too. There were over 30 Raiders players from those teams.*

Me: *I talked to a lot of them. John Vella, Gus Otto, Ben Davidson. Ben Davidson, by the way, refused to stand up, if I'm not mistaken. I mean, you had to tell him twice.*

John: *He wanted to sit down. Usually those guys would stand up and they were hams. And then today, they had a moment in the sun. I said, "Take your moment. Stand up. Don't sit down." You know, they all just wanted to stand up, do a little wave, and sit down. I wanted them to stand up and stay up.*

Me: *These guys still aren't listening to you. I mean, you're in the Hall of Fame and they still won't listen.*

John: *No, they listened. When I told them to stand back up and stay up, they stood back up.*

Me: *But genuinely, every one of them was so thrilled for you. John Robinson was out there. These people, your whole life was out there.*

John: *Yeah, right. That's the thing. And when you go in as late in life as I am, you have a whole lot out there. I mean, when you go back to childhood and then you have high school and college and then you have the pros and you have coaching—college coaching and pro coaching—and then television and life after. I mean, there's just so much living that you've done that you kind of have to get it all in there one way or another. And even though you can't mention everyone and everything, they know. I mean, they're here to celebrate it and they're all part of it.*

Me: *All right. We're recording this conversation on Saturday afternoon. Tonight will be the first time your bust, if I'm not mistaken, will have the chance to have that conversation that you've been talking about with the other busts. What have you told your bust to tell the other busts?*

John: *Just enjoy it. I mean, I think that those conversations are going to be so great. I was talking to Merlin Olsen afterwards and he said, "You know, I believe that." He said, "I think they do talk to each other." And I said, "I believe that, too." I can't wait to get in there and have my bust talk to the old coaches. Find out what it was like for them, how they got started. Like I said, the Knute Rocknes, George Halases, Vince Lombardis, those guys that went before me that I followed.*

A few hours later, John and Virginia were hosting one of the happiest parties I've ever attended. All those people who'd arrived on the Madden charter flight were there, plus many more. John's buddy Dominic Mercurio and his barbecue crew handled the feeding at a country club in Canton and everyone was thrilled for the guy in whose honor we'd gathered.

"I wanted to have fun. I wanted to include as many people as I could. And I wanted everyone to make a memory. I know that I sure as heck did. It was the greatest weekend and each day was the greatest day of my life."

I honestly don't know how he pulled it off, but he *did* make it to his NBC Sports premiere with Al Michaels that Sunday, launching the final act of his television career as the Raiders beat the Eagles. He'd been up late the night before; it was almost Sunday morning at the party when he took the microphone to thank everyone for coming.

"I thought, 'Well, if you haven't made a memory by now, midnight on Saturday night, you got a little time left, but you better go make one, right now.'"

I'd seen it in person in Canton, and my colleague Hal Ramey was handling morning sports duties the following Monday when he mentioned the same thing. "John, throughout the day and night, when you were down on the field, that smile on your face," Hal observed, "anybody who's been around you, they'd know that you were enjoying it pretty well."

"Yeah, that's something you can't hide. I mean, it's either there, or it's not there. And believe me, it was there for me and it's still there. I mean, you keep saying, 'It was great, it was great,' but it's very real. I mean, it's real. It is. It's real and it's emotional and it's passionate. That's raw. It's the best time of my life. You really don't want to lose it or leave it. I know I was the first guy in on Wednesday, and I'm probably the last guy to leave because whatever's here, I want to soak it in."

Not once did I ever pick up a sense of bitterness from John over the obvious injustice of his long wait for Hall of Fame honors. When the long-overdue honor came, he approached it with pure, unadulterated joy, reveling in each moment.

And while there's no way to prove it, I believe his bust *is* having those nighttime conversations with those of the other legends of pro football. Knowing John, I'll bet his bust is the first one talking each night when they turn off the lights and lock the doors, and it's the one that slips in the last word before the staff arrives in the morning.

CHAPTER 13

The Soul of Pro Football

Any discussion of the most valuable sports leagues in the world begins with the runaway leader: the National Football League. With annual revenue exceeding $18 billion, the NFL dwarfs every other league on the planet.

That's a hard, irrefutable fact. You might start an argument by asserting that this person or that person was most responsible for the NFL's stratospheric value, but no sane person would claim that John Madden's name doesn't belong in that discussion.

The old saying, "Do what you love and you'll never work a day in your life," applies to John as well as anyone I've ever met. He truly lived for football, as he told me on the morning in June 2005 when word broke that he'd be switching to NBC for its new *Sunday Night Football* broadcast the following year.

"I've been lucky. I say this and I say it humbly: I'm not a smartass, but I've always figured that I'm the luckiest guy in the world because life to me has been recess. From playing in grammar school and high school and college and then pro and then coaching it and then broadcasting it…I've had a football season all my

life since I don't know when. I started playing on Madden's Lot on Knowles Avenue in Daly City, probably when I was six or seven years old."

But it was more than this sense of good fortune that kept him wedded to the sport. Coach was fueled by football; it gave him energy and purpose.

"You know, you do it for half of every year and as the season goes on, the games get more exciting and more meaningful and bigger. And then, of course, you have the big game at the end, the Super Bowl, then you have six months off, six months to sit around and think about it. After three or four months, like right now, I'm ready to go. I mean, I've had enough of this 'no football' stuff. So I'm ready for football. And I still have to wait another couple of months before we start. And that has always been in my life. It's never gone away."

A man with that level of investment in something is doing more than just going to work. He's all-in, a part of the thing itself. Football was clearly in John Madden's soul, but I'd argue that he more than returned the favor, becoming one of the most important figures in the history of America's number one sport.

NFL Commissioner Roger Goodell's words on the day of John's death ring true. "Nobody loved football more than Coach," Goodell's statement read. "He was football. He was an incredible sounding board to me and so many others. There will never be another John Madden, and we will forever be indebted to him for all he did to make football and the NFL what it is today."

Years before Coach's death, his lifelong friend John Robinson told me, "It's so impressive to me to see him in this role. I think I've always seen him as the face of the NFL in recent years. I've got a grandson who's eight years old and he plays the *Madden* video game. I mean, he knows John Madden more than he knows his teachers in school because he loves playing that game. So there's so much about the NFL that John has a big impact on."

How did this happen? How did one man who never played a down of professional football, who never owned a team, and whose professional coaching career spanned barely a decade come to mean so much to the sport and the league? Let's start with Coach's role as a broadcaster.

From the 1981 NFL season through the 2008 season, concluding with Super Bowl XLIII in February 2009, John *was* pro football on TV in America. He appeared on all four over-the-air networks (CBS, Fox, ABC, and NBC) and amassed a streak of 476 consecutive in-season weekends working the featured NFL telecast.

He was ubiquitous and instantly recognizable. In an industry full of competent yet interchangeable talent, there was ever only one John Madden. But it wasn't just his singularity that helped him propel the growth of the NFL juggernaut. It was also the fact that he brought new people to the party and made football accessible to folks who never tried to separate the "X's" from the "O's" on a locker room chalkboard.

Coach's success as a broadcaster may have been accidental in the sense that it wasn't a career he pursued. But what he did on the air didn't just *happen*. His folksy demeanor and verbal theatrics may have hidden the serious thought and hard work that fueled his performances. He questioned *everything* about the way football was presented on TV and fueled numerous changes that are now part and parcel of every game you watch.

When John was inducted into the Sports Broadcasting Hall of Fame, his longtime director Sandy Grossman said, "When there's a book written about directing football, there needs to be an entire chapter dedicated to directing for John Madden because he changed the way things are done."

One morning, I mentioned the fact that my wife had been watching the previous night's Chiefs-Titans telecast and at one point had marveled at how quickly and concisely John could analyze what had just happened, using language that even a first-time football viewer could grasp. He recalled the play instantly.

"Well, I just saw it. I mean, I just saw the end wide and I saw Willy Roaf kind of fake to him, the left tackle, and then go up on Keith Bulluck. And I knew that they were in a shotgun and Larry Johnson was next to Trent Green's right. And it was a draw play. And again, I thought the big thing was that because the end was so wide, they didn't have to block him. So that led to the tackle getting on

the second level and then they got the block there. So that automatically put the running back to the third level."

Got it. I think. His analysis of what he said on the air was much more detailed and far less accessible to the casual observer than what he told viewers like my wife during the telecast. Of course, a television broadcast is more than just one smart guy watching the game and describing what he just saw, so I asked how he knew what pictures would be on the screen when it came time for him to pick a play apart.

"All they do is tell you what angle it's coming from. You know, end zone camera, or SkyCam, whatever. And there are certain things. I mean, everyone knows if it's a running play that runs inside the tackle, between the guard and tackle, you know that you have to have the offensive guard and the tackle and then you know, if you get the offensive tackle, you have to have the defensive end. So there's very little communication required."

At that point, sports anchor Steve Bitker jumped in. "I don't think anyone has ever been as good at analyzing a play that is coming up on replay," said Steve, who watches a lot of televised sports, "and you've had no time to see the replay. I mean, it's just amazing to me."

"Yeah. Yeah. You have to see it. You have to see the play because there's no time to see a replay before the audience sees it. And so, again, you have to know *what just happened. You have to pick it apart."*

What he's saying here is that he saw what was about to happen, watched it happen, and then was able to quickly explain to millions of viewers what *had* just happened and why. It's no surprise that many people say they learned the game of football from John Madden.

Steve had one more observation, and I think it's key to understanding the genius of John Madden: so many football analysts belabor the obvious. You'll hear, "He overthrew that receiver!" Well, yeah, I could see that for myself. Coach was usually content to let the action speak for itself when warranted.

"Yeah, yeah. That's what you have to do, but sometimes you're forced to talk about those plays. I mean, I've had it where, as the analyst, if the producer or director gives you replays, you have to comment on them. And then sometimes, you

get multiple replays and you'll get your second or third look at something and you go wall to wall to wall. And pretty soon you get tired of yourself."

There's not much evidence that the audience ever got tired of that guy.

Coach's mastery of the telestrator is a significant part of his legend and was also a key element in his ability to broaden the appeal of pro football. In typical "aw, shucks" fashion, he took our radio audience back to the beginning.

"I was one of the first ones that ever did it, I guess. At the start, I would just throw slop up at it. You know, if you worry about penmanship and stuff, you're not gonna do it. You don't have time. You have to locate where everyone is or remember what they did on that last play when you saw them do it and then you have to diagram it."

He broadcast more than 500 NFL games, and Coach never sat down.

"I've always stood the entire broadcast. That was one of those things, when I was a player, obviously you always stand, or when you're a coach, you always stand. And when I started broadcasting, I just always thought football is your life. It's not something you sit down and do."

John's ascendancy to household name and cultural phenomenon came at the side of CBS Sports colleague Pat Summerall, a former NFL player with a sparse, deadpan style that meshed perfectly with Coach's voluble approach. The two wound up working 22 seasons together at CBS and Fox. Summerall's death at age 82 jolted Coach, who nevertheless joined us the following morning to talk about his old partner and friend.

"He was just a guy's guy. If we'd be leaving at 10:00 in the morning and the bus would be down there, I would get on the bus at like five minutes to 10. Pat would get there at 8:30, 9:00, and he'd drink coffee and sit and talk to the drivers. And he loved that. I mean, he just loved hanging out, sitting and telling stories. He's just the greatest guy. He's everything that you would want in a friend and everything that you'd want in a man."

Our conversation that morning rambled, as will happen when people gather to remember someone who's passed away. At some point, I told Coach how I would never forget the programming announcements Summerall read at the end of Sunday afternoon games on CBS. "Stay tuned after the game,"

Summerall would intone, "except on the West Coast, for *60 Minutes* and *Murder, She Wrote.*"

"Yeah, and the thing he did is, he kind of did it his way. The show name was Murder*, comma,* She Wrote*. And Pat was an English teacher, so back when he started, a lot of people just called the show* Murder She Wrote*. And Pat said, 'There's a comma in there. It's not* Murder She Wrote*. It's* Murder*, [pause]* She Wrote*, the way he said it. And then over the years, that pause became a thing and the pause became longer and longer. And finally it was,* Murder *[four-second pause],* She Wrote*."*

The mystery drama starring Angela Lansbury was the top-rated TV drama for nine consecutive seasons. Having Pat Summerall, John Madden, and the NFL's featured game as the lead-in every week might have helped a bit.

For all the innovations that John Madden championed and/or embraced, there were a few that he could never quite pull into the broadcast to his satisfaction. One was the miked-up player or coach. He wanted more than the NFL was willing to give.

"If a player is miked, we don't hear it. I've always asked for that. Just to know what a guy says, like after a quarterback throws an interception, if he says, 'Well, I didn't see that safety,' you'd like to just hear what he said. But they [the NFL] won't let us listen, nor will they give us anything they don't approve to go on the air."

I'd assumed the NFL was playing the role of censor, protecting its image by filtering what was captured on those player and coach microphones. John had heard enough locker-room and sideline language, so he didn't care about that. He *did* care about building a better, smarter broadcast.

"A lot of times you think *you see something. You see a coverage and you think that's what they did. And then you wonder why the quarterback didn't see that, or what he was looking at, and you'd just like to hear that. Or a linebacker, what'd he read that got him in the hole so quickly or what a receiver did, was it an option route? All the things that you kind of have to imagine and just look at the pictures, if you just had a few words to go with them, sometimes that would help."*

Again, it was John seeking not just the "what?" but also the "why?" of what was unfolding on the field. It was a common theme in his football life.

John was already looking way downfield as he transitioned from coaching into broadcasting. The idea that would evolve into the blockbuster *Madden* video game first came to his mind not as entertainment, but as a tool for teaching and analyzing football.

"That was the original idea. That was my idea because I didn't know anything about computers. But, you know, we're going back to 1980, so not a lot of people did know much about computers. So that's what I was thinking: if I could take these football plays and put them in against a defense to see their chance of success against a computer, that would save a lot of time in practice. You could take your game plan and play it against the other team's defense before you played the game. So that was my idea, that this thing would be a teaching tool. I had no idea that it was going to be a video game."

It was a few years later that John and Electronic Arts founder Trip Hawkins had their famous train ride, sketching out the idea for a product that would take another four years to come to market.

"Trip Hawkins, who started EA, said that someday everyone's going to have a computer and they're going to want to do things on it other than just business or schoolwork. He said they're going to want to play games. So that was his goal, to make games for computers. So when they became what they are today, you could play these games on them. Of course, then the video games came out and all the new hardware came out and we had a head start on the software. So we just adjusted and adapted all the software."

Madden NFL has spent more than two decades as America's best-selling sports video game title. Millions of people play it, and more than a few NFL players have credited the game with teaching them the game of football—not the blocking and tackling, but the formations and strategy that are so crucial to the sport.

In the process, some of these *Madden* players began to reinvent the game itself, a case of life imitating art. In the first game of the 2009 NFL season, the Denver Broncos pulled off a miraculous win over the Cincinnati Bengals. With less than 30 seconds on the clock, Denver quarterback Kyle Orton threw the ball deep. It bounced off a defender and was grabbed by wide receiver Brandon Stokley.

It was what Stokley did next, and his explanation of that act, that cemented the video game's reputation as a meaningful element of modern football. Stokley headed for the end zone, poised to score the go-ahead touchdown, but then veered to run *across* the field, parallel to the goal line. He was burning time off the clock, decreasing the odds of the Bengals having enough time to re-take the lead.

Nobody had seen anything like it before, but Stokley knew full well what he was doing. He later told reporters it was a move he'd used many times while playing *Madden*. The play is known in Bronco fan lore as "The Immaculate Deflection," and it was a harbinger of things to come.

After the New Orleans Saints beat the Indianapolis Colts in Super Bowl XLIV, Coach realized what he and EA Sports had wrought.

"The Saints' Sean Payton played the game like a video game. I mean, doing those things like going for it on fourth down? I would have kicked the field goal. And then the onside kick [to open the second half]? The whole thing is a video game. I mean, those aren't things you do in the Super Bowl. That was a gutsy call, but that's what you do in a video game; you don't want to give the other guy the ball. You just want to keep the ball. So they go for it on fourth down all the time, which he did, you do the onside kick so you don't have to give them back the ball, which he did. I mean they do all these things in the game and then you say, 'You can't do it that way. That's not how they play the game.' And now you look at it and that is *how they play the game."*

In 2011, Raheem Morris, then the 35-year-old head coach of the Tampa Bay Buccaneers, said half-jokingly that he'd majored in *Madden* while a student at Hofstra University. That didn't surprise the man whose name was on the box.

"That's right, and he credits the game for him being able to become a head coach at such a young age and know how to organize a team because that's in the video game, too."

In our media-saturated society, John's visibility on the air and as the force behind that video game guaranteed his influence would be felt. Beyond that, though, I'd argue that Coach's importance to the NFL is based, as well, on his institutional knowledge and his deep passion for the sport and everything around it.

Pick any aspect of pro football and Coach could tell you a story about it. He knew the history of the game and the business of pro football, both from study and from personal experience. For example, the annual hullabaloo around the NFL Draft could trigger a story from his coaching days with the Raiders.

"Ron Wolf was our director of player personnel and Ron Wolf was great. He had a photographic memory and he knew every player in the country in his head. He had all the books and all the charts and all the stuff and everything. So now it's the day of the draft. We'd start at 6:00 in the morning, I think, because it was starting in New York at 9:00. Anyway, it's the day of the draft and we've been working for months to get ready. Everyone's there, but no Ron Wolf and we don't hear from him. So we call his house thinking he overslept or something. He's not there. He left and he didn't get to where he was going. And he lived in Alameda."

I suddenly knew where this story was going because my hometown, Alameda, is an island city separated from Oakland by a couple of tunnels and three drawbridges.

"This is the day of the draft and this is before cell phones and stuff. So we're getting ready to draft now. You need your guy. I mean, Ron Wolf is like the encyclopedia. So we don't have our encyclopedia there. And you know what happened? He was coming in. I mean, of all days, just imagine, this has to be a director of player personnel's nightmare who lives in Alameda, but he had to cross the bridge and the bridge went up and he got stuck at the bridge."

Coach didn't just sit around and tell stories about the good old days. He worried about the future of pro football. The guy who grew up choosing pickup sides on Madden's Lot and listening to sports broadcasts on the radio was worried about the current generation of young Americans and their attachment to football.

"We are losing viewers and we're losing them every year. And to me, we're losing kids because they can't go to games anymore. It's all corporate. Families can't go to games. We've been losing them for 15 years. So, someone who was 10 years old 15 years ago is now 25 years old. It's that whole group that I think we lost. We have to do new things in order to get some of these people back."

If there was any place that represented the vision of pro football that fired Coach's imagination, it was Green Bay, Wisconsin.

"If you don't do a Sunday at Lambeau Field, it's not pro football. I say this to every fan, 'If you're ever going to take a trip and watch a game in another stadium, the place to choose is Green Bay and Lambeau Field.'"

John was more than just an admirer of the Green Bay football scene. He became part of it in a typically Maddenesque way.

"Three or four years ago, I was listening at half time and they had this drawing for the seat that you were in. There was all this excitement and then it went silent. They drew, like the number is Seat S-148. And the whole crowd went crazy and the guy won a year's supply of brats. The whole place went nuts. I mean, it was like they just won a Super Bowl. And so I mentioned it in the second half. I said, 'How do you know what's a year's supply of brats?' I mean, do you get them daily, weekly, monthly? Do you have some truck drive up and just dump them in your yard? So anyway, it turns out a year's supply is a case per month. So then the company said that they would give me a case per month. So I said, 'Don't send me any brats. Just leave them right there in Green Bay and whenever I come, I'll pick them up.'"

And that's exactly what he did. For many years, whenever Coach's broadcast assignment would take him to Green Bay, he'd round up his supply of bratwursts, organize a cooking squad, and host a big-time brat fry behind the stadium. There'd be pregame brats, halftime brats, and postgame brats.

One year, I made the pilgrimage along with KCBS colleagues Steve Bitker, Mike Sugerman, and Doug Sovern. We got to cook 500 brats at Lambeau Field and serve them to everyone from the broadcast crew to stadium security personnel to the Marine color guard. It was an unforgettable experience and let the record note that Sovern ate brat No. 500 that evening.

Aside from his role as pro football's greatest booster, where John Madden *really* made a difference was in his dogged insistence that people take player safety more seriously. He was a realist about the very nature of the sport.

"You have to admit it's a violent game. I mean, when big, strong, fast guys run into each other at full speed, that's a violent act. That's a collision. So you can't say it's not a violent game. It is a violent game. Now, within that, then you can try and make it safer."

And so he did. From the beginning of our conversations together, he was outspoken about the damage football did to the people who played it.

"That's a serious thing that has really never been studied and was for years kind of taken as a joke. You didn't even use the word 'concussion.' You would just say, 'Well, what's happened? Oh, he just got dinged,' and you'd usually put 'just' in front of it, and then 'dinged,' you know, 'He just got dinged; he'll be okay in a minute.' And then you gave him some smelling salts. Once the smelling salts shakes their head, then they were okay, and then they'd go back and play. Everyone did it. The number of concussions that these guys have had over the years, some players, I'm sure, not only had one concussion in their career. I mean, I think everyone's had a concussion in their career, but some of them had like one a game. What's that going to do later? And I've always said, and this is true, 'If you play one down of football in the NFL, your body will never be normal the rest of your life.' And that's just one down we're talking about now."

Even for a guy who'd grown up in the sport and coached it successfully at the highest level, the modern game astonished John Madden. He went on that morning to relate the story of the day, while working as a broadcaster, that he returned to the sidelines.

"I forgot myself and I went to a scrimmage. It's when the Raiders were in training camp in Oxnard and I was standing there on the sideline while they had a full scrimmage and I thought, 'I forgot. I forgot how hard they hit.' There's no way, unless you're down there and you get in it, you have no idea. People say, 'Football's a violent game.' No kidding, it's a violent game. You get guys running

into each other that weigh 320 pounds and lift weights all week. They're as strong as a truck running into each other at full speed. That's a violent act."

That conversation took place in May 2001. It took the NFL many more years to fully acknowledge the toll repeated head trauma was taking on the men who played the game and built the business into the behemoth it is today.

Coach made it his mission to change the conversation about head injuries. He called me on the carpet one morning when I made reference to Brett Favre's "slight concussion" suffered in the previous week's game.

"Where did you get 'slight concussion'? How come everyone puts 'slight' in front of the word 'concussion'? I just don't think you take concussions this lightly. He may be okay by Monday, but I don't know how they know that now. I preface this again, as you know, I'm not a doctor, but I don't know how they know the day after a game that he's going to be okay on Monday with a concussion. I don't know that. The thing that we don't study enough in football is concussions. And I think that's probably the thing that we know least about."

As a broadcaster, John discarded terminology like "he got dinged" or "he got his bell rung" to call concussions what they are: brain injuries.

"You bruise the brain is what you do. I've always felt this way: we don't take that seriously enough. You know that in boxing, which is, I've said this before, in the dark ages as a major sport, if a guy gets knocked out, he can't fight for a month. In football, we say, 'the day after.' I'm not sure that there's much science behind that."

Pro football remains a violent, dangerous enterprise, but few would disagree with the notion that John Madden's voice was an important one in moving the NFL toward a greater acknowledgment of the price being paid by its players.

In the years after his television career ended, John immersed himself in the workings of the NFL. At a time in his life when he could have just hung around the house or given a few speeches, he played an active role on player-safety and rules issues. His final act with pro football came about as he approached his first NFL season without a real job and found himself talking with a former television colleague.

"The more we talked, the more excited I got and I said, 'Doggone, I know I'm all ready to go, but I don't have any place to go.' And so I have to do something. I really do. This isn't buyer's remorse, either. But it was interesting, when Walter Cronkite passed away the other day, they had all these stories on him. He had done a thing in his later years about retirement. He said, 'People ask me about retirement. What do you do in retirement? How should you approach retirement?' And his answer was, 'Don't do it.' Well, I thought, 'Where were you six months ago, Walter?'"

Coach got back to work, serving as an unpaid adviser to Commissioner Roger Goodell. He pushed for the creation of the Coaches Subcommittee to the NFL's Competition Committee and wasn't content just to see the subcommittee be created; he went on to actively chair what came to be known as "the Madden Committee."

It wasn't long before Coach went beyond his regular conference calls with Goodell and hosted him as a passenger on the Madden Cruiser.

"I've been going to training camps all my life, and he likes to go to training camps and talk to players and see what's going on and all that stuff. So that's what we're doing now. We're getting on the bus and we're riding to these training camps and we're going to watch practice and eat and talk to players and just see what the heck's going on there. Just learn by observing."

Coach was proud of the progress he'd seen and knew there was work left to be done. He watched as other sports evolved around similar issues. One morning in 2014, when some fans were protesting the National Hockey League's toughened stance on hits to the head by wearing pink hats to games, Coach praised hockey's overseers.

"The league has to step in and provide the protocol and say this isn't acceptable. Those guys who make fun of it, the pink hats and stuff, either they've never taken a real shot to the head or they've taken too many shots to the head."

Coach's influence and relentless search for a better version of the game he loved led to numerous rules changes, including what some call "the Madden rule": a player diagnosed with a probable concussion has to be taken off the field, monitored by medical personnel, and can't return to play that day. A brain-trauma specialist who's not affiliated with the team is part of the process.

Hard as he worked and outspoken as he was, John didn't win 'em all. In one of our final on-air conversations in 2018, he expressed dismay at what he saw as a looming threat to the NFL and sports in general: widespread gambling.

"I'm really against it. I've always said we in sports can overcome most things if we just stay with it. We've had a scandal here and a scandal there, drugs and so on, but the one that would take your sport down is gambling. I mean, if gambling ever got into the sport where games were fixed in any way, that would be the end of it, because that takes away the whole thing. If anyone feels that everything's not legitimate, you're not going to care about it or you're not going to watch it. I've always worried about gambling. If it does get in there, I think it's a big, big mistake."

After John's death, the NFL chose to give Coach's favorite football day a new name: the *John Madden Thanksgiving Celebration.* In announcing the honor, Commissioner Goodell said, "No one cared more or contributed more to our game than John Madden." Hard to argue with that.

CHAPTER 14

Maddenisms

A HUNDRED YEARS BEFORE JOHN MADDEN, ANOTHER GREAT AMERICAN commentator amused people with memorable turns of phrase. Upon further inspection, it seems that many of the things Mark Twain supposedly said or wrote were actually somebody else's words. This fact doesn't diminish Twain's brilliance in the least. To me, it's evidence that whenever people ran across something clever, their first assumption was, "Mark Twain *must* have been the source!"

In the case of John Madden, there's no need to put other people's words in his mouth. It's all right here in the record. Many of Coach's memorable sayings got recycled frequently; he obviously knew a good one when he found it. Some are quite easy to decipher while others require some explanation.

In my long broadcasting career, I never came across anyone whose on-air comments seemed to "stick" the way Coach's did. I long ago lost track of the number of times people have recounted to me something John said on one of our broadcasts, remembering a story or a phrase in great detail. Now, with the transcription of our archive, I can see that they didn't just remember the gist of the thing. They often recalled the exact words.

Television director Drew Esocoff, who worked with John at NBC Sports, saw the same thing. "John would say something on the air that would take 12 seconds, and people would still be talking about it 40 years later," Esocoff told Sam Farmer of the *Los Angeles Times* in 2022.

It still happens. An acquaintance of mine, after hearing that I'd be writing this book, said, "Man, if you could find that episode where he talked about 'taking it in in Oakland and letting it out in San Francisco' [a beer-drinker's description of the two-city doubleheaders played in the old Pacific Coast League], that would be awesome!" Well, I did find it, and my friend had remembered it word for word, *two decades after he heard it.*

My own family has adopted a Maddenism to describe those situations where you were just innocently hanging out when something went awry. John's common preface, "I was just sitting there, minding my own business, not bothering anyone…" has opened many a story in our household.

As you've read Coach's quotes in this book, you've seen a few that started with the word "no" repeated several times. This was classically Coach: a denial or correction of something said by someone else wouldn't just start with one "no," but a string of them. They were always paired, so you'd get at least a "no no." But the more amped-up he was, the more pairs you'd get. I think the record was four pairs: "No no, no no, no no, no no!"

I should note another of Coach's verbal habits. To be honest, it escaped my attention during our daily conversations but leaped out at me when I saw those exchanges transcribed into text. John often exchanged the second-person pronoun "you" for the first-person pronoun "I" when telling a story about himself. Thus, he'd say things like, "There's just so much living that you've done that you kind of have to get it all in there one way or another" when analyzing the challenge of his Hall of Fame induction speech.

I'm indebted to the many KCBS listeners who responded to my social media posts shortly after Coach's death. I asked them to send me their favorite Maddenisms. I was struck not just by the sheer number of submissions, but by the breadth of the replies. There were a few repeats, but for the most part, each listener's response signified a separate Madden saying that had taken hold in his or her life.

So let's dig in. As I mentioned, some of what Coach said was straightforward. Some needs a bit of explication, which I've attempted to supply. Feel free to adopt any Maddenism you see here and use it in your own life!

"If you're going to eat cherries in the orchard, make sure they are worth the stomachache."

Taken literally, Coach is talking about what happens if you can't wait to dig into a bag of freshly picked cherries, something he loved to do when he'd take the grandkids to the orchard he and his buddy Dominic Mercurio owned. But scratch a bit deeper and you have a classic Maddenism: a reminder that short-term gains sometimes bring long-term pains.

"Even when I could do something like that, I couldn't do it."

A reminder here to every weekend warrior: you're not getting any younger, and even when you *were* younger, you weren't all that.

"If I can't do it, it's a sport."

How many arguments have centered around this question: "Is that *really* a sport?" Some divide the world of competition into "sports" and "games" but don't we call them "games" when football, basketball, or baseball players play them? My head hurts already. Coach cut to the chase on this matter: as he got older, he recognized the harsh reality. Sports are (usually) for the young.

"It has to start with the parents."

We had many conversations about the toxic, win-at-all-costs atmosphere that was becoming more obvious all the time in youth sports. John saw coaching as a form of teaching. He was certainly not averse to winning; in fact, he hated to lose. He also hated seeing kid sports co-opted by people who really didn't have the best interests of young people at heart. He felt strongly that the answer was at home.

"Don't let the hose out until you know where the fire is."

Honest admission: the first time Coach rolled this one out, I had to stop to figure it out. Now, it's one of my favorite admonitions, maybe because I used to be more of a "ready, fire, aim" guy.

"Don't worry about the horse being blind, just load the wagon."

On the other hand (see above), Coach had no trouble rallying the troops by telling everyone the destination might be unclear, but the journey required effort. I once asked him if he'd come up with this one on his own. He said he'd heard it somewhere and liked it, although he really didn't know exactly what it meant. But he used to wrap up his pregame pep talks to the Raiders with it, and he sprung it on his former player Dave Casper shortly before Casper's induction into the Pro Football Hall of Fame in 2002.

"Always a good day when football starts."

No explanation needed here, but for Coach, he meant the start of training camp. These days, that's in mid-to-late July, but over our years together, I could tell his sap was starting to rise around the Fourth of July. I strongly suspect he'd have supported a constitutional amendment guaranteeing 13 months of football every calendar year.

"Never arm-wrestle a one-armed guy."

A solid coaching and management philosophy here: it's good to play to your strengths, but it's really important to know your opponent's strengths as well.

"When you say you are going to retire, you have *retired."*

Coach didn't believe in "farewell tours." He made all three of his own retirement decisions (from the Raiders, from NBC Sports, and from KCBS) after taking some time to ponder his plans. When he said he was done, he was done, and there were no comeback tours either.

"I was just sitting there, minding my own business, not bothering anyone…"

The story you're about to tell is a good one, because whatever happened next was totally unexpected.

"Winning is the best deodorant."

This may be the best-known of the sports maxims Coach employed on a regular basis. He'd often trot it out when a team was on a losing streak or a player was in a slump. A couple of base hits or a win could suddenly make everything smell good.

"If you have two quarterbacks, you don't have a quarterback."

"Quarterback controversies" are part and parcel of football, but the Madden view of these situations was simple: you wouldn't have a controversy if one of your quarterbacks was the obvious starter. Substitute "favorite restaurant" or "preferred vacation destination" if you like; it's a way of thinking that cuts a clear path through ambivalence.

"Your guy is your guy until you find someone better."

This one speaks to the harsh truth of professional sports: you're only as good as your last performance. A winning organization may show loyalty, but ultimately, it's always looking for a winning edge.

"If you played one down in the NFL, your body will never be normal."

John Madden's coaching career was kickstarted by a knee injury. He saw the violence of the game firsthand as a player and a coach and while he loved the sport of football, he was keenly aware of the toll it took on those who played it. This Maddenism was in use long before the devastation of repeated head trauma became common knowledge; it's no surprise that John pushed hard for the NFL to improve player safety.

"If you don't do a Sunday at Lambeau Field, it's not pro football"

There's no other place in the NFL like the Green Bay Packers' home stadium. It sits in an actual neighborhood in what is by far the smallest city to hold an NFL franchise. It's been the scene of many memorable games, some played in truly brutal weather (and there's no roof on *this* stadium). I was lucky enough to make two pilgrimages to Lambeau with my KCBS colleagues Steve Bitker, Mike Sugerman, and Doug Sovern. Coach hooked us up with the tickets and I think he enjoyed hearing about our experiences as much as we did having them.

"It's a weird sport, coached and played by weird people."

I guess it takes one to know one!

"Always start without the blanket. It's easier to put it on than take it off."

An example of how a casual bit of Coach's advice would stick with people. When I tracked this one down in the archive, I realized it came from a conversation we had in 2001, and was still locked in one listener's memory 20 years later. As to the merits of his argument, I'm not completely convinced. To each his own, perhaps.

"He who knows that he can do something well will always be the first to want to do the thing that he does well."

This gem came as Coach described a gathering where a bunch of competitive guys started doing the old "I bet you can't do *this*" bit.

"If they have that kind of money to pay, what have they been doing with that money before they paid that money?"

Salaries for athletes and coaches are a common part of any sports-related conversation. Coach never begrudged a professional player or coach getting what he could, suggesting in this Maddenism that any owner who could afford to pay those salaries must have had more where it came from.

"I would pick Derek Jeter first and then we'll decide the game later."

I'll bet if Coach was alive today, he'd *still* pick Jeter first. John was a sports fan, first and foremost, and the Pride of the Yankees fascinated him.

"Golf, it's your game. Tennis, it's your game. Football, it's not your game... it's a team game."

A straightforward statement about the dividing line between individual sports and team sports. Coach didn't care if you were the star quarterback or the second-string left tackle: you were part of a team.

"If you're going to play golf and you're not any good, don't take it seriously or you'll just get frustrated."

Would that the vast majority of us who struggle at golf could keep this one in mind!

"The bigger the event, the worse the fans."

By "worse," he meant "less knowledgeable." It didn't matter how famous or wealthy John became: he was still the Daly City kid who'd sneak into Seals Stadium to watch minor-league baseball. He appreciated *real* fans, not the people who only show up when the stakes get high.

"If you put Tabasco and ketchup on it, you can eat anything."

Don't bet that he didn't.

"Don't have your last one be a bad one."

From a coach's perspective, it's an admonition to work at it in practice until you get it right. From a performer's perspective, it's a reminder that the audience will always remember the grand finale.

"Always get ready for things before they become the thing."

The John Madden version of the Boy Scout motto: "Be Prepared."

"I can't get dark chocolate. It's like they started to make chocolate and right in the middle of it, they went the other way."

It probably won't surprise you to learn that there was no designer chocolate aboard the Madden Cruiser. He didn't go for single-origin organic 85 percent cocoa bars; he served M&M's.

"There's no sport that I know of that you can be good at it if you can't bend your knees."

Any argument on this one?

"If you have a turducken, you won't go back."

Warning: it won't be a light snack.

"If you have to get up early to do something, I won't do it."

The first time I heard Coach say this, I thought, "Wait a minute. You're up every weekday morning to do our radio show." Upon further consideration, it hit me: he spent a good portion of every year in time zones east of ours, often gaining three hours on us. And even when he was at home, being ready to chat on the radio at 8:15 didn't require an insanely early wakeup time.

"Sometimes in life, you just get stuck on stupid."

We've all had those days. Or weeks. Or months

"Sometimes, stuck on stupid is good."

I'm going to say this is Madden-speak for the old saying "ignorance is bliss."

"If you didn't know how old you were, how old would you say you were?"

Coach's version of "You're only as old as you feel."

"There are physical geniuses and there are mental geniuses—they're just not in the same body."

Coach used many variations on this theme over the years. My favorite was the label he applied to quarterback Jeff George, a top NFL draft pick whose career fell short of expectations. "Good hardware, bad software" was the Madden assessment.

"You always think you can do something until you watch someone who can really do it. Then you realize you can't do it."

Keep this one in mind the next time you're ready to boo a Major League hitter for swinging through a nasty slider.

"Coaching is the type of thing that you shouldn't do unless you can't live without it."

I never heard John express any doubts, regrets, or second thoughts about walking away from coaching at the age of 42. He'd learned—the hard way—enough about himself to realize he couldn't continue down that road. Conversely, his boyhood friend John Robinson was 75 years old when he signed on as a high school defensive coordinator.

"There's not a place you can go to buy a can of quarterbacks to open before every game."

John's way of pointing out a couple of obvious truths about the game of football: without a good quarterback, it's hard to win, and good quarterbacks are hard to find.

"Golf has too many bendovers. You go through the day trying to limit your bendovers."

I'd never thought there was a noun to describe the act of bending over until I met Coach. I can recall how he lit up once as I told him about watching some elderly gentlemen playing the French boules game of pétanque. They were using little magnets on the ends of strings to hoist the ball from the ground before each shot, eliminating the need for a bendover. He was quite impressed with the concept.

"Why do they always give the guy who wins the long-drive contest a driver? The last thing he needs is a driver!"

Classic Coach. The world is full of stuff that doesn't make sense upon closer examination.

I suppose that if we'd been more clever, we'd have created a "Madden Quote of the Day" calendar or sold T-shirts with some of his wisdom imprinted on them. The truth is, we were just playing it one day at a time, carrying on a long-running conversation. Only occasionally did we realize the depth of the connection between John and KCBS listeners.

One such occasion was when Coach made news in April 2009, announcing his decision to step away from NFL telecasts. You'll find a full recounting of that big day in Chapter 22, "The Fourth Quarter." Suffice it to say, the decision to close such an important chapter in his life was an important and emotional one for John.

It turns out that it was an emotional day for many of our listeners as well. Unlike athletes, stage actors, or musicians who perform live, radio folks get no immediate feedback. We spout our words out into the ether and rely upon a highly imprecise ratings system to tell us if anyone is actually paying attention. Yes, of course things are changing as streaming services grow in popularity, but more than 80 percent of Americans aged 12 and older still listen to good old radio every week.

That percentage was even higher in 2009, and I'll honestly admit I was not expecting the immediate outpouring of appreciation for John Madden, nor did *he* expect some of the reaction. Apparently, his own family thought maybe he was shutting it all down.

"[Grandson] Sam asked [John's son] Joe yesterday if that means that Grandpa won't be famous anymore. Even my mother said, 'What does this mean? You're not going to be at KCBS?' That was the thing that she was worried about. I said, 'No, no, no, no. I'm still going to be there.' You know she listens every morning. Hi, Mom."

I told him, "It's amazing. You probably weren't aware of this, but we had a forum up on the station website. A number of people wrote in to say wonderful things about what you have done for them in their understanding of football. Here's one who's an immigrant who says you taught him to know and love the game. There are a lot of women who say your work on TV is what turned them into sports fans and that your explanations of the game allowed them to hold their own in dinner-table conversations."

Co-anchor Susan Leigh Taylor and sports anchor Steve Bitker then joined me.

Susan: "Everybody knows that David Letterman has made the 'Top 10 List' famous. And one of our very, very bright, witty listeners came up with their own Top 10 List. So here we go. The Top 10 Things I've Learned from John Madden. Number 10: No one cries during 'My Old Kentucky Home' anymore."

Me: "Number nine, hitting fungoes is harder than it looks."

Steve: "Number eight, ballroom dancing is not for everyone."

Susan: "Number seven, there's no difference between high def and regular def."

Me: "Number six, an NFL playoff game at Lambeau Field is as good as it gets."

Steve: "Number five, it's fun to eat your lunch while sitting on your breakfast."

Susan: "Number four, John Robinson gets bored by the time we get to Stockton."

Me: "Number three, always take Serena and Tiger versus the field."

Steve: "Number two, Newfies talk."

Susan: "And number one, Don Shula *bought* his golf game."

Coach's reply?

"That's pretty good. But that is someone that listens. I don't know why."

If he and the rest of us didn't know it until then, it was becoming pretty damned clear: our daily radio chat might have just seemed like a throwaway, a nice 10-minute diversion from our relentless torrent of news and information. That's how we saw it, anyway. To our listeners, it was much, much more. It was an intensely personal connection with a guy who probably never fully realized the extent of his impact on the lives of people he would never meet in person.

That's when I told him about the email I'd gotten from a listener who said she was glad the previous day's retirement conversation hadn't gotten any more emotional. She told me she'd teared up while driving and was afraid she'd crash the car. Coach's reply came in an uncharacteristically husky voice.

"Well, I'm, you know, it's emotional for me, too. It's, it's just a tough thing to do, you know, and to hear stuff like that."

Steve Bitker then popped back in, saying, "In fact, John, I should add that at the end of that Top 10 List, this listener said, 'John Madden, he's from here.'"

I wish I could personally thank the listener who sent in that list. She or he unwittingly provided a quick point of departure for tracking down many memorable "Mornings with Madden"—every item on that list found its way into this book in some form.

The audio console from which I ran our broadcast in KCBS Studio A for all those years had a set of those big VU meters in front of me. Those are the gauges that tell an audio engineer if the sound level is being properly maintained. Thus, I knew the needle was always moving when we were speaking.

But "moving the needle" has a deeper meaning in the modern vernacular. It refers to making a noticeable change. Viewed that way, and proven by the audience response to what John Madden said on the air, he most definitely moved the needle.

CHAPTER 15

Man's Best Friend

FULL DISCLOSURE RIGHT OFF THE TOP: WHEN IT COMES TO THE DIVIDING line between "dog people" and "cat people," I'm over here with the canines. And given his oversized body and persona, it's probably not going to shock you to learn that John Madden was a dog guy as well.

Further full disclosure: I'm pretty sure it was Virginia Madden who did most of the heavy lifting when it came to the dog-management duties *Chez Madden.*

Long before I got connected with Coach, the Maddens had a couple of big bulldogs named Boss and Tug. During our radio years together, there were Newfoundlands with names like Joey, Sweetie, Bubba, Yogi, and Boo-Boo.

The Madden dogs didn't travel on the bus with John the way John Steinbeck's poodle Charley roamed America with the great writer, but we got a lot of mileage out of those Newfoundlands when Coach was at home.

Living with big dogs requires certain adjustments. One morning, I told Coach I'd seen someone driving a small sports car through San Francisco with a Newfoundland hanging over the windowsill. It seemed to me there was about as much dog outside the car as there was in it. I asked how the Maddens handled car rides with their big pooches.

"They have their own car. It's like a van or whatever with no seats in the back. It's kind of a low thing so they can get up into it. And whenever we take them anywhere they have only that one car they go into. You can't share your car with a Newfoundland. Especially when you have two. I mean they take up from the front of the van all the way to the back. They take it all up, two of them."

Makes sense that a larger-than-life figure like John would wind up with larger-than-average dogs in his life.

"You can't beat a Newfoundland. They behave better than anyone."

There's behavior, and then there's hygiene. My co-anchor Susan Leigh Taylor once offered to keep an eye on Bubba the Newfie, if Coach would make sure she had a towel to handle the drool.

"No, no, no, no. With the Newfoundland, you can't worry about that stuff. If you worry about that stuff, then you have to get a Chihuahua or something. I mean, you can get white pants and after a while they're not white anymore, but they have that character to them. You say, 'Oh, boy, look at those pants. Now you're talking!' You got to jump in with both feet in these deals."

We were often privy to conversations Coach claimed to be having with his big dogs. He was a prodigious newspaper reader, combing several papers every day, and once, he'd spotted Newfie news.

"I was telling Bubba and Sweetie this morning that I looked in today's Chronicle *and I see someone that has four Newfs, and my two think* they're *a handful. I said, 'Look at this. Here's someone who has four.' Big photo, four Newfs just laying right out there. They're docile. I was showing it to mine. I said, 'See, this is how you're supposed to be.'"*

I asked Coach if the story had any suggestions as to how someone would manage a whole herd of giant dogs. It turned out the article was about a couple who had installed a lot of solar panels and storage batteries at their home. Aside from the photo and a reference to "pony-size dogs," the Newfoundlands really had no role in the story.

"The dogs are just a prop. I was looking for a story on the dogs. But the dogs are just a prop. They're just laying there. They must have just been fed or something. Just laying there. Is it 'lay' or 'lie'?"

This was one of the many times in our years together where Coach would test my level of education. "Lying there," I said. "If you could pick one of them up, you would 'lay' it down."

"Okay, 'lying.' Anyway, mine don't lie around like that when people are taking pictures and stuff. They want snacks."

There was a lot of woofing at the Madden house when an irrepressible Newfoundland named Josh won "Best in Show" at the 2004 Westminster Kennel Club Dog Show, charming the Madison Square Garden crowd with his loud barking and playful demeanor. There was also some salivating, which Newfies are pretty good at.

"If you worry about slobber, if you're not a slobber lover, if slobber is not okay, if you hate slobber, then you don't like Newfoundlands. I was just talking to Sweetie about this this morning. When you get a Newfoundland, then in your mind, you have to say that slobber is okay. And then I said, 'You guys slobber all the time.' Well, slobber is okay if you get a Newfoundland. And then she reminded me about the Westminster Dog Show where the Newfoundland had just won. The best dog in the whole world. I mean, they're the champions of the world. It's like with people, when their team wins the Super Bowl, wins the World Series, wins the NCAA, the NBA, wins those types of things, then they talk about it for a year."

A year later, Coach and the dogs were wrapping up their 12 months of superiority as the Westminster show headed for its final night.

"We're still defending champions until someone beats us."

I brought up a newspaper article about the outgoing champion Josh, which said he'd retired to New Jersey where he lived with his girlfriends and worked as a therapy dog.

"I will tell Bubba. Bubba knows Josh, because you know, they're brothers. But I know that they didn't even win their group last night, so I know that the title is going to go someplace else. I wasn't sure Josh wasn't in it, but the Newfoundland was beaten anyway by a Great Pyrenees. That's why Bubba and Sweetie came in this morning and didn't feel good. They got up and went back outside and they're out there lying in the rain. That's what it is. They heard the news."

Coach then realized he might be able to cheer Bubba up a bit.

"I don't think Bubba knows that news about Josh and his girlfriends. I'll tell him. And the part about being a therapy dog, they're good at that. I mean, they do spread good cheer if you can take the slobber. If you can't take the slobber, then you don't belong around them."

John Madden didn't like losing. In his telling, his dogs didn't like it either.

"A German shorthaired pointer won. But what was interesting is that the woman who handled the Newfoundland that won last year also handled the German shorthair that won last night. Bubba and Sweetie were saying, 'What's up with that?' They wanted to know where the loyalty was because they kind of thought that she was part of the Newfoundland deal. And then, lo and behold, she switches from the Newfoundland to the German shorthair."

It was clear that those two big Newfies had gotten their noses out of joint.

"Last night, I brought them in to watch the dog show and when they went to lie down, they turned the other way. They said, 'There's no Newfies,' so they don't care. They don't care about other dogs. They don't even want to sniff."

A year after that conversation, Coach revealed a Newfoundland population explosion at his place. Maybe that *San Francisco Chronicle* story he'd mentioned in an earlier broadcast had gotten him and Virginia thinking about expanding the tribe.

"We have two new puppies that are from the one that was the champion, Josh. They're Josh's people. We got Yogi and then another one came, a female. She's called Boo-Boo. Are you kidding me?"

I was flabbergasted, having shared a house with three dogs for a while but never any dogs as big as Newfies. Four of them!

"It's probably against some law. You know, they had a thing down here where someone had too many chickens in their backyard. I don't know if they have a dog catcher still around that comes to your house to count your dogs."

Yogi quickly became part of the annual Westminster dog show Newfie disappointment story.

"The dogs came in and they were looking at the TV. They didn't see any Newfoundlands in the final so they just went back to sleep. I mean, they don't have to win it all the time. Yogi would say, 'We won it a few years ago and we don't

have to win it every year. But if we could just be in the final, just to have some representation, that's all we want.'"

The Newfoundlands and their antics became a fairly constant thread in our radio conversations. One thing Coach knew plenty about was food, and there was certainly an intersection.

"You have to reward them all the time with food. To get a dog to do anything, you have to either give them a treat or offer them a treat. And that's how we get them in and out and all that stuff. Doesn't have to be big. They don't know the difference. They just know you have something in your hand and as long as they know it, then you're good. Sometimes they get disappointed, but I mean, they don't enjoy their food. They just take it and go 'gulp' and it's gone. You say, 'You have to chew it, you have to enjoy it.' No, no, no. It's just poof, it's gone."

Speaking of dining habits, as far as I know, the Madden dogs never were subjected to a "home remedy" for dogs that Coach read about somewhere.

"These dogs had upset stomachs and then they ate rotten fish and they got better. So I was just telling my dogs, 'If you guys get sick, I'm going to give you rotten fish.' They just turned their heads. But I don't know where to go get rotten fish. Every place you go, it's got fresh fish. No one says, 'We got rotten fish.' Anyway, that's what I'm telling my dogs, 'If you guys get sick, I'm going to give you some rotten fish. That'll make you better.'"

It turns out Newfies are among the breeds with a higher risk for ruptures of their canine cruciate ligaments. The CCL is basically a dog's version of the anterior cruciate ligament (ACL), which many an athlete has ruptured (and many a non-athlete as well; mine due to an ill-advised ski stunt).

Yogi the Newfie wound up with a CCL injury that put him on the PUP list. I couldn't help myself on that one: the Physically Unable to Perform (PUP) list is one of the NFL's designations for injured players.

Just like a star running back, Yogi got sent to physical rehabilitation. Coach would keep us posted on the big pooch's progress until he had good news one morning.

"Got a Yogi update. He's right here, just walking by as I'm talking about him. He's going to his last day of rehab. He graduates from rehab today. He looks pretty

good. I don't know if he gets a diploma or not. That's something these days. You have to go to all these graduations now, when kids graduate from preschool and kindergarten and everything's a party. So I don't know if Yogi gets one of those. I don't think so."

At that point, John hollered to the big dog.

"You know, you don't get anything!"

"He's disappointed, I can tell," I said.

"Nah, he's looking for a treat. Begging. Begging for treats."

One morning the conversation was focused on athletes who'd come back from ACL repairs seemingly no worse for the wear, the result of skilled surgeons and focused rehabilitation work. Susan picked the perfect moment to slide from athletes to dogs, asking, "I was wondering if Yogi had any better talents after his ACL repair?"

"It's interesting that you ask about that, but he climbs the hill. I mean, we have a hill in the backyard and he likes to jump up and run up it. And I think that's where he got the injury because going up *the hill everything was okay, but when he came down and started going down the stairs, he'd jump off the ledge to the ground. See, it's good when you jump, but it's bad when you land and you're landing with all that stuff. So I noticed there for a while he wouldn't go up. And then yesterday there he was, running all around the hill."*

Another athlete back in action thanks to modern medicine.

The Madden Newfies got their share of airtime but that wasn't where their celebrity ended. Coach's friend Tony La Russa and his wife, Elaine, founded the nonprofit Animal Rescue Foundation (ARF) after La Russa rounded up a stray cat on the field while managing the Oakland A's (La Russa and his family have since cut ties with the group). One year, La Russa came to Coach with a request.

"They're doing a calendar and for his calendar, he wants a picture with me and my four Newfoundlands. I mean, imagine four Newfoundlands, two of them are puppies, and this picture is never going to make any calendar. I mean, how in the heck!? Here's me and four big dogs that look like bears and the photographer wants them to pose. She wants a portrait, you know, like, 'Why don't we have two

of them lying down at your feet and two of them…' Heck, you can't get four of them to do any *one thing! They're dogs. They're puppies. It's just, 'stand,' 'sit.' If you can just get them all looking straight ahead, you've got a thing."*

I'm not laughing *at* Coach. I'm laughing *with* him, having struggled more than once to get our family's two flat-coated retrievers to pose for the annual holiday greeting card snapshot. You'd need to have at least four arms to wrangle all his dogs.

"That's exactly what I was doing. I mean, I had a chain on one while I was trying to wrestle another, and she's talking about a portrait? Then she said, 'Well, I'll just have you with one.' Yeah, well, then that loses the thing. You wanted to take a portrait of me and my dogs. You know, guys that don't have tailors don't take portraits."

Anyone who's ever tried to get a good photo of a black dog knows how light just seems to vanish into them. You wind up with featureless blobs on your image. I mentioned that to John.

"Right, and then multiply that by four. That's what I got. And then add me. You got five big blobs."

I think it actually came as a surprise to Coach that the family portrait made the cut for the 2007 ARF calendar. La Russa delivered the news himself one morning. "It's the most beautiful picture you've ever seen in your life," La Russa began. "No, I'm not talking about John. I'm talking about these four gorgeous dogs. They sent me the calendar that's going to print, and John's in there, and they got all four of the dogs in one picture. It's a gorgeous picture."

Coach couldn't let go of his memories of the chaotic photo shoot.

"They tried to get 'em to pose. They wanted, like, two in front, two in the back, two on either side. One was drinking out of the water bowl behind me and wanted to go over on the other side. So didn't we end up with three on one side and one on the other?"

La Russa confirmed the unbalanced lineup and said they'd used a little digital trickery to improve the layout. "I just saw it," he told us. "They sent me the copy and I just FedEx'ed it so Elaine will get it this morning so she can take a look at it."

"Did you okay it? Did you put 'Okay' on it or did you write 'Drop this'?"

Listening back to the segment, I'm pretty sure Coach thought La Russa was setting him up for a prank, but true to La Russa's word, the calendar really did come out with the Madden dog pack included. I wrapped things up that morning by asking if we could get the dogs to autograph a copy once the calendar shipped.

"Yeah, they'll do anything. They don't care."

Call him a dog-whisperer if you like, but Coach often seemed to know exactly what those big Newfies were thinking. At least, that's what he told us. On the occasion of yet another televised dog show, he filled us in on what he was picking up from his pooches.

"They look for flaws and they just kind of shake their heads. Then I think when they drool, I think that means that they don't like what they're seeing. So they go to sleep. The dogs really didn't give a darn because they had all those little dogs on TV. They look like bait to them. To be serious, they don't count them as dogs. They look at them and think they're like a toy or something that they don't pay any attention to. They'll look up and then put their heads back down and then they sleep right through it."

Figuring I was speaking in sympathy with several hundred pounds of Madden Newfoundlands, I then referred to the winner of yet another edition of the Westminster Kennel Club show as "a dinky Pekingese."

"You are going to get in trouble that way. What did you call that Pekingese?"

I tried to weasel my way out of trouble, saying, "It was Susan. She referred to it as 'a little dust bunny.'" Coach was having none of it.

"No, no, no. You called it 'dinky.' *Just so everyone knows who said what. I'm just saying what my dogs said about little dogs. You know, I enjoy all dogs. My dogs won't even look up. They won't even watch the TV. They said, 'They don't even count as dogs.' I said, 'Give them a chance. They're dogs too.' Yeah, that's what I say to them. 'Look, they're dogs,' but* they *look and think, 'They're not dogs.'"*

John's dogs might have picked up a bit of big-dog bias from the Master of the House himself. In yet another dog show analysis conversation, he put it out there.

"I prefer the bigger dogs, like I've always liked bulldogs. Any kind of bulldog, anything in that group there, I kind of like. But I don't know half those dogs they're showing. I mean, I didn't know half those dogs were dogs before I saw they were dogs last night."

As you've read, John got a lot of mileage out of his joking claim to have competed in the Iditarod Trail Sled Dog Race in Alaska. He had, in fact, covered the race for CBS Sports once, early in his broadcasting career, but his professed memories of tough days on the frozen trail were all bogus. From time to time over our years on the radio, I'd bring it up again and we'd get fresh laughs out of old material. One year, Coach was the one who tossed the Iditarod into the mix, mentioning Mitch Seavey's win.

"I was talking to Bubba about it this morning, and the dogs don't like it because, you know, they never give the dogs credit. I mean, it's 'Mitch Seavey this and Mitch Seavey that,' while Mitch Seavey, all he did is ride the sled. All he did was mush. They never mention the dogs. Like in a horse race, they'll mention the winner, they'll mention the horse, they'll mention the jockey, they'll mention the trainer, and they'll mention the owner. They all get in a circle after they win and kiss and stuff."

"So is that why you haven't gone back to the Iditarod," I asked, "because your own dogs are kind of giving you grief about it?"

"Yeah, they don't like it. They don't like the way they treat the dogs. They don't like the fact that they never get mentioned."

It is a fact that after that broadcast, John Madden never again rode a dog sled on the Iditarod trail. Now you know why.

Even when Coach wasn't telling us what the Newfies were up to, he seemed to be on alert for dog-related content. One morning, Susan made reference to a freeway tie-up, calling it a "bad, bad situation," a few minutes before I introduced John. He jumped right in.

"You know what Susan just did? She just did a 'double-bad.' She said, 'Bad, bad.' And that's usually saved for dogs. Like when your animals jump up, you say, 'Get down. Bad, bad.' And Susan, I haven't heard a good 'bad, bad' like that, that didn't refer to a dog jumping up, in a long time."

Susan, our resident cat lady, came back with, "I got some practice this morning. One of the cats jumped on a table and knocked something off and broke it."

"I was thinking, I swear, when I heard you say 'Bad, bad,' I knew that you had a problem with one of your cats. I swear I did. That's saved for cats and dogs."

The big Newfies weren't the only dogs in Coach's life. His arrival aboard the Madden Cruiser at high-profile, high-security events like Super Bowl games meant he had to undergo the full screening protocol.

"They would always send the dogs on the bus, and that would kind of offend me, you know. What do they think I'm going to do? What they think I have in here? And they're saying, 'Someone could put something in your stuff knowing you're going in, blah, blah, blah.' So then it became a good thing."

I wanted to know if the trained security dogs ever showed any interest in the bowls of M&M's that were always kept replenished aboard the bus.

"No, no. The dogs are pros. I mean, they know what they're doing, what they're looking for, what they're sniffing for. And if it's not something they're looking for or sniffing for, they don't go for it."

One of my favorite exchanges with Coach involved yet another riff on the Iditarod race. He claimed that his two Newfoundlands were upset about the nomenclature of the sport.

"I was talking to Bubba and Sweetie, and they were upset. They wanted to know why in the hell the 'sled' got put in front of the 'dog.' They said they don't want any part of it, if they're going to put the word 'sled' in front of the word 'dog.'"

What Coach did next took the segment from "funny" to "unforgettable." He slipped into the voice of a bloviating political orator.

"And I'll tell you, all dogs in this country and in other countries are upset about this. See, I learned how to talk like a senator: 'And all dogs in this *country... pause...and raise your voice...and* other *countries are upset about this! And we're going to do something...Right! Now!'"*

He had my vote.

CHAPTER 16

Team Player

It would have been easy for John Madden to just jump on the air every morning, spout a few provocative words, and get on with his busy life. We've all heard radio contributors like that.

That's not how he rolled. Coach may have been the perennial All-Star, but he still approached the gig like a hustling rookie trying to stick with the squad. He was the consummate team player.

As I said earlier, KCBS wasn't the obvious place for a raconteur. The fast-paced, all-news format didn't appear to leave a lot of room for warmth and bonhomie. John Madden started changing that the day he first appeared on the station in 1997.

My predecessor (and hero) Al Hart was a lovely man with a warm, approachable style. He didn't know an awful lot about sports but that was fine with John. Al's co-anchor Susan Leigh Taylor would become my broadcast partner for 20 years, making us the longest-tenured morning duo in the century-plus history of the station.

Steve Bitker was the morning sports guy. Steve had a challenging role: lead into "the Madden Segment" with a quick round of sports headlines, then take part in a conversation that often ranged far away from the world of sports.

But Steve had an even bigger challenge. In order to maximize our use of John Madden's gigantic brand, KCBS would replay a slice of the morning Madden conversation during afternoon sportscasts. Steve had to figure a way to pull out something sports-related for later replay.

Trust me: there were many mornings when we'd be far, far away from sports as the clock wound toward that moment when I'd have to wrap things up and move on to the next traffic and weather report. I can still see the anguish on Steve's face as he tried to figure how to derail the runaway train so he could ask about the latest quarterback controversy or free-agent signing.

John was keenly aware of every bit of this, though no one ever told him anything directly. He had an innate ability to read the room and read between the lines. It helped make for terrific moments on the air.

Part of the joy of writing this book has been unearthing broadcasts that occurred during the three years between when John joined KCBS and my return to the station in 2000, when I replaced Al Hart upon his retirement. This one played out just after Al welcomed Coach one spring morning.

"I don't mean to start any trouble. I'm not that kind of guy. I'm really not. So I'm driving in my truck yesterday afternoon, and for some reason Steve is doing the afternoon sports. So I'm listening to Steve. I think it's either 2:15 or 2:45. You can check your tapes. He calls the other people, you know, the afternoon gang in there, he calls them 'sweet.' He says that they're sweet. Now, I have never, ever, ever heard Steve ever call you or Susan 'sweet.'"

Al replied, "I guess there's a reason for that."

"Well, I don't know what it is. I don't know what's going on here. I mean, when he's with you, it's just 'old Al and Susan,' right? And then he goes on in the afternoon and he's telling them how sweet they are. I don't mean to start any trouble. I was just driving in my truck, not bothering anyone. I heard that and my seatbelt kind of jerked."

Time for Steve to explain himself. "I just felt I needed to ingratiate myself to my new partners for the day."

"What'd you call them? 'Sweet?'"

"I think I did."

"Yeah, you did. You did. I heard it with my ears. My raw ears. I'm driving around. Maybe, Steve, you oughta call Al and Susan sweet."

I'm betting this: of all the news stories, traffic reports, weather forecasts, and financial updates that ran on KCBS that morning, the odds are very good that the thing listeners remembered all day was John Madden and the word "sweet."

Looking back on my radio career, I realize that life was always better with a dance partner. You *can* dance like nobody's watching, as the saying goes, but they also say it takes two to tango. Maybe not surprisingly for a guy who actually taught ballroom dancing once upon a time, John Madden could effortlessly join the dance.

Often, it was just a quick little move, like the morning I had to jump in after introducing him because I'd forgotten to read what we call the "sponsorship billboard."

"I should remind our listeners," I said, "these next few minutes of whatever we're going to give you is sponsored by the State Compensation Insurance Fund."

Coach was right there. *"Verbiage. You know, a lot of people say 'verbage.'"*

Back to me. "Yeah. They miss the 'i' in there."

Coach's turn. *"Yeah, yeah. Verbiage."*

Bing, bang, done. John had followed my lead, added a little sparkle, and we moved on. He'd also, by the way, reminded us of his love for language.

In the early 2000s, a vocabulary-improvement course called "Verbal Advantage" was running a lot of radio commercials. They were hard to ignore. John knew about them; he'd listen to KCBS at all times of day when he was in the Bay Area.

One morning, we'd had a far-ranging chat about the way football blocking was taught back in John's years on the sidelines. I was in "let's wrap this up" mode and Coach did something he loved to do: extend the conversation, often with a thought from deep-left field.

"The other thing, you know, those old cowboy movies, you always hear the guys say that they're going to go have some vittles. How do you think you spell 'vittles'?"

Caught off guard, about all I could muster was, "With two t's?"

"No, no. I saw it spelled the other day. It's spelled v-i-c-t-u-a-l-s. I always thought, 'Yeah, yeah, yeah. Let's get some grub. Let's go get some vittles.' I always thought it was like v-i-t or v-i-d or something. Who would have thought? That's why you need 'Verbal Advantage.'"

John had been practicing that "and one more thing" bit from the very first day he appeared on KCBS. As I mentioned earlier, his arrival at the station created a definite "square peg/round hole" situation. KCBS, like all of the CBS-owned, all-news stations, had long based its format on strict adherence to the clock. Sports happened at :15 and :45 past the hour, traffic and weather reports came around "on the 8s," and so on.

I wasn't around for that first John Madden/KCBS broadcast in 1997, but Coach's son Mike remembers it clearly. He was sitting with his dad when the call came from the KCBS newsroom.

As Mike tells it, the KCBS producer (no doubt with station management nervously lurking nearby) greeted Coach and said something along the lines of, "Now remember, we have a very tight format here so this will be just a five-minute segment."

At that point, Mike says his dad replied, "Okay, got it," then covered the mouthpiece of the phone, turned to Mike, and said, "Watch this."

Al Hart introduced Coach, a conversation ensued, and the five-minute mark was rapidly approaching. Al started trying to wrap things up, and that's when John looked over at Mike, winked, and said, "Yeah, Al, and another thing…"

"Another thing" from John almost always turned out to be worth the extra few seconds.

As an aside here, I should tell you about the internal clock radio announcers tend to develop. If you spend enough time in a fast-paced radio format, your brain just knows when 15 seconds or 30 seconds has passed. Coach seemed to possess this skill too; I suspect he perfected it during those NFL broadcasts when he had a very short time to sum things up before the next play started. His ability to lock into the rhythm of our broadcasts made him not just a guest, but one of us.

Coach seemed to really light up when he could get involved in something going on around the radio station. Remember, this is a guy who *never visited KCBS* in the 20-plus years he was associated with the station. Thus, he had to develop his camaraderie with the on-air and off-air staff through brief phone conversations and our on-air chats.

One morning, we were gently mocking my co-anchor Susan. She'd brought in a birthday cake for one of our newsroom staffers and things had not gone according to plan. John jumped on this.

"What happened to Susan's cake for Angela's birthday? Happy birthday, Angela."

Susan, who would shamelessly beg for John's wife to make her acclaimed chocolate cake for the annual KCBS/Madden Barbecue, said, "Virginia would not be proud of me. It just went all wrong. It looked like a five-year-old made it. Something happened to my frosting. And on the way to work, the top layer slid off of the bottom layer and it broke in half. It was just a wreck."

"Wait a minute. The top half slid off, and then broke in half? The top half broke in half again?"

At this point, Susan's ever-sympathetic studio partners chime in. "I thought it was abstract art," Steve offered.

"It wasn't pretty, but it did taste good," I verified.

"Not gonna win any beauty contest, though," Susan said glumly.

"Yeah, well, how did it look when you left the house?"

Susan admitted, "Not a whole lot better, frankly, than when I got here."

"So it didn't look good. Didn't look good coming out. You had good ingredients though? Did it rise?"

Back to Susan. "It rose. The problem was with the frosting. It's a frosting with whipped cream and sour cream. And for some reason, it wasn't fluffy. It came out really runny. It looked like I just kind of dumped a carton of milk on top of the cake."

By now, I'm thinking the topic has probably run its course with Coach, who's a serious eater but not a guy you expect to see in the kitchen. But he's not finished just yet.

"This looks like a job for Narsai David [the longtime Bay Area restaurateur and KCBS Food and Wine Editor], because there's some ingredient you could put in there that would thicken it up. If it were stew, I'd tell you to put some more flour in."

The exchange didn't solve any world problems, but it did showcase John's desire to be a part of the team. At times like this, I often wished that he *did* come into the studios for his segment, but then I'd see the problem: if John Madden was hanging around the newsroom, nobody would get any work done.

One of John's great teammate talents was to engage with everyone on our broadcast crew. I introduced him and ushered him off the air every morning, Steve would always get in a sports-related question or two, but Susan would often be cut out of the deal for days at a time. When her turn did come around, John was always ready.

Every year, Coach would mock Susan's insistence that the playing of "My Old Kentucky Home" at Churchill Downs on Kentucky Derby day caused everyone in attendance to cry.

"They always say 'My Old Kentucky Home,' there's never a dry eye in the house. I've looked. I would watch, and I would say that I couldn't find a wet *eye in the house."*

Susan stood her ground year after year, until we finally agreed to a test. Susan brought in two guests who were Derby Day regulars, our colleague Al Hart sang "My Old Kentucky Home," and Coach said he'd pay a hundred dollars for each person who cried.

Newsroom producer Ted Goldberg was called in to judge. "I saw one official tear coming from Susan Leigh Taylor," Ted reported. "As for the other folks in the room, I can be honest about this. They became increasingly emotional. They were touched. I did not see any eye precipitation."

Coach wasn't going to concede to Susan on this one, despite her best efforts.

"I was listening to the lyrics and stuff, and I thought, 'Oh, man, how long is this thing going to go on?' And I yawned. And then you kind of get a little moisture there, when you yawn. So maybe they were yawning."

"The Madden Segment," of course, rotated around John. But since we never drew any plays up in the dirt before launching the daily conversation, Coach often had to improvise. He did it many times with guests we'd spring on him—again, he would have zero prep time but, in football parlance, would adjust his pattern on the fly.

One of many examples involved Chris Wondolowski, who remains the leading career goal-scorer in Major League Soccer history. "Wondo" is a Bay Area native and spent most of his professional career with the San Jose Earthquakes.

The Earthquakes were "playing out the string," a few weeks away from the end of a season in which they would fail to make the playoffs. Coach may not have known a lot about soccer, but he understood athletes enough to frame a question for Wondolowski.

"You know, I've never met any athlete that could turn it on and off, that needed a reason to win. And therefore, when there's no reason, you're not going to win. I've always thought that's a bunch of baloney. There's a game and there's only one way to play it, and you go out and play it to win. And it'll be interesting what Chris thinks about this. I think it's fans who say, 'Oh, you have nothing to play for anymore. Why do you go out there and play?' Because there's a game. I'm a player. I'm a pro. That's what it is. How do you feel about that, Chris?"

Not surprisingly, we got a thoughtful answer from Chris Wondolowski.

Coach could roll with surprise guests who weren't pro athletes. One morning, a fellow who'd won a charity auction item allowing him to visit the KCBS studios showed up with a pair of brothers, aged 10 and 12, in tow. My colleague Al Hart wanted to make their day special, so he brought them into the studio. When it was "Madden Time," Al introduced them, saying, "Hey, we have some special guests who are big fans of yours. We have Kevin Swimmer and Blake Swimmer sitting here and hanging on your every word today."

"What are they doing there?"

Al replied, "Oh, they just want to bask in the glow of the Madden show."

I chipped in, "And you should see Kevin and Blake. John, these two young guys are wearing suits and ties this morning. They're all scrubbed up. I got to tell you, you'd be proud to see your grandkids look like this."

"So they're all scrubbed up? They take a bath?"

That would have been enough of a memory for two young Bay Area kids to tell *their* grandkids about someday: John Madden noticed them! But this story gets better.

Somehow, the conversation that morning wound around to physical fitness and Coach wanted to know if any of us could drop down and do a few pushups. I demurred (after all, *somebody* has to stay at the audio control panel, right?) but Al was cajoled into performing. And not just Al.

"Can those kids do pushups in their suits?"

The boys didn't have headphones on, and when studio microphones are on, the studio monitor speakers are muted, meaning they couldn't hear Coach's question. I had to inform them that John Madden wanted them to drop down and do three pushups.

They eagerly hit the floor and nailed their pushups while Al may have wobbled a bit on his last one.

"Ties on the ground?"

I confirmed the boys' neckties had indeed brushed the floor. Laughs all around, including from the KCBS newsroom staffers who'd crowded against the studio window to watch the exhibition. Coach has built an even better memory for those two youngsters. But there's still more to the story.

Four years later, one of the Swimmer boys is playing high school freshman football. His school is playing a squad coached by John's son Mike. John was a regular at these games. After the game, Kevin approaches Coach and asks if he might remember him as one of the Swimmer kids who did pushups on KCBS.

Without missing a beat, John said, "Oh yeah. The Swimmer kids. Ties on the ground, right?" I have trouble remembering what I had for lunch yesterday, but he immediately remembered the details of a segment from four years before. Broadcasters work tirelessly to give listeners a reason to tune in regularly. In that brief encounter, Coach locked in the Swimmer family, and everyone they know, for life.

As big a deal as he was, when Coach called in to our show, he was just one of the gang. Of course, I'd describe him as *"Primus inter pares"* (First among equals). One year, the Associated Press Television-Radio Association (APTRA) decided to bestow the equivalent of a Lifetime Achievement Award on John.

Roberta Gonzales is a meteorologist who, at the time, was working at the CBS television station KPIX, whose building we shared. Part of her gig was to pop in with us a few times each morning for a live weather segment.

She was the vice president of APTRA, and told reporters, "Like everyone else, I see John Madden on national television and on the cover of my children's video games. But I also have the privilege of working on the same radio show as John and there is no one else in his league."

The group's awards dinner was being held at Universal Studios in Hollywood. As would happen many times over the years, we had to let the organizers know that Coach was unlikely to attend, though he would record a video greeting. In this case, I was named "designated hitter," tasked with picking up the award for Coach and saying a few words on his behalf.

The day before the event, I told Coach, "I need some instructions from you because they're telling me I might have to go and pick up a trophy for you. So if I'm in the role of John Madden, how do I handle this? What do I do? What should I say?"

"You know, just say, 'Thank you.'"

"That's it?" I replied. "Just say, 'thank you'?" And that's when John Madden, The Team Player, kicked in.

"Here's what I think—and I really believe this. Any time that you receive an award as an individual, when you work with a lot of other people on a team, you're receiving it as part of that team. That's not just baloney. I mean, I really feel that way because no one in this business or just about any business does anything by themselves. And so when you get an award for yourself, you have to include the

other people that you work with and work for you. Those people are a big part of it.”

Sweet words to hear. Of course, we were never far from a joke, so I then said, “I’m going to get up there and tell everyone that Susan suggested I say it exactly like this, when the applause dies down: ‘I’m only speaking for John because John couldn’t be here tonight. He’s a very busy man, but I’d like to accept the 2007 Stan Chambers Award for Extraordinary Achievement, with special thanks to Susan Leigh Taylor for making it all possible.’”

“Yeah, yeah, yeah. That’s good. Susan Leigh Taylor. And name yourself and name Steve. And then name Ed [Cavagnaro, the longtime news and program director] and name them all, everyone in the newsroom.”

I wrapped things up by reminding our audience that this honor was coming from a broadcast journalists’ organization, saying, “They consider John one of their own, which I think is pretty cool. Because you *are* a reporter.”

“Well, you know, sometimes I go out on assignments.”

We had a hell of a run at KCBS. I mentioned the 20 years Susan Leigh Taylor and I shared the studio as the morning news anchors. Sports guy Steve Bitker was part of the morning crew for over 25 years. By the time of my 2021 retirement, the “new guy” among our on-air crew was financial editor Jason Brooks, who’d been there for a dozen years.

John Madden’s piece of that team history spanned parts of three decades. In sports parlance, he was a steady clubhouse presence, even though he never actually set foot in the radio station. Of course, the regular arrival of boxes of See’s Candies chocolates to mark holidays like Christmas and Valentine’s Day helped cement Coach’s reputation among the troops, while also providing fodder for a classic observation about what happens when children are in the same room with a box of candy.

“If people that tell you that kids don’t do this, they’re not watching their kids. They’ll take a bite, because they don’t know. They’ll take a bite. And if it’s one they don’t like, then they’ll just put it back and then go get another one. But my son Mike somehow memorized every one of them. He can look at a box of See’s candy

and define every piece. But most kids, it's trial and error. You know, take a bite. You don't like it, throw it back."

Good teammates share in each other's successes and failures. But no team lasts forever; it's in the nature of the team concept that new players arrive and others move on.

Our beloved colleague Al Hart was one who left the starting lineup, and a few years later, the team itself.

Al had started at KCBS in 1966, two years before the station's conversion to the all-news format that turned it into the powerhouse it is today. Al's original role was to be a producer and sidekick for another Bay Area radio legend, Dave McElhatton. When the switch to all-news happened, Al became a broadcast journalist, practically overnight.

For several years, he served as a news editor and afternoon news anchor. When McElhatton jumped to television in 1976, Al became the steady voice that defined morning news programming on KCBS for most of the years until 2000.

He was in that slot in 1997 when John Madden made his decision to leave KNBR and join KCBS. The chemistry between Al and Coach was instant and relatable. The two seemed like they could carry their daily chats on forever without the act getting old.

But away from the radio station, Al was facing an enormous challenge. His wife, Sally, was battling ALS. At the time, Al told reporters, "With that disease, she may live six months, she may live 10 years. You just don't know, so I'm not going to take a chance."

Al's unexpected decision to retire left KCBS management with a challenging decision. Let's not forget, John Madden had become a key player in the station's ratings battle against longtime rival KGO. Let's also not forget that John was only *on* KCBS because he'd had a bad experience with a guy who replaced another broadcast legend, Frank Dill, at KNBR.

I'll never forget receiving a call from KCBS news manager Paul Hosley, asking if I'd be interested in discussing a return to the station where I'd worked for 10 years before heading off to other ventures. I was about to park my car outside San Francisco's KRON-TV, where I was having a blast working on a syndicated show covering the Silicon Valley technology scene.

We worked out a deal, and I rejoined KCBS in July 2000. I can only imagine the anxiety among KCBS management. What if I screwed up the Madden relationship? Fortunately, it didn't work out that way. As the "new guy" on the team, I was very fortunate that Coach gave me some slack, and we quickly fell into our own rhythm.

I mention all of this because Al Hart got to have a last lap. After Sally passed away in 2002, a deal was worked out to bring Al back as a participant in the Madden conversations, one morning a week. His task was to do the "toss" to Coach after Steve Bitker's 8:15 sports segment. Al would usually do something over the top like, "Stand back because here he comes…it's the big man himself, Johnnnnnn Maddennnnn!" If anyone else had done that, it would have flopped. With Al, it worked.

Al would spend seven more years coming back to the radio station for this Wednesday moment. To be honest, he wasn't the guy he once was, but who among us is? Yes, there were moments when there were eye rolls as he seemed to lose his place, but not unlike having an aging parent still in the game, it was a blessing to have Al with us.

Coach always had an extra spark on Wednesdays when Al brought him in, and that's why it was fitting that he be the one to sum up Al's career. By 2009, it was time for Al to step away from the microphone for good.

His final day was a bittersweet experience (accent on the "sweet" because Al, as he often did, had brought in a load of homemade snickerdoodle cookies). We played back a few great on-air bits, like the time Coach got Al to pantomime hitting the seven-man blocking sled. We got one more laugh out of it as the coach in Coach came out.

"Was he any good? I don't know, 'cause I couldn't see his bucket. Did he have his bucket low?"

I assured John that rail-thin Al Hart didn't have a discernible bucket, and then John wrapped it up that morning, speaking the way a team leader speaks.

"All the years I've been with Al Hart, he was one of the reasons that I really came to KCBS originally. I never heard anyone ever say a bad word about him. I mean, all of us have people saying, you know, 'I hate that guy. I don't like that guy.' But no one doesn't like Al Hart. If you put all the good guys in the world together in a room, Al Hart would be in that room. It's not going to be the same. I mean, I'm going to miss you so much. And I know more importantly that everyone who listens is going to miss Al Hart because there was no one better. I mean, just think of KCBS and radio and greatness and, my man, that is you."

We called him Coach, and coaching was where John Madden first made his mark. Plenty of players become great coaches, but John was an example of a coach who moved on to become a terrific teammate.

CHAPTER 17

Always Competing

To the tens of millions of people who knew John Madden from weekly NFL broadcasts or specials like his "All-Madden Team," he was a friendly, quirky fellow who knew and loved football. Anyone old enough to have watched him coach the Oakland Raiders also knew he was a fierce competitor, a guy who really, *really* hated to lose.

Age may have cooled his competitive fires a bit, but we heard enough stories from him to know those fires were not fully extinguished.

We've established that Coach wasn't a great golfer and took a rather cavalier approach to the game. That didn't keep him from teeing it up in competitive rounds. I can't recall him often reporting good news after these outings, but there was one memorable morning where an innocent, "So how'd the golf thing go?" truly teed him off.

"I was 18th. I was dead last."

He spat those last two words out like they were pieces of rotten food.

Sports anchor Steve Bitker: "I thought with your handicap, you might finish much higher."

"I know. I mean, even with my handicap, I was lower. Dead last. Dead last. Not second to last. Not third to last. Not fourth to last. Didn't win. Didn't come in second. Didn't come in third. Didn't come in fourth. Dead last."

As I listened back to this segment some 20 years after it was broadcast, I was struck by something: nobody in the studio laughed. Certainly Coach didn't expect to *win* this little tournament, but he was baring his soul.

"I never want to be last. That's terrible, to be last. But then you don't like to win these things because then they all call you a cheater. It's, 'You cheated, you sandbagged, you did this and that.' But when you come in last, no one even looks at you. You're like nothing. I mean, you're like sawdust on the floor or something. Dead last. You hear me? Dead last."

You can easily conjure up an image of the Daly City neighborhood battles played out on what Coach called "Madden's Lot," a sandy patch near his boyhood home. Does little John Madden sound like the kid who just shrugged it off when his pickup team lost? One morning, amid a chat about childhood competition, we brought up Coach's lifelong friend John Robinson, suggesting those two probably still battled it out.

"Well, yeah, but he doesn't play golf. You know, I still do compete with him, pitching pennies or anything."

When Coach *did* win at something, he was like a kid who burst in the door from school with news of a straight-A report card. One Monday morning started with my greeting. "Good morning, John. How are you doing? How was your weekend?"

"My weekend was good. I never win at golf and I won. I won two matches."

"How'd that happen?"

"I don't know. The first time you think, 'Holy moly, I won,' and then the second time or whatever, I always lose, so I don't care. But that's the thing. If you're not going to get frustrated, then you have to not care. And then that's the point that I got to."

It seemed that Coach's oft-stated golf philosophy—caring only leads to frustration—might have been turned on its head. Maybe *not* caring freed his mind and grooved his golf swing. In any case, we had to know who he'd beaten.

"Well, one's Dominic. I got Dominic on Friday, and then I'll just use first names, Frank and Jim, on Saturday. Two days in a row, back to back to back to back to back to back."

You counted correctly: in his giddiness, Coach claimed six wins but only named three opponents. That's a guy who was ready to do some bragging.

We had a very revealing conversation one morning while John was still working on NFL broadcasts. It started with an item about baseball's All-Star Game. Coach's friend Tony La Russa was managing the National League team and John observed that La Russa would want to win at anything. Anyone who's spent any time around La Russa is nodding in agreement.

But Coach had more to say about competitiveness.

"I had an experience the other day. For years and years and years, I've played Don Shula at golf and he and I are about the same. So he's the only guy that I really compete with in golf. The last time we played was like four or five years ago. And I ran into him on Friday. So we played. He'd been waiting for me because like I said, the last time we played was four or five years ago when I won and then I kind of ditched him for a little while so that I could keep that victory. And I thought, you know, four or five years, maybe he'll slow down. Maybe he won't be as competitive. He's more competitive. Anyway, he beat me, so I lost to Shula. Shula, Tony La Russa, you know, they're the same guy. I mean, great coaches could coach any sport and be the best and have the strongest competitive drive you'll ever see."

I had to know, so I asked, "Are you in that category? I mean, do you consider yourself a guy who *has* to win?"

"Uh, no, because there comes a point. Yeah, I mean I have to win. But not if I'm not good enough. I mean, you can't put that pressure on yourself. You can't if you're not good enough to compete, if you're not good enough to get mad. I mean, I see guys with 20 handicaps. They get mad. And I tell 'em, 'You're not good enough to get mad.' I mean, you're supposed to hit bad shots. That's why you're a 20 handicap. And you know, I've kind of accepted that, that I'm not good enough to get mad. I'm really not good enough to compete. But having said that, I have competed against Don Shula all my life. And then when I get to him, I'm the same as he is. I mean, I'm not good enough to compete with other people, but I'm still good enough to compete with Don Shula. But again, having said that, this guy's playing every day."

I can tell that a loss to fellow coaching legend Shula galls him, so I rub it in a bit, saying, "He's got a private instructor, you know that?"

"Yeah. And I'm still working."

The record shows there were eight NFL games (including regular-season and playoff matchups) in which our two golf combatants faced each other. John had the edge, 5–3. That version of their rivalry ended with his football retirement in 1979, but they were still butting heads on the golf course 30 years later.

A key to the Madden approach to competition emerged during our many conversations about Don Shula: if you win one against a superior opponent, just stop playing against him. That way, you're the current champion.

This eventually caught up to Coach. He would occasionally dump on Shula over the years until the former Dolphins coach finally got a rematch. Not that our Coach slowed down on the needling.

"He's a hack. A complete hack. The difference between me and Don Shula is Don Shula has had a lot of lessons. He still has a lousy game. He's no better than I am, but he's a little smoother because he's had lessons. Yeah, Don Shula bought his game. I earned mine. I mean, he's had Jack Nicklaus work on his game. He bought it. He has a trained game. I have no training in my game."

And that's when I welcomed Shula to the broadcast, "Don Shula. Good morning. How you doing, coach?"

In his unmistakable voice, Shula answered, "I'm doing great. I'm glad that I've heard the reason that I can beat Madden's butt every time we play."

"Well, what happened to my butt the last time we played?"

Shula quickly replied, "I think I won. I think I was like 16 and 0 against you in golf matches. And then you finally won one and you jumped all the way. Your vertical is only about two inches. You get about two inches off the ground. Then I wanted to play you again. And you said, 'Never.'"

"Well, I bluffed the first time. You said, 'Okay, tomorrow.' And I said, 'Well, let me think about it. I'll call you.' Well, you never got a call. Never is a long time."

It was obvious that these two had enjoyed a lot of laughs amid their competition. Shula repeated his observation about John's victory celebration, saying, "I'll never forget that vertical, when you were so happy you jumped those two inches."

"Yeah, but that vertical was the same as when I could *have done a vertical."*

I moved to wrap things up, saying, "Just like our John Madden. He finally wins and then he just doesn't want to play anymore. I think we've heard this before."

"Well, yeah, yeah. When you finally win, then you keep that win and you just go away with it and you don't let the other guy get back."

There turned out to be a bit more to the story of Shula's return to victory. As he explained, the long-dodged rematch happened in Las Vegas. "We went down to the last hole and we both had to hit over water," Shula said. "So John hits first and he hits it in the water and I'm laughing. And then I hit and I hit it in the water. We both kept dunking it in the water."

By now, both are laughing as they tell the story, and John gets the last say with his version of the tale.

"Then I hit and I hit in the water again. And then he hits and he hits it in the water again. Then I hit and I hit the water again. Then he hits and he hits in the water again. And I hit the water again. And then he hits the ball on the green. And I just drove right to the clubhouse and watched. I didn't do anything. I just drove in. So he didn't beat me. I quit."

The takeaway: "If you can't beat 'em, head for the clubhouse."

A few years before I returned to KCBS to begin my association with Coach, he had gotten into bocce. Well-known Bay Area developer Jim Ghielmetti was the driving force behind Ruby Hill in the Madden family's hometown of Pleasanton. Ruby Hill featured fancy homes, a high-end golf course…and some bocce courts.

Coach met Ghielmetti, became a Ruby Hill member, and was smitten by bocce. His friendship with Ghielmetti produced plenty of funny stories on the air, but his bocce exploits could probably merit a book of their own.

For John Madden at this point in his life, bocce checked a lot of boxes: a social game that almost anyone, regardless of age or athleticism, can become good enough at to compete. A match usually involves food and drink, too. And there's ample room for trash-talking. In short, a game made for Madden.

He didn't necessarily dominate the sport.

"I'll tell you how bad I played in the last bocce league tournament. I went over there last night just to check in on everyone. I wasn't going to play. And one of the guys said, 'Oh, come on, you got to get back on the horse.' I didn't realize I played that lousy. Holy moly, I must have really been bad. So I said I wouldn't play, I'll sit it out, and no one tried to talk me out of it. I'm that bad."

Coach's golf nemesis Don Shula slipped into his bocce world, too.

"We played bocce last night, and he didn't even know what a bocce ball was. But then he was on the winning team so I had to pay him money. You know how when Muhammad Ali would win a fight, knock a guy out? He was doing that, both hands in the air, jumping up and down. Sometimes in life you forget how to compete. You remember how you used to compete and then you forget. But Shula's a guy that has never forgotten how to compete. He doesn't have the greatest skills in the world, but he does know how to compete. And then when he beats you, you have to live with it."

At around the time that Coach started rolling bocce balls at Ruby Hill, he and then-49ers head coach Steve Mariucci launched a charity bocce event. Anyone who's ever suffered through the day-long agony of a charity golf tournament could see the advantage of a bocce event immediately. You hung around, schmoozed, played a few 30-minute matches, ate, drank, ate some more, and got home at a reasonable hour without a sunburn. The Madden-Mariucci Charity Bocce event (known as the Coach Mooch Battle of the Bay since John's death) has raised millions of dollars for Bay Area charities over its quarter-century run.

Coach's ups and downs at his weekly bocce league events coupled with his natural tendency toward gamesmanship created plenty of memorable on-air conversations. As we approached the early June Madden-Mariucci tournament each year, the dial on bragging, taunting, and needling would get turned up to "high."

"My team had a practice Monday night and we look like we don't even need it. I swear. I mean, I hate to say this. I'd like to keep these things back, but we look like we haven't missed a beat. I mean, we're so good, I just can't help myself blurting it out."

After several years of enjoying all this vicariously, I and several KCBS colleagues got dragged right into the middle of the fray. We were entered in the Madden-Mariucci tournament.

Regrettably, the recordings of our conversations surrounding that 2007 event are among those lost to history, but I remember it all quite clearly. The KCBS squad included me, co-anchor Susan Leigh Taylor, sports anchor Steve Bitker, traffic anchor Kim Wonderley, plus several of our newsroom support staff. Some of us got an hour of coaching from some competitive bocce players.

As fate would have it—or more likely, The Hand of Madden was involved—we were matched up against Coach's team in the first round. As the 30-minute buzzer sounded, the score was tied. This meant a one-ball rolloff was in order; closest to the target wins the match.

Coach grabbed a ball, looked me in the eye, and said, *"Mano à mano."* Showdown time. He rolled first and put his ball maybe two feet past the target. Not a bad shot. With video cameras rolling to capture it all for posterity, my shot ran right up onto the target ball and stopped.

And as I said earlier, I was so excited that I skipped down the court, looking for people to high-five. In my celebration, however, I managed to miss the hand Coach was extending in congratulations. As you might imagine, the snub did not go unnoticed.

Fast-forward a few years. The KCBS team has become a fixture at the bocce tournament. We've never threatened to win it all but we've had our moments. And this year, we've recruited overnight sports anchor Dave Lewis to join the squad.

Dave showed up for a practice session with an unorthodox but effective way of rolling the bocce ball. I described it for Coach. "It's granny style. He gets down on one knee and then he takes the ball and instead of going out-board of his knee, he swings it between his two legs."

"Oh, no. Oh, he's a joke. The guys will laugh at him."

I acknowledged, "Yeah, it does look kind of like the belly putter of bocce, I'll be honest with you about that. But I'm telling you, Steve has video evidence." Steve added, "Results are telling."

"Well, that's to be determined."

That led me to pose an existential question to Coach. If you could come up with a silly-looking way to play bocce that would lead to mockery but also lead to victory, would you try it?

"The thing is, I've never thought that I've walked around in splendor. I mean, I don't think I ever hear, 'Now that guy really dresses well.' So for me to dress down isn't hard. So I mean, if I had to really look stupid, I think I probably look kind of stupid all the time."

Pressing the issue, I asked, "If they told you, 'Just throw it like this, you got to spin three times sideways and then stand on your left foot and then throw it behind your back,' but every ball was perfect, you'd do it, right?"

"Yeah, I'd do it. Because I'm not any good. It would make me good."

As it happened, when exposed to the heat of competition, Dave Lewis' style not only looked bad but *was* bad. The KCBS team had another under-whelming run at that year's "Madden-Mariucci," but somebody on the morning team had a bit of bragging to do the morning after the tournament.

"We've been up all night. We didn't go to sleep."

We all knew how much this mattered to John. "Winning the tournament with your own name on it…does it get better than that?" I asked.

"No, it doesn't. But it gives you the opportunity to practice humility. This is a humble thing. It was all about guys working hard, preparing, working together, being a team. It's all about your teammates."

He might have been roughly 20 percent serious. And then it took him about 20 seconds to train his sights on the other tournament sponsor, Steve Mariucci.

"Poor old Mooch didn't even make the playoffs. He was really downtrodden, and he's a good little player and a good guy. When we were leaving the facilities, his wife was driving. They're parked next to me, so first of all, he tells her, 'Watch out for John, he's right behind you.' And then he said, 'Oh the heck with it, run over his big butt.' Yeah, Mooch took it a little hard. Humility out the door, you know? You know how sometimes you can't help yourself? When we were getting ready to play the championship game, I told Mooch, 'You go ahead and get ready for the championship trophy presentation. You're going to have to do it by yourself.' Because usually, he and I would present the trophy to the winners but he had to do it by himself."

The respected Pew Research Center says about one of every five adult Americans engages in some form of sports wagering every year. The majority of those bets are with friends and family, whether in an office pool, a fantasy league, or a casual bet. It's another form of competition that attracted John Madden.

We had a long-running bit: whenever an athlete became dominant, Coach would demand to know if Steve and/or I wanted *that* athlete or "the field" (everyone else) in a given event. There was never any money on the line, just our reputations.

For many of our radio years, golfer Tiger Woods and tennis player Serena Williams ruled their respective sports. It didn't even have to be the U.S. Open for Coach to demand some action. It could be an ordinary event like the 2007 Sony Ericsson Open tennis tournament, which was underway on this particular March morning. "Let's say good morning to John Madden," I said. "How you doing, coach?"

"I'm doing fine, Stan. And I take Serena."

Steve immediately replied, "No, no, no. I already got Serena."

"No, no, no, no. You always gave me Serena the whole time, and then she was injured there. You made me take her anyway. So now that she's back and on top of that tournament, I get to have her again because I've had her all that time."

I said, "So this is like claiming 'permanent shotgun,' is it?"

"Yeah, I just pick Serena and I always have, through good and bad. Some people have been known to jump on bandwagons, and then when things go bad, they jump off."

"I'm just writing this down," I said. "'Lifetime Serena for John,' right?"

"Yeah. Steve gave me that years ago. I stuck with her through the injuries. Even when she didn't show up. She was going to play in one tournament but she didn't get to the tournament. Steve still told me I had Serena. As Weeb Ewbank [another pro football coaching legend] used to say, 'I just want my fair advantage.'"

Some guys enjoyed the role of underdog. Coach preferred to be the top dog.

One morning, we had a free-flowing conversation with guest Russell Baze, the Bay Area–based horse racing jockey. At the time, Baze had just posted his 9,000th win in a career that would eventually produce 12,844 wins, still the North American record.

It's impossible to discuss thoroughbred racing without talking about betting. Coach made it clear that he wasn't a serious gambler, but he also made it clear that he had a firm philosophy about wagering.

"I think any time you have a horse or anyone you believe is going to win, you just bet on them. And then, if the odds are good, you're going to make more money. If the odds aren't, you're going to make less money, but at least you're betting on who you think's going to win and not some longshot all the time. But there are some people that just play longshots. I mean, their whole life, it's like the people who buy lottery tickets. They're the same group of people. You know, they bet on the longshots or buy the lottery tickets. They really think that bet's going to come in."

It's not as if Coach's approach to wagering on the Sport of Kings always worked out. In the spring of 2008, a colt named Big Brown became one of the biggest stories in sports. He'd won the Kentucky Derby and the Preakness Stakes and was the odds-on favorite to complete the Triple Crown with a win at the Belmont Stakes. It didn't happen; in a shocking performance, Big Brown stopped running at the final turn and finished last. Coach was as shocked as anyone.

"I got snookered into a bet at the KCBS barbecue on Friday by some medical doctor. He came up to me and said, 'For charity, I'll make a bet with you and you

can have Big Brown and I'll take the field.' And I, being cocky and stupid, I said, 'You're on.' And he said, 'No, more, it's for charity, let's do more.' So we did. So I stepped into it. He probably knew something, you know, because he's a medical doctor. And I mean, he's not a horse doctor, but these guys, they know a heck of a lot more about kinesiology and stuff. He was probably taking biology classes when I was at recess. So I think he took advantage of me is what I'm saying. He's a medical doctor. I'm a P.E. teacher and, you know, I was out cleaning the erasers while he was in there dissecting frogs."

A footnote to the story: "Dr. Jim" had managed to get Coach to increase their wager from $50 to $200. When it came time to pay up, the designated charity got a check for $500. Even a loser can look like a winner.

Let's turn to poker, a game at which one can compete without breaking a sweat. John loved poker, probably because it represented another opportunity to hang out, swap insults, and do some eating while competing. Of course, we'd inquire about his luck each time he got together with his regulars on the Monterey Peninsula. A typical report follows.

"I kind of finished in the mid-top. Out of 32, I came in ninth."

Knowing just above nothing about how competitive poker works, I offered, "That's not bad."

"It's not good, though. There's only one, two, three, four places that count. I was out of the money, but I was in until after dinner. I played for probably nine hours. In a tournament, you get one set amount of money, and then when you lose that money, you're out. There's no add-ons or anything like that."

It was only after Coach's death that I learned the inside story of his poker arrangement. In my mind, I'd envisioned real money being thrown around, the way former Bay Area resident and NBA coach Don Nelson does when he plays with folks like Willie Nelson, Woody Harrelson, and Owen Wilson at his Maui home. Not quite.

Coach's friend Dominic Mercurio set me straight on the genesis of the Madden poker party. Soon after John decided Dominic's Cafe Fina clam chowder passed muster, Coach had another challenge.

"He asked me if I like to play poker," Dominic recalled. "I said, 'Yeah, I play poker because I fished in Alaska. That's what we did in our downtime.' So he says, 'You got guys?' I go, 'Yeah, I got guys.' He goes, 'Well, I got some guys. Why don't I get my guys and you get your guys and we'll see if we can get a friendly game going.' I said, 'Okay.' And now in my head, I'm going, 'Wait a minute. The restaurant's brand new. I got two babies. I'm fighting for my life to stay open.' You know what I mean?"

Dominic was thinking exactly what I thought: surely a multimillionaire celebrity with an expensive home in Carmel plays poker for big bucks. "And then he goes, '$40 buy-in,'" and that's how then-struggling restaurateur Dominic Mercurio became part of the game, helping round up some locals and arranging for the catering.

As with many things Madden, his poker gathering grew its own set of rules and customs, especially when their annual all-day poker fest came around.

"We have a deal that the first guy out is Bozo and we have a big hat they have to wear and a big trophy and all that. I've been the Bozo. So now the tournament starts, I swear, with everyone just playing Bozo defense. They just don't want to be Bozo. And since Carl Panattoni and I put on the tournament, we kind of rule it. I have a new rule this year. I'm going to have a Bozo table where all ex-Bozos play at the same table and are exempt from being Bozo."

"Oh, kind of like a loser's bracket," I suggested.

"Well, no, it's just a celebration of having been a Bozo and it's such a great opportunity for others that we want others to be able to experience what we've experienced before we have to experience it again. They may argue about it, but they'll lose. Because once a Bozo, you're always a Bozo. So you don't have to be a Bozo again to be a Bozo. And if they don't like it, they can go home."

As far as I can tell, Coach never won his annual tournament, but all our poker talk triggered a priceless memory. A listener called to suggest we ask Coach about his days playing poker in Grays Harbor, Washington, where he'd landed at the community college after a redshirt season and an injury at the University of Oregon.

"*That's where I broke into poker. I had a job there. I was a shill at the Mint Cafe. You need five players to start a game. So if you only have one or two players from the outside, the house provides three and then as more players come in, you get out. That's all you are, a game starter. In those days, the game was five card stud, and to this day, I'm a pretty good five card stud player.*"

Unfortunately for Coach, his regular poker buddies took a pass on five card stud and played the popular poker version known as Texas hold 'em.

You might get the impression that John, after a lifetime around sports, would compete at anything. Pretty much true, but he drew some lines around what he considered to be a "sport." The annual hullabaloo regarding the Nathan's Famous International Hot Dog Eating Contest in Coney Island really got him going.

"*I think they get a little carried away with that. I should* be on the side of, *'Oh, you know, eating belongs up there as a sport.' But come on. They lead with it on ESPN and the local sports news. And to me, it's not even eating. It's stuffing. They're just stuffing it down their throats. I'm not a fan of that.*"

I needed some clarification, so I followed up with, "So your concern is not so much that competitive eating is not a sport. What you're saying is that those fellows aren't actually *eating.*"

"*No, no, no, no. They're not eating. Now, if it was a steak-eating contest or something like 'how much you can eat in an hour' or something like that, that would be an eating contest where you're really eating. These guys are just stuffing.*"

Coach, who knew a bit about eating, wrapped it up that morning with some local color.

"*Out at the Alameda County Fairgrounds in Pleasanton [a couple of miles from his house], they made the biggest hamburger in the world. So now that, to me, would be eating. I mean, if someone got up there and took a whack at* that, *that would be something.*"

Anyone want to set the odds on that?

CHAPTER 18

An Old Coach and Technology

IT WOULD BE EASY TO ASSUME THAT A GUY BORN IN 1936 MIGHT HAVE A hard time adapting to modern technology. Not true in the case of John Madden, who famously turned the telestrator into a magic wand that changed the way football was broadcast on television.

Coach was a guy who absolutely got the big picture when it came to technology. In addition to the telestrator, he championed the use of the first-down overlay on TV broadcasts. That innovation has become so much a part of the televised football experience that it's weird to watch old videos from *before* its existence.

There was also the *Madden NFL* video game. While Coach certainly didn't write any computer code, he was well ahead of the curve in seeing what *could* be done with computers and video. I once sat next to John and several developers from EA Sports as Coach went through NFL game video, pointing out the elements that needed to be improved in the next release of the video game. The computer guys could barely keep up.

But as with the rest of us, technology sometimes got the upper hand with John Madden. I'd barely said, "Good morning, John" one day when Coach jumped right in.

"Man, do I have a dilemma. You know how there's some things you just shouldn't mess with? That's a cell phone. You're always right on the verge of something going awry. I'm reading Peter King's 'Monday Morning Quarterback' column on my phone. And the next thing I know, audio breaks out."

At this point, anyone who's ever landed on a website and had *really loud sound* blast from the speakers knows exactly how Coach feels.

"I'm on my phone, so I don't want it. I can't turn it off. I can't switch and I can't get out of it. So now I've got voices. I'm hearing a podcast and I can't turn my phone off. I can't turn the sound off. There's still someone talking. So I just stuck it down—you know how there's room in between the seat and the chair?"

He's painting quite a word picture, so I offer, "You did a wedge job with it?"

"I just did a wedgie, yeah, yeah, yeah. And I stuck it in there and then I covered it up with a blanket to shut it up because it gets louder and louder. But you know it's down there still. You can hear it."

He was right. We *could* hear it.

"How long does this guy talk?"

This is when sports anchor Steve Bitker and I inform Coach that our own podcast often burned past the half-hour mark. It's probably not what a guy with his cell phone wedged into his chair cushions wants to hear.

"I mean, shouldn't you be able, when you're in the middle of a good read and a podcast jumps out, shouldn't you be able to turn it off?"

There was also the time when John's TV pre-production schedule had him sitting in an NFL head coach's office for a chat at precisely the time our broadcast was scheduled. No problem; he just commandeered the coach's desk phone and settled in for our conversation.

At some point, we could tell he was a little distracted and we thought we could hear a cell phone ringing.

"That one I had in my pocket and I kept looking at everyone else to see if they heard it too. Because if you have something in your pocket, you don't know if it's just you hearing it. But I guess everyone heard that one, huh? And were you guys checking your own pockets?"

Yes, we were!

One topic that amused our studio crew for years was the arrival of high-definition television. Younger readers, please ask your parents what TV was like back before 8K and 4K and streaming this and DVR that.

For a guy who was earning millions from the world of television, it was amazing. Coach couldn't seem to see the difference between the old standard-definition broadcasts and the new high-def content. A typical exchange went like this.

"I was over last night at Floyd the Barber's house. We went over this high-def and I can't tell the difference. He's saying, 'Well, here's regular and then here's regular stretched and then here's high-def.' I swear, I don't know the difference."

This being a matter of some contention at my house, I popped in. "You and my wife. I mean, I'll sit down and I'll say, 'Look, here's the ballgame' and then we'll switch over to high-def. And she's going, 'Well, maybe it looks wider.' It's not only wider, it's crisper."

"But I can't tell the difference. I swear I can't. I don't even know how to get it, you know? You have to go to channel 700-something or 200-something to get the thing. And then when I get there it's supposed to be high-def. But if it's not high-def, it's that other thing. And it can't be the other thing without being high-def."

Considering how often our morning conversations took place while Coach was somewhere far from a solid telephone connection, we were generally pretty fortunate. His standard procedure when the bus was out in the middle of nowhere was to look for a solid cellular signal, then pull over to make sure the connection would remain solid.

It didn't always work. One morning, as Coach headed out for the first training camp visit of the summer, the phone call dropped out right as our conversation started. We got him back on the line pretty quickly. He told us they'd just had the bus inspected top to bottom. Then, he delivered an analysis that had us all nodding in agreement.

"You know, sometimes what happens in life, people come in and there's a little something wrong with something, or nothing *wrong with something, and they work on it and then there's a lot wrong with it."*

I'm fairly sure that many listeners felt vindicated by some of Coach's technological stumbles. He admitted one spring morning that the shift to Daylight Saving Time would allow him to be more punctual while driving his pickup truck.

"My clock was always an hour ahead, and I couldn't set it back, and everyone would try to set the clock back for me, and I couldn't set it back. So I was an hour off for six months. And then yesterday morning I got up and I was right on time. I was an hour off for everything and I mean, I pushed every button. I just started pushing buttons and then everyone else would say, 'Oh, I know how to do that. Let me get in.' And they'd try and no one knew how to do it. So my clock stayed like that forever. And then, lo and behold, yesterday I got in and it was right."

She probably won't be happy that it's now in print for the world to see, but my wife's car has functioned exactly like that for years. The difference is, my wife *knows* when the car's clock is an hour off and does the mental math.

When I first started chatting with Coach on KCBS, the digital video recorder (DVR) was just hitting the market. At the beginning, there were two competitors, ReplayTV and TiVo.

It may seem crazy to today's readers, but back in 2000, a lot of people had trouble wrapping their heads around the idea that you could "pause" a live television broadcast. Up until then, if you wanted to record, say, a baseball game, you needed a videotape that could hold a whole ballgame. You tuned in the right channel, hit "Record," and *only* when the whole game had been recorded could you hit "Rewind" to go back to the first inning and start watching.

It didn't take long before morning sports anchor Steve Bitker and I fell in love with the DVR technology. We appreciated the fact that we were no longer slaves to the starting times of sports events. We also found joy in the ability to skim through recorded games, watching for significant moments (my son and I learned how to "goal troll" through San Jose Sharks games when we were short on time, watching for the little score graphic to change so we could roll back and watch scoring plays).

Try as we might, we could never convince John that this was a good thing.

"Nah, I never get back to TiVo. I'm not good at that. I mean, I TiVo stuff and then never watch it again the rest of my life. I'm a 'live' guy. And if it's over, I'm not that interested in it."

Steve and I kept hammering at him over the years, and once I thought we might have broken through. Coach started our conversation one morning with a question.

"I was going to ask you about yesterday. You said you didn't watch a game live, you TiVo'ed it and watched it later. But when you watched it later, did you know what had happened? Or were you just oblivious?"

I told him I was oblivious to the outcome when I sat down to play back the game in question.

"You know what? I could do it that way."

It felt like a big moment: John Madden was going to join the growing legions of sports fans who used their DVRs to improve their lives! But I felt I needed to warn Coach about the one big problem with living the TiVo life: friends who don't obey the rules. "You're going to have friends like Steve," I said, "who will text you. You'll pick the text message up and it'll say, 'Wow, this first quarter is amazing!' But sometimes they're not that clever. They'll say, 'Raiders already down two TDs,' or something like that, and it can really foul your day up."

And that's where I think I lost him. I'm guessing he had too many people in his network who would blow the whole thing with one ill-advised message.

"Because I've been thinking about that since you said that yesterday. I couldn't do it if I knew what was going to happen. I love fights, for example, and I can watch a fight live. But if I already know who won, I have very, very little interest, because the suspense of what's just around the corner is eliminated. There's no suspense."

A year or so before our final broadcast together, Coach had finally come around. Sort of. He tried to use the DVR to help him do two things at once:

go to a high school game in which his grandson Jesse was playing and his son Mike coaching while *also* recording a Thursday night NFL game so he could watch it later.

"So I go to the high school game. I record the first half of the Raiders game, get home, watch the second half live, and then I go to watch the first half. And I don't know how to watch on a recorder. I'm trying to get through the commercials. So I push something, and now I'm at the end of the game. It's the same old stuff. I never did see the game in its entirety."

There were other ways for a traveling man to miss a football game. As far back as the turn of the century (this century, not the last one!), Coach had the Madden Cruiser fitted out with a satellite dish. That way, he could tune in games while he traveled.

It didn't always work. For many years, the NFL operated under a strict blackout policy: if a home team didn't sell enough tickets, the national broadcast would be unavailable in that team's local market.

Coach learned the minute details of this process the hard way one weekend when he *thought* he'd be able to watch an Oakland Raiders game after wrapping up a broadcast in Minneapolis.

"I have the satellite on my bus. And for some reason that game was blacked out on my satellite. I know I paid the bill so that's not it. And that was the only game that was blacked out."

Once we confirmed that the game had been blacked out in the Bay Area because the Raiders missed the ticket sales threshold, we sorted it out: the satellite dish and the black box that goes with it are locked into your billing address ZIP code, meaning the Madden Cruiser might as well have been parked in Coach's driveway.

"I'm dragging my blackout with me. I've dragged things all over this country, and I didn't know I was dragging my blackout."

Yep. Years before we started having rolling blackouts in California, Coach was already experiencing them. When we *did* begin to experience rolling power blackouts, a new set of problems arose.

"*Stan's always talking about the rolling blackouts and where you look to find out what grid you're in. Al, I bet you know what grid you're in, don't you?*"

My predecessor Al Hart was in the studio for his regular Wednesday visit, and he laughingly replied that his wife handled that sort of information. Coach wasn't going to let this go.

"*I think you look at the lower left-hand corner of your bill, but I don't know what grid I'm in. But the toughest thing for me is, I know when I've had a rolling blackout because I don't know how to fix blinking 12s. I got some places where a clock will stop and I don't know how to fix it. I can't find where you reset it. I can't even get that, so I'm stuck with blinking 12s. I'm dead with the blinking 12.*"

Even when the alarm clock was showing the proper time, issues could arise for Coach. There was the morning where Steve Bitker apparently had a problem with his headphones. He began his sportscast, then stopped with a puzzled look on his face to ask, "Am I on?" I assured him that tens of thousands of KCBS listeners were waiting to hear what he had to say and that his microphone was working just fine.

Moments later, I introduced Coach by jokingly asking, "Are you on, John?"

"*Yeah, I'm on. I just* got *on when I heard Steve saying, 'Am I on? Am I on?' Did he blow into his mike? That's the thing most people do. You'll see someone will get up to the mike and they'll go 'Am I on?' And they'll blow into it like this: WHOOSH, WHOOSH. Then they'll go 'Am I on? Am I on?' And they'll tap it like this: TAP, TAP. Well, you just have to say it once.*"

While this was playing out, one of our KCBS engineers was in the next studio, cringing as we talked about blowing into and tapping on expensive broadcast microphones. It was an unusually dark, foggy morning.

"*I just woke up and I don't know what happened because I set the alarm. I'll work on that later and find out what happened. And then you get up and it's foggy, and then the first thing you hear is, 'Am I on? Am I on?' You know, you're off your axis. Things just get a little discombobulated.*"

I was incredulous. Coach was telling us that he'd awakened just moments before going on the air and yet here he was, pulling off a sharp riff on how people behave around microphones. He had one final point to make.

"They always keep asking, 'Is my mike working?' You know, they always say it louder, too."

Tell me he's not right on *that* one.

John knew how to tell a story that could get people smiling and nodding, saying, "Yep, I know *exactly* what he's talking about."

"I got a dilemma. You know how you get used to these cell phones? You always look around and you think, 'Where did all these people with cell phones come from and why do they have them?' Then you lose yours and you can't live without it because you got all your numbers and speed dial in there. And do you know, because I did this, the number one way that people lose their cell phone? Well, not lose it, but break it?"

The KCBS studio crew fumbled around for the answer, finally deciding the most likely way to decommission a cellular phone was to drop it on the sidewalk.

"No. Fumbled in the toilet! That's where I dropped mine. I turned it off and I was going to plug it in and I dropped it in the toilet. I swear it was off. And I reached my hand in and I go FOOM! Yeah, because it's just a reaction I'm talking about. I go FOOM and I pull it out. It's off now and then it starts to vibrate and then red and blue lights start coming on. I think this is just the thing dying. And everyone tells me, 'Dry it off.' I dry it off. I have a guy that takes a hair dryer and blow-dries it but it never came back to life."

There was some general commiserating about what a pain it is to have to go through the whole phone-replacement process. That's when Coach made it clear he'd crossed the digital divide and was having trouble going without his connectivity.

"I haven't had a cell phone for like five days and I don't have any numbers. I don't know if anyone is calling me. I don't have anything. I mean, that's the thing. I always laugh at people about this, you know, 'What did people do before cell phones? Why is everyone always talking on the cell phone, blah, blah, blah? Why

do you need one, why does it ring all the time,' and all that stuff? And then you get one and you become one of them. And then you find without it, it's like not having a body part or something."

Hands up if you still peck out your text messages with your index finger (welcome to my team). Here's an example of where an old football coach got on board with the new way of doing things.

When I first saw him sending text messages, it was sort of painful to watch. He used the technique I just mentioned, but with his big hands, things didn't work so well. Some time later, we were sitting together and I watched as he grabbed his phone, spoke his intended message, and hit "Send." I told him I thought it was pretty cool that he was using the speech-recognition function.

He asked, "Don't you do that?" I told him I felt weird speaking my messages out loud so I just stuck with the old screen-poke technique. His response? *"You need to figure this stuff out or you'll get left behind."*

Touché. And the fact is, as we look at a world where it sometimes feels like our tech has taken control of our lives, Coach had it pretty well figured out.

"I have an iPad with limited use. I mean, I can just do a few things on it. And I got a Kindle and an iPhone. I mean, I have all the things and I'm just not real good at them. But I still don't email. I don't want to answer it. I mean, that's the thing. It's like 'tag.' If someone sends you an email, then you're 'it,' you know, and you have to answer. I just didn't want to get into that, so I don't email."

Tell the boss John Madden gave you a lifetime pass on the email.

CHAPTER 19

He's From Where We're From

John Madden's birth certificate lists him as a native of Minnesota, born in Spam's hometown, Austin, on April 10, 1936. But make no mistake about it: John was a San Francisco Bay Area guy.

It's not one of those deals where a place claims somebody famous just because he or she spent some time there. In John's case, it was the other way around. He embraced the Bay Area, and it hugged him back.

John grew up in Daly City, a fogbound, windswept place just across the city limit line from San Francisco. His father was a mechanic and John would later describe the family as poor, but his childhood was rich with the sort of adventures kids of that era were allowed to experience.

Coach never lost track of his boyhood memories. One June morning, the Bay Area was baking in a heat wave. The high in San Francisco would reach 89 degrees, which is a good 20 degrees above normal. So naturally, our conversation began with me asking, "How are you enjoying the weather?"

"It's so hot, you can see Cliff Melton. That's before your time."

Two thoughts here. First, yes, quite a bit before my time. Cliff Melton pitched for the hometown minor league San Francisco Seals from 1946 to 1950. Second, go back and repeat John's line out loud.

"You're going to need to explain that one to the youngsters here," I said.

"Yeah, probably to everyone. But it's one of the funniest things I think I ever heard as a kid. You know how you remember things as a kid and maybe they never were funny, but at that time when you were that age, you thought it was funny. I was out at Seals Stadium, 16ᵗʰ and Bryant Streets, and it was one of these hot days like this in San Francisco and the Seals had a pitcher named Cliff Melton. Some guy was in the bathroom saying, 'It's so hot out there, you can see Cliff Melton.' That was funny to me."

He wasn't done summoning up youthful ballpark memories.

"In those days, they used to have doubleheaders with the Oakland Oaks playing the San Francisco Seals, and they'd play the first game in the morning in Oakland and then play the second game in San Francisco or vice versa. I never got to go. But the other funny thing I remember all these years, it probably isn't funny now, but at the time we thought it was. I was in the bathroom there at Seals Stadium and a guy was saying, 'Take it in in Oakland, let it out in San Francisco.' Hot day, San Francisco. Those are the things that jump through your mind."

Both of those minor league teams are long gone, pushed aside by the arrival of Major League Baseball on the West Coast. Neither Seals Stadium nor the Oaks' ballpark in Emeryville survived. Coach's recollection of the Cliff Melton gag was indelible, though Melton's last year on the mound for the Seals was when John Madden was 14 years old.

Those Seals memories ran deep for Coach. This was, after all, his hometown team in an era where Major League Baseball only reached as far west as St. Louis. Sports anchor Steve Bitker once asked if John had any memories of Bobby Thomson's "Shot Heard 'Round the World," the 1951 playoff home run that lifted the New York Giants over the Brooklyn Dodgers.

"No, I don't really remember anything. When you were a kid in this area in those days, you really weren't a Major League fan because everything was so regional. I was a Seals fan. Everything I knew about baseball was the San

Francisco Seals and the Pacific Coast League. And to be honest, we didn't pay a lot of attention, other than to players that had played in the Pacific Coast League and went on to Major League Baseball. In our stories, the Pacific Coast League was as good as the Major Leagues and the Seals could beat most of the Major League teams. And [San Francisco–born baseball legend] Lefty O'Doul was as good a manager as there was in baseball. Those were our thought processes."

KCBS remains a powerful connection between the Bay Area's past and its present. It is America's first broadcasting station, a claim cemented in the historical record of Dr. Charles Herrold's transmissions from San Jose that began in 1909. Herrold later received the call letters KQW, which were changed to KCBS when CBS completed its purchase of the station in 1949.

As we've seen, a young John Madden growing up in a Bay Area where television hadn't yet dominated the media landscape was a keen fan of radio. He understood the medium, but more important to our story, he understood the intimate connection between a local station and the place it serves.

This allowed him to play an important role on the modern KCBS, linking the present-day Bay Area to the one in which he was raised. This was valuable to the station; as new arrivals crowded into the growing region, KCBS sought to maintain its historic role as a reliable source of information. Having a beloved and trusted figure like John Madden create links to our past was a big win for us.

That he could perform this role subtly only added to his value. It might have been easy to slip into the role of the old guy telling "way back when" stories, but Coach always seemed to be aware of the trap of living in the past. Note how this exchange during yet another heat wave ends.

"Going back to my days in Daly City when we used to have an ice man. You'd get up early in the morning, you'd get a block of ice, and then you'd carry the block of ice around with you. When it was big, you'd sit on it and then later in the day, you'd put it on your head."

I mocked the notion that frosty Daly City ever got that hot, an easy swipe to take for a kid who'd grown up 50 miles away in balmier San Jose.

"Well, right. But we did have an ice man. I wondered, 'What the hell did they have an ice man for?' He used to come around with blocks of ice. They didn't have refrigerators. The guy with the big tongs would come by and give you ice and you'd put your ice in your icebox."

Aware that some of our coveted younger listeners might be tuning out as two old guys rambled on about a past no one under retirement age could comprehend, I said, "You realize that half the people listening right now, John, have no idea what we're talking about."

"Three quarters of the people, I hope, have no idea."

In other words, he was happy to share the memories, but also understood that a radio station only maintains its relevance by adding younger listeners to the mix. In our case, the coveted demographic is people between 25 and 54 years of age. Not many 25-year-olds have ever seen an icebox!

Coach came from an era in which kids still organized their own games and activities. You read earlier about how he recalled the radio announcer for his hometown San Francisco Seals. He did more than listen to Jack Macdonald on radio station KYA. He also tried to emulate Macdonald's home run call, "It's out Aunt Maggie's window!"

"We used to play in Madden's Lot, which was right next to my house. We would hit one, it would break my window, and we thought that was cute. We'd always call my window 'Aunt Maggie's window.' It was a foul ball in Madden's Lot, but we'd still hit it up there and we'd yell, 'It's out Aunt Maggie's window!' It would break the doggone window. And then they finally put a screen up there."

Coach's long Bay Area history gave him plenty of material with which to work. You never knew when he'd head down Memory Lane or where that detour would end up. On this particular morning, Jim Gentile's name was in the news. The San Francisco native was a power-hitting first baseman who had a few big years in the Major Leagues (note to baseball stats freaks: go look up Gentile's 1961 season).

"He was ahead of me in school and he was playing at Sacred Heart High School. In those days, he was a pitcher, and he could really throw the ball. I mean, he was a hard-throwing left-hander. I played against him in The City.

When we got to high school, John Robinson went to Serra. I went to Jefferson. Serra played Sacred Heart. Robinson was either a freshman or a sophomore and was playing against Jim Gentile when Gentile was a senior. So I saw Robinson that night and he said, 'I hit Gentile.' I said, 'No, you didn't.' And he said, 'Yeah, I hit him.' And I said, 'How many hits did you get?' He said, 'None.' I said, 'Well, what did you do?' He said, 'I struck out every time, but I got two foul balls.' I swear he went on for like two hours to talk about those two foul balls that he hit off Jim Gentile, and he's still proud of it to this day. I swear I'm not making this up here. I mean, John Robinson doesn't have a lot of athletic achievements, but he would put at the top of the list that he hit two foul balls off Jim Gentile in high school."

Another hard-throwing lefty was a frequent topic during our years on the radio. Randy Johnson's exploits were often newsworthy as "The Big Unit" won Cy Young Awards, threw no-hitters (including a perfect game), climbed the career strikeout list, and became what I'm betting will be the last pitcher ever to record 300 wins in a Major League career.

Plus, there was the weekend day in 2001 when, during a Cactus League game in Tucson, Johnson managed to kill a bird with a pitch. The hapless dove was in the wrong place at the wrong time as Johnson, then playing for the Arizona Diamondbacks, delivered a pitch to Calvin Murray of the San Francisco Giants.

It was an unavoidable topic of conversation the following Monday morning. And your author fell into a trap when Coach responded by pointing out that Johnson was a local guy, from Livermore.

Mr. Know-It-All affirmed Johnson's upbringing in Livermore and gave a shout-out to Granada High School. Unfortunately for me, of the two public high schools in Livermore, I'd chosen the wrong one. Angry listener response ensued, and the next day, Coach washed his hands of the whole matter.

"That's why you don't do that. I mean, I just started out the thing by saying he was from Livermore. He played high school ball in Livermore. And then you said, 'Granada.' You gotta leave the Granada–Livermore High thing up to the people. Let the whole city of Livermore claim Randy Johnson."

Lesson learned, straight from the master. Easy enough to say "Livermore's Own" without getting caught up in the details.

Coach's adopted hometown of Pleasanton is right next door to Livermore. Both cities are over the East Bay hills from Oakland, where John's coaching career reached its pinnacle. The Madden connections to Pleasanton date to the mid-60s, when John and Virginia settled there.

While Coach kept track of many athletes from his neck of the woods, there was one whose story intertwined remarkably with the Maddens. John's sons Mike and Joe both graduated from Pleasanton's Foothill High School and Mike returned to spend many years coaching the freshman football team there. He had a pretty good quarterback one year named Brandon Crawford.

It turned out Brandon's real athletic calling was baseball. I can't recall if his first mention on KCBS came while he played shortstop at UCLA, or when he was drafted by the San Francisco Giants, or when he played minor league ball for the nearby San Jose Giants, or when he made the big club. I do know he was a frequent topic of conversation in the "he's from where we're from" category.

And then it got even better, because Coach clued us in one morning to a fact about Brandon's mom, Lynn Crawford. She taught at Vintage Hills Elementary School in Pleasanton and guess whose grandson was in her class?

"The Giants have to win, because then she's in a better mood. And Brandon Crawford has to do well, because then she's in a better mood. So he watches every play when Brandon's playing in the infield, if he makes a double-play, or doesn't make a double-play. If he gets a hit, I mean, my grandson can tell you what he's doing, right up to date."

We proceeded to get a lot of mileage out of the "Mrs. Crawford" bit, considering the fact that her boy wound up playing more games at short-stop than anyone in the history of the Giants franchise, New York or San Francisco. One of us would often refer to him as "Mrs. Crawford's son" the morning after Brandon made another spectacular defensive play or delivered a memorable hit like the 2014 Wild Card Game grand slam that turned a raucous Pittsburgh crowd into silent, sullen spectators.

Coach did eventually make it clear that Brandon Crawford's mom, a fifth-grade teacher, was no pushover.

"She doesn't give a lot, you know. When you look at your teacher at the beginning of school, you don't say, 'Oh boy, I got an easy one this year.' She's not an easy one. Fifth grade is when they start, you know, hardening it up a little bit. And that's exactly what she does. She does a great job at it."

Another Bay Area athlete has had a pretty good run, but this guy was almost a household name before he even left high school. Jason Kidd's exploits at St. Joseph Notre Dame High School in Alameda, followed by two stellar years at the University of California in Berkeley, provided plenty of fodder for conversation long before his lengthy career as an NBA player and coach. Late in his playing career, Coach reflected on Kidd's long résumé.

"He's been a terrific player for a long time. He's just a great competitor. He knows how to play the game and he knows how to play it at a high level. You just get the feeling that his competitiveness is the thing that's so special. I remember when he was at St Joseph's High School in Alameda. Seems like it was about five years ago [in fact, Kidd had graduated from high school almost 20 years earlier]. *When you go all the way back to his high school days and his Cal days and his pro days, it seems like we've been talking about Jason Kidd in basketball for 30 or 40 years."*

The Bay Area has produced plenty of superstars. You can run out names like Joe DiMaggio, Bill Russell, Ken Venturi, Tom Brady, and Barry Bonds for starters. But Coach often got a kick out of tracking the less-celebrated. Take someone like Josh Johnson, the record-setting NFL quarterback. By "record-setting," I mean he's drawn a paycheck from more NFL teams (14) than anyone else in the league's history.

Johnson's from Oakland and, in fact, stayed in Oakland and raised his family there despite his nomadic work life. Johnson's built a career largely out of being available, but Coach was always a fan.

"I liked him. I was impressed with him. He throws pretty well and he runs very well. I've had coaches tell me that today you need a quarterback to pick up three or four first downs a game for you and he looks like a guy that could pick up three or four first downs a game just running with the ball."

While John loved to point out Bay Area connections, the region and the state of California were proud to claim him as an adopted son. He once told us a terrific story from his past, about the day yet another famous adopted Californian wanted to talk with him.

"You can't believe this thing. One day I'm at a restaurant for lunch, and I get a call from my office, and they say, 'The White House is trying to get ahold of you.' So I figure this would be something like sign an Easter egg. I mean, I'd done a few things like that in my life, so I told them where I was. Then I get another call and it's 'White House Operator 2' that's calling. She says, 'President Reagan wants to talk to you.' So I'm sitting there and I'm thinking, 'I've never talked to a president.' As luck would have it, the night before, he'd given the State of the Union speech and someone called him Mr. Reagan. And I was saying to myself, 'That's wrong. He's either Mr. President or President Reagan, but he's not Mr. Reagan.' So now I'm thinking there's something not to call him."

Remember, the guy telling this story may not have been the leader of the free world, but he was a massively popular figure, welcomed into millions of American households every Sunday during football season.

"I don't know what the heck I'm supposed to say. Then she says, 'Are you ready to talk to the president? The next voice you'll hear will be the president.' I don't know how you get ready to talk to the president. I was sitting there, so I stood up and I just kind of bent my knees a little, and I go, 'Okay!' I didn't stand at attention. I stood there bending my knees, like a hitting position, like I was going to block or something.

"So now he gets on the phone and says, 'Hi John, this is Ronald Reagan.' So now I'm not sure what I'm supposed to call him, but I don't want to call him the wrong thing. So I don't call him anything. The first word out of my mouth, I swear, you know what it was? 'Hey.' And then the next thing was, 'How ya doin?' And that was my salutation, because I didn't want to make a mistake."

It turned out President Reagan was doing some recruiting, asking Coach if he'd be willing to appear with flying ace and record-setting test pilot General Chuck Yeager in a public service announcement for the Space Foundation. John said, "Sure," and that was the extent of his conversation with President Reagan.

"I said, 'Thanks for calling.' People always say, 'Just be yourself.' So I guess that's all I could think of is, if you're not going to have some reverence about it, then you may as well be yourself. You know, like if someone calls up and says, 'Hey, John, this is Bob,' you say, 'Hey, Bob, how ya doin?' That's what I'd say. Hey, at least I didn't say 'Ron' or 'Gipper' or something. I said, 'Hey, how ya doin?' I didn't even put a 'g' on the end of 'doing.'"

The PSA with Yeager was part of a campaign featuring "opposites." In this case, it was the first pilot to break the sound barrier paired with the guy who didn't fly. Both were later honored with induction into the California Hall of Fame, giving Coach another chance to hang out with a hero.

"I get to introduce Chuck Yeager. That's really good. It gives me a lot of pride to be introducing Chuck Yeager."

Like Ronald Reagan and Chuck Yeager, John Madden was a guy born elsewhere who became a celebrated son of California.

The peripatetic nature of Coach's work schedule during the television broadcasting years often left me asking him where he was when I greeted him in the morning. On this occasion, he settled that issue and explained his ability to become a sort of geographic chameleon.

"I'm not on the road. I'm at home. You know, you're always kind of moving around, but you always end up in a place. So whatever place you end up in is where you're from. I learned that years ago. It's easier to say, like, if you're in New York, instead of saying you're from California, just say, 'I'm from New York.' You're always from there and whatever town you're in, you like that local team and all those local things, and then you don't have any fights or arguing. Yeah, you're always from where you are."

He may have used that philosophy to avoid territorial disputes while traveling, but Coach understood the value of place. He lived through an era in which the gulf between pro athletes and the fans who supported them wasn't as wide as it is today.

"That was when fans and the players all lived in the same communities. I remember when someone like the Kiwanis would have a crab feed. Half the team would go because they'd get a free meal. And [colorful Raiders defensive end] Ben Davidson would be the first guy there, the last guy to leave, and eat the most."

If there was a sure-fire way to get Coach fired up, it was simply to mention Oakland. He didn't live long enough to see the last of the city's three big-league teams leave town, but he watched the Raiders bail out twice and didn't like the idea of the Warriors decamping from Oakland's Oracle Arena for a new basketball palace in San Francisco.

"I wonder about the Warriors. I mean, you know how great the fans are. I hear it. I see it every night, the fans and Oakland and Oracle and the whole thing going crazy. And now we're going to move them. What? What's that all about?"

Steve Bitker and I tried to discuss the economics of modern sports, how the Warriors' new arena would enhance the value of the franchise, generate more revenue, blah, blah, blah. We were talking to the wrong guy.

"I don't know. I don't know. I don't know that that's true. You know, they sell the place out now. They have everything. And like I always say, Oakland needs a win, too. It just can't be, 'Oh, we want to get out of here.' I mean, if everyone wants to get out of here, we're not going to have any Oakland. How about Oakland?"

In the 2000s, two of Coach's favorite things intersected: Oakland and boxing. The city produced a terrific young fighter who was beginning what would become an undefeated, multi-championship professional career the day we discussed him in 2005.

"He's a local guy, Andre Ward. He has the only gold medal that we won in boxing at the [2004] Olympics. And he's ours. We haven't had real boxing in the Bay Area for so long that I don't even remember the last time we had it. I guess it was when George Foreman was training here. And I remember [San Francisco heavyweight] Henry Clark fought a couple of fights in Oakland. And we really haven't had much here since those days. I think Andre Ward is our shot."

Coach had been waiting a long time for a local boxing hero. Foreman's and Clark's local exploits were a good 30 years in the past at the time of our conversation.

"Sometimes, you know, there'll be a fighter from someplace else, and you try and bring him in and make him a local guy. But he's not truly a local guy. Andre Ward, in this case, is a local guy. He's from Oakland. He was an amateur here. He went to the Olympics from here. And now that he's a pro from here, that'll be good. I leave Friday for my next trip and as I go across the country, then I can always say, 'I'm from where he's from.'"

Coach reminded me a bit of folks my family and I met during a three-year stay in North Texas. There were plenty of native Texans, of course, but the rest of us often bought bumper stickers or T-shirts bearing the slogan "I wasn't born in Texas but I got here as fast as I could." Same with Coach and Oakland; he wasn't a native son but he loved the place deeply. He'll be there forever, too, because that's where he's buried.

CHAPTER 20

John Madden, M.D.

Since John Madden's central expertise was in the world of sports, specifically football, and since the radio station had seen fit to schedule his daily visit with us at 15 minutes past the hour ("Sports at :15 and :45" was one of the many KCBS programming mantras), it made sense that injuries, health, and sports psychology would be regular topics of conversation.

Coach had more than a few views on these topics, often preceded by a phrase that became a catchphrase.

"I should always preface that with the statement, 'I'm not a doctor...but,' and then you go on from there. Just start with, 'I'm not a doctor...but.'"

Of course, once the disclaimer had been offered, Coach could proceed with all sorts of advice, not all of which was necessarily endorsed by the medical establishment. In point of fact, Coach *was* a doctor, having received an honorary Doctor of Humane Letters degree from his alma mater, California Polytechnic State University, San Luis Obispo (Cal Poly). I never heard anyone call him "Doc," though; "Coach" sufficed.

Office hours were always available. Sports anchor Steve Bitker was scuffling through a bad case of the sniffles when I asked Coach if he had any suggestions.

"Yeah, I do. We're in Georgia now, and as we're going through Georgia, they got what they call red dirt. And my driver Willie Yarbrough's telling me that as a kid he used to go out with a spoon, they'd send him out to get red dirt. His mother told him to get clean red dirt. They'd put it in little cans, and then the guys used it for snuff. So what I'll do is, I'll get some red dirt and I'll send it. He can put red dirt between his lips and then stick some up his nose."

Steve appeared dubious, suggesting that maybe a better remedy would be to go to Kauai in search of red soil, and while there, just flop down on a beach.

"No, you need the red dirt from here. Willie's mother said the cleanest dirt was next to the root of a tree. Okay, now we'll have to go and get red dirt, but not only red dirt, clean red dirt. Willie knows how to do it. I don't know how to do it. I've never used red dirt so much. But we'll get it, don't worry. It's in the mail."

One morning, I was the "patient." I greeted John by telling him I had a bit of a frog in my throat and wondered if he had any remedies.

"Yeah. Yeah. What you do is you stick your hand down your mouth to your elbow. Don't put it in any deeper than your elbow and then bend your knees and turn your toes out. And then put your head between your knees and pull everything out. That'll work."

"And does this work for you, John?" I wondered, trying to sort out the various physical impossibilities he'd just described.

"Yeah, that's what I do. But I think you sound good. I think it's not a bad frog. I mean, if it's a frog, it's a little frog. It's not even worth worrying about."

Coach's "prescription" probably should have come with a legal disclaimer: "Don't try this at home. Side effects may include...." As fate would have it, a few months after this episode, the tables were turned. John was the one with a husky voice.

It was the Monday of Thanksgiving week, meaning he'd be doing three games in eight days. There was no way he was going to miss a Thanksgiving Day broadcast. He didn't sound too good as he talked to us at 8:15. By the 9:15 segment, help was on the way.

Steve Bitker started his sports report leading into Coach's arrival by saying, "A loyal listener just called and reminded us that when one of us had a bad cold a few months ago, John had the solution. He said, 'Sit in the chair and stick your head between your knees.'"

Co-anchor Susan Leigh Taylor chimed in, "Coach, heal thyself."

"I tried that one, you know, then I came back up too fast. I think that works over time, but it's not an immediate fix. There are all those remedies, but none of them have worked yet. I'm gonna have to call my doctor. He's listening."

I suggested that Coach's physician, presumably an *actual* M.D., could call the KCBS newsroom and we'd link him up with Coach.

"Dr. Linfoot, John Linfoot. Yeah, he'll be listening. Because he can hear me right now, then he can play it back and he can do a diagnosis. And then after he gets his diagnosis right, he gives the Rx."

This generated a mental image for me. "I can see it now," I said. "A whole team of guys in white coats gathered around the speaker saying, 'No, I don't think it's that. It could be this.'"

"There's probably a lot of people listening that are doctors and lots that are not doctors. They're all saying, 'I know what he's got!' Because I don't have any other symptoms now. I mean, there's no headache. There's no cold. There's no stomach trouble. There's no nothing. There's just this. What you hear is all I have. I don't have anything else."

Because we had a standing 8:15 AM appointment, we got an update from the patient 24 hours later. I thought he sounded a little bit better.

"No, no, I think I'm a lot *bit better. Yesterday was a struggle, and I think today is going to be a lot better. The only thing that everyone seemed to say was to drink warm stuff. You know, drink tea and lemon and honey, and rest your voice. And other than rest your voice, I did most of them."*

Inquiring minds wanted to know what sort of tea he preferred, since he had always been a coffee guy.

"They usually give you a whole basket of them now. I just open them up and I don't even know what they are. I mean, I just grabbed the closest one. What I think is, the tea is a bluff. I think it's the hot water because I put lemon and honey in. I think it's the hot water and the lemon and the honey that do the job. I think your tea is just along for a free ride."

Two days later, John broadcast a thrilling Thanksgiving Day game in Detroit that saw the Packers hold off the Lions 29–27. He sounded great.

We morning radio people had a bit of an inside joke. If you got a bunch of us together at a party, the conversation would not be about money, real estate, sex, or even sports. It would be about sleep, since none of us ever got enough of it. I was fortunate to "sleep in" compared to some of my colleagues; my alarm was set for 4:03 AM (and I kept my clock set 20 minutes fast, just to ease the psychic pain of seeing "3:43" when the alarm sounded).

Coach didn't have to get up that early, but he wasn't a natural early riser either. Like me, he needed some caffeine to get cranking.

"Don't ask me too many hard questions. It's too early on a Monday morning. I haven't had a second cup of coffee here. Because you know, when you sleep at night, your brain sleeps too. So then when you awaken, then your brain awakens slowly and you don't just get out of sleep, jump out of bed, and have your brain working."

At this point, he was warming to the topic (and maybe that first cup of coffee was kicking in).

"Your brain only works at like 10 percent efficiency anyway, you know? So when your brain is fully working, it's only at 10 percent and when it's not, it's about like a half a percent. And then finally by around 10, 11, 12 o'clock, then you got your whole 10 percent or whatever you get."

We once had a conversation about sleep that revealed a lot about Coach. He'd taken a few days off after the end of the football season, and I welcomed him back by asking if he'd done anything fun.

"I didn't go anywhere. The only thing I did is, I went to bed at night without an alarm clock. And guess what? Because I always wondered what time I'd wake up if I didn't have to wake up at some time."

I took a wild guess. "Was it like a half hour after you wake up with the alarm clock?" I asked.

"No. No. Longer. An hour and 45 minutes."

As a fellow member of the Association of the Chronically Sleep-Deprived, I had an observation. "If you add up all those hour and 45s that you've been costing yourself, that's a lot of days of your life."

"I know it. Oh man, I know. But the other side of that coin is that if you slept, you missed a lot. That's why, even as a kid, I always had a tough time going to sleep early because I was always afraid I was going to miss something. I still have a little of that. I want to watch the news and I want to watch the other news. I want to watch Seinfeld *in between the news. I want to watch Letterman. I want to make sure that I don't miss anything before I go to sleep."*

The annual switch to Daylight Saving Time occasioned many a conversation about the hour of sleep we'd just "lost."

"It's always tough at the start. Everyone's, 'Oh boy, I'm tired this morning.' I'm tired as well because you're off your axis, that's all. I mean, you're just a little off-kilter and you're tilted a little to one side more than the other. And then lo and behold, in like three and a half weeks, you get back in your normal groove."

The notion of being "off your axis" was a theme Coach returned to many times over the years. Probably best to let *him* explain the cause and effect when it came to Daylight Saving Time.

"What you do is you just have to get back on your axis, because you do get a little crooked. It's like, the tide is controlled by the moon. So the moon kind of pulls the ocean. And then that forms the tide. So then the moon pulls on the ocean, forming the tides, and the tide pools and all those other things that go with tides also have that extra hour in them. So when you understand that the moon is pulling to make the tides, then that's the answer."

I'm not sure Neil deGrasse Tyson or Bill Nye the Science Guy would certify Coach's explanation, but he definitely believed that one's axis was an important part of a healthy life.

"That's one of the great excuses. You can use that, like kids in school when something happens. They ought to just say, 'I'm off my axis,' because no one knows what to do about it. I mean, a teacher wouldn't know. A principal or a doctor doesn't know. No one would know what you mean when you just say you're off your axis."

"Doctor" Madden's observations about health and the human body could pop up at any time. One morning, the great Brazilian race-car driver Hélio Castroneves had joined us as an added guest. Somewhere in his description of life in the cockpit of an Indy car, Castroneves mentioned a recent event where he'd gotten a cramp in his right leg. Coach perked right up.

"I was just thinking when you said that one thing, 'getting a cramp,' that that would have to be the worst thing that can happen to you, huh? I mean, I was just imagining, when you said that, I just felt one coming on myself. And when you feel one coming on, you stand up. But when you're doing what you do, you can't stand up, can you?"

Castroneves assured us he'd managed to fight his way through the cramp without crashing his car, and John had his own cramp story to share.

"Years ago when I was in training camp, I got on a roller coaster and we had just started up the hill, just started to rise. You talk about the most miserable time of my life, a cramp right then. You know, any time you get a cramp in your leg, everyone will say, 'Well, just stand up.' That's what you do. But if you can't stand up, I'll tell you, you just have to sit there and live with it. I don't think there's anything more painful. When he said, 'I got a cramp,' I just imagined that cramp that I got on that roller coaster."

Coach would often be asked to weigh in on the various training regimens being employed by big-name athletes. Bay Area fans may recall "The Hill," a brutal uphill run in Redwood City's Edgewood County Park. San Francisco 49ers stars Roger Craig and Jerry Rice put this steep two-and-a-half mile trail on the map. It wasn't a place you'd ever find John Madden, but he had some thoughts about the benefits of training on it.

"It's strength. That's why you have inclines on treadmills. It's just a tougher thing to do. It exercises different parts of your legs and you get burns in different places. But again, you're talking about a guy that couldn't have done it when he could have done it. I mean, I never, never ran hills, although I had a theory one time. It wasn't my theory, but there was one going around that I did mess around with. I love to run downhill. And the theory was that if you could run fast downhill, you could lengthen your stride and run faster."

I can recall looking across the studio at my colleague Holly Quan and watching her eyes grow larger. Holly was an avid runner and she may have been imagining a relaxing run on a quiet trail when suddenly, big old John Madden came barreling down the hill from behind.

"I enjoyed running downhill. Started as a kid. We used to roll downhill and then throw dirt clods at the end of the hill when you got down there. But then running downhill and trying to keep your balance was fun. Now what Jerry and those guys do isn't *fun. I mean, when you run uphill and then you leave your breakfast up there at the end of it, that can't be a fun thing, I wouldn't think. But it does get you in condition."*

Since Coach's full-time job for many of our years together on the radio involved broadcasting NFL games, we were never short of athletic injuries to discuss. His own potential NFL playing career had been derailed by a serious knee injury suffered in training camp with the Philadelphia Eagles, and John had watched many a modern player battle back from the sorts of orthopedic nightmares that a generation earlier would have led to an outcome like his.

And then there were our *own* knee injuries. Steve Bitker, our sports anchor, was also my daily carpool partner. Steve spent years coaching and refereeing youth soccer and managed to pile up three anterior cruciate ligament tears, each requiring ACL reconstruction surgery. I joined the torn ACL club with a clumsy fall on the ski slopes, and Coach couldn't wait to get involved in my case.

"Do you have to have surgery?"

I told him I was waiting to see my orthopedic surgeon, who was on vacation, but it didn't look good, based on what I'd heard from the emergency doctor at the ski area.

"Well, if you really tore it, you're going to have to operate. I mean, those things don't grow back together. Unless it's partially torn. Are you limping around?"

At this point, I sensed a certain lack of sympathy. My suspicions were confirmed when the details of my mishap emerged: I'd talked my hungry son into one last run before lunch so I could ski past a photographer. My attempt to nail a big turn right in front of her led to me catching a tip and falling. Coach was howling with laughter.

"Vanity trumps hunger. I can't believe this. Wait till Dominic and the boys hear about that.*"*

Some bedside manner.

After I underwent the MRI exam that confirmed the nature of my injury, Coach pointed out just how routine this diagnostic procedure had become.

"You play a game and you stuff them through an MRI and then you play another game. That's gotten to be more of the norm."

Steve looked across at me in Studio A and smiled, saying, "We know what that's like, to be stuffed through an MRI."

"No, no, I wouldn't do it. I'm claustrophobic, so I always said if I ever have to go in an MRI, take what you think *it is and treat that. Take the worst thing you think it is and say, 'Okay, that's what it is,' and treat it. I'm not going through one of those tubes. I don't even know if I'd fit in one."*

A few weeks later, after the ACL reconstruction surgery Coach had predicted, he wanted to know about my rehab program. Listening back to the recording today, I realize how "into" the topic he was; he wanted all the details.

"Oh, you had the ligament and *the meniscus?"*

I replied, "Yeah, I had the ACL, a little meniscus trouble, and I think there was a little fracture in there, too. It was like the triple play."

"Holy moly, you really got that thing! So what do you have on it now? I mean, they don't immobilize anymore, do they?"

I've often heard there's nothing worse than a bunch of golfers sitting around the clubhouse, replaying every shot. I think this may apply to knee-injury patients as well. I proceeded to explain, in great detail, the ice-therapy device, the post-surgical brace, and the continuous passive-motion machine, each of which had velcro straps that seemed to get caught on my sweater.

"I don't think you need a sweater when you're doing your rehab. If you need a sweater, you're not working hard enough. How's your pain?"

It occurred to me later that there might have been a healthy dose of wistfulness fueling Coach's curiosity about my knee injury and the process of recovery. I had the good fortune to suffer it more than 50 years after a certain

21st-round draft choice out of Cal Poly destroyed his knee in training camp, ending his NFL career before it began.

Before that knee injury, John had not only been a prized football lineman but also a pretty good catcher on his high school and college baseball teams. One morning, a discussion of how catchers get into a squat got things rolling.

"You have to be able to hunker. You have to be able to bend your knees. Some guys can sit like that, sit on their heels."

My own athletic capabilities are decidedly modest but one thing I *can* do is hunker down and stay there. Coach was incredulous as I told him I was going to get into a squat and stay there for the rest of our conversation.

"My dad used to be able to do that. I couldn't do that. I mean, that hurts my knees just thinking about you doing that. My dad used to hunker down like that and smoke a cigarette when he got down there. That was his position to smoke a cigarette."

Except for the fact that I remained in my squat, the rest of the segment was pretty normal; we meandered from one thing to another until we got to the topic of boxer Archie Moore. That triggered a memory for me of the night I got his autograph at a minor league baseball game in San Jose without actually knowing who he was. All the other kids were grabbing this guy's autograph so I figured he had to be someone important.

Coach listened to this memory resurface, then filled in details about Archie Moore's work with heavyweight champion George Foreman. I thanked him for rounding out my long-forgotten memory about the Moore autograph, and he responded with a classic piece of Madden medical "knowledge."

"Well, you know what happens is, when you get in a hunker, what that does is that takes all the blood and it gets more blood going through your system and the blood carries oxygen. And that oxygenates your brain. And then you remember things that were in the back part of your brain, at the bottom of the gray matter pool."

If you say so, Coach.

Maybe you've noticed this as well: it sure seems like modern athletes have a lot of trouble with their oblique muscles. On one of the many occasions when a star athlete was out of commission with a strained oblique, I asked our resident medical expert to give the listeners some details.

"The oblique? You know, if you can find it, you're doing pretty well. I think it's in the back somewhere, isn't it?"

We kicked it around a bit, deciding a better description might be "those muscles on your side."

"I thought it was more around the back because I was doing an exercise once at a health club in Chicago. I thought it was for an oblique something. It was a machine that tells you what it's for, but I didn't know where that was so I didn't know where it was supposed to hurt."

One of the most basic human reflexes is a nightmare-in-waiting for broadcasters. I'm talking about the sneeze. Coach told us many times that he often started his day with a bunch of sneezes. Once, we almost heard them.

"This is as close to sneezing on the air as I've ever come. I mean, I think I just finished my last sneeze, like, two seconds ago. It was right down to the wire. I thought it was going to be over *the wire, where you barely say, 'Hello' and then that big sneeze comes out. And I never know. You're not supposed to hold it back, right? You're supposed to let it out? It just doesn't feel right when you hold it in."*

There was general agreement in Studio A that stifling a sneeze is probably not a good idea. Then we wanted to know if he was following the modern advice: sneeze into the inside of your elbow rather than your hands, as many of us had been taught as children.

"I have trouble remembering that. I know you're supposed to do it, and I see people doing it, and I think, 'Well, they finally have that.' I don't have that one yet. You always think afterwards, 'Man, you know, I'm too old-fashioned.' I mean, this isn't the way you do it now. And then you see someone put their arm up, go in like that, and sneeze, and you think, 'The next time I sneeze, I'm going to do that.' And then when the next time you sneeze comes up, you forget."

Must have been a high pollen count one July morning when *both* John and I had been sneezing.

"I always get at least three. I don't know where they come from or why. And everyone closes their eyes. You can't keep your eyes open and sneeze."

I told him my urge to sneeze had come at an extremely inopportune time during my drive to work, as I found myself in a narrow lane between a big rig and a concrete construction barrier.

"You gotta hold it then, for a while, but you do *have to close your eyes when you sneeze."*

It could have been worse. I got through my freeway sneeze-fest unscathed, but Coach had more to report.

"I have a friend. The other day he went to open his car door, and he sneezed and hit his head. He cut his head on the car door. He kind of wobbled and had to get some first aid."

I didn't have the heart to ask whether his friend had remembered to sneeze into his elbow.

A lifetime around contact sports have John a pretty good feel for what didn't feel good as well as for how athletes dealt with pain. During the 2010 NBA Playoffs, Phoenix Suns star Steve Nash memorably broke his nose in a collision. It hurt just to watch it happen, but what *really* hurt was seeing Nash try to re-set his damaged schnozz.

"That's what you try to do. You try to set it yourself. But when you touch it, it hurts. Oh, it's really sore, that's the thing. You try to handle the pain and hope you don't get hit square on it again. The one thing it does, it affects your tear ducts. And so seeing could be a problem. I know it is with fighters. And then concentration's the other thing. It's harder to concentrate when you have something like that, especially a fresh one."

Though not an official man of medicine, Coach did have a way of distilling complex health issues to their essence. His take on NFL quarterback Joey Harrington's irregular heartbeat, treated with a cardiac catheter ablation procedure, was an example.

"It's not the plumbing in the heart and it's not the heart itself, but it's the electrical part. They go in there and they just burn one of these things that spark off. So it's a wiring job. You always have to preface this stuff with the fact you're not a doctor. Like someone would listen to me and ever think that I was a doctor. You

know, I really don't know what I'm talking about, but I have seen, in football and in other sports, I have seen cases of this with young people."

"I say this with all respect to you," I responded, "but I would have serious concerns about anyone who listened to you and thought you were a doctor."

"Well, especially a surgeon. I mean, I'm the same guy that dropped his telephone in the toilet. And you'd come in and say, 'This guy is going to do surgery?' and you'd have no idea where your parts would wind up."

CHAPTER 21

Hanging Out
With Coach

PEOPLE WOULD OFTEN ASK ME, "WHAT'S JOHN MADDEN REALLY LIKE?" For many years, my pat answer was something along the lines of, "Just listen to the radio. That's the John Madden I know."

A more considered answer, though, would include the time I spent with him off the air. Much of my in-person contact with Coach, at least in the early years of our working relationship, revolved around events. There'd be the KCBS/Madden Barbecues and the Madden-Mariucci Bocce Tournaments and an occasional sponsor-driven appearance together. In these settings, we were both "on," to a certain extent: aware that we were surrounded by listeners and sponsors and donors.

But there were a couple of other regular (and repeated) chances to hang out with an unfiltered version of Coach. One evolved as an adjunct to the annual barbecue event at the Madden production facility near his home. We'll get to that in a bit.

The other chance to spend time with John came every Sunday after he'd retired from his television career. It didn't really hit me until I sat down to write this book, but of the time I spent on the air with him, half of the years were while he was still working on television and the other half were after that phase of his working life ended.

Coach may have stopped drawing a paycheck to pay attention to the NFL when he left TV in 2009, but he didn't end his love affair with pro football. Sundays were still High Holy Days in Madden-land.

John and Virginia Madden, their sons, and their grandchildren were regulars at Oakland Raiders home games until John's health began to falter (and of course, the Raiders bailed out of Oakland in 2020, relocating to Las Vegas).

When the Raiders were on the road, Sundays meant football-watching parties at Goal Line Studios, the facility originally built so John could produce things like his annual "All-Madden Team" TV special without having to travel. This was no hobby studio; it was the Bay Area's largest sound stage.

It became the setting for a sort of man cave on steroids. The Maddens rigged the place with a huge wall consisting of eight big video panels flanking an even bigger center projection screen. They filled the whole thing with football.

It was another example of John Madden seeing over the horizon. He first floated the idea to us while he was still doing weekly *Sunday Night Football* broadcasts.

"I think I'm going to do it at my soundstage. I'm starting to work on that now. I think I'm going to set it up there and I'm going to get all the monitors and then it'll be like a studio thing where I can see all the games."

In my mind's eye, I saw something like a TV control room, with a producer and director calling the shots, looking at a bunch of live feeds and deciding what to show on the main screen. That's not how Coach saw it. Once again, he had the *idea* for something and left it to the experts to fill in the blanks.

"No, no, no. I'm not going to have that. I'm going to do it myself or have them all on, and just have the sound up on one, or something. I don't know how to do that because I've never done it. I mean, I've always been live at the events. I know there's a way to do it and I just haven't done it yet, but I'm going to have a wall.

I'm going to have all the games up there because Dick Ebersol at NBC Sports has a trailer. And in his trailer he has a setup like that where he can watch all the games. I mean, all the games are on smaller monitors and you have one big screen that you can pop it to. So that's my model right now."

A year later, Coach's only work commitment was our morning radio broadcast. He'd stepped away from NBC Sports and a few weeks before the start of the 2009 NFL season, he had his Sunday football setup ready to rock. It involved nine screens, with the featured screen in the center flanked by a column of four screens on each side.

"So the one in the middle will be Number One. Then to the right of the middle, Number Two. Number Three to the left of the middle, Four down below on the right, Five down below on the left. And then Six, Seven, Eight, Nine. And then I took the first week's games. You know, I'm crazy. I already numbered the first game since I put the game that I like best on Number One, the main screen. So I'll rate every game and then put them in the grid where I want them. Then there's always going to be someone there, maybe it's a Detroit-Tampa game and the guy's from Detroit and he wants that to be his main game. Well, he's going to have to go and get a headset and watch on Screen Nine."

The Madden Great Wall of Football had already evolved. Coach had concluded he wanted the speakers cranked up with the sound from his preferred game, the one on Screen One. Anyone else who cared about a different game had to grab a wireless headset and dial up the appropriate feed. It was a little like the barroom scene in *Star Wars*, if the bar had been a sports bar.

"It's crazy. I mean, I didn't even think it was a little crazy until I started to say that I did it and then I thought, 'Man, you're goofy.'"

The Friday before the NFL season kicked off, we checked in with Coach. "You got the barn all fired up, TV screens tested, salty snacks, and beverages at the ready?" I asked. His excitement was almost childlike as he answered.

"Yep. It's all ready. It's ready to go. In fact, if they were to sneak in and start early, we'd be ready to catch them. Yeah, if they played today and they said, 'We're not going to wait until Sunday,' we'd be there. We'll be ready."

It had taken me a while to realize that I didn't need to wait for an invitation from Coach to show up for the Sunday festivities. I'd been there often enough to get the rhythm down: wander in, try to adjust to the reality of several games happening at once, grab something to eat and drink, and check in with Coach. He had a big chair, front and center, flanked by a handful of other (usually empty) seats.

Kevin Radich, who'd first met John back in the mid-90s at KNBR, was handling afternoon sports duties at KCBS in these years. He knew the Sunday drill too. "I always felt at home going to those things," Kevin recalled. "Remember when you, Steve Bitker, and I would go watch football games? He would always make a point of letting us sit next to him and talk. And, you know, he liked that part of it. He liked our observations."

It was a privilege shared by the lucky few of us who were inside the ropes with Coach. There might be a few dozen friends and neighbors. His sons, Mike and Joe, were usually there. Mike's son Jesse, a future University of Michigan player, would be showing off his football mind while still in grade school.

Late in Coach's life, I wandered in one Sunday to see another elderly fellow sitting next to John. "Stan," he said, "you know John Burton?"

Everyone who'd followed Bay Area politics certainly knew *of* John Burton, a larger-than-life Democratic powerhouse who served in both houses of the California Legislature as well as in the House of Representatives. Burton's everyday speech would make a sailor blush, and he and Coach quickly got into a battle over their respective youthful athletic exploits.

Burton was born four years before Coach and starred in basketball at San Francisco's Lincoln High School and then at our mutual alma mater, San Francisco State. Coach was mocking Burton's forcefully mounted claim that he'd once scored 20 points in a game against Bill Russell's University of San Francisco team. I don't know that the two ever settled their debate, but I walked away amazed at having been part of the conversation as these two lions in winter relived the exploits of their Bay Area youth.

Since none of our listeners would ever have the full Madden Man Cave experience, I once used our radio conversation to bring up the one job you wouldn't want: Carl Moxley's. He was the man at the video switcher, tasked with keeping the main screen full of football.

I said, "I always love the poor guy in charge of making sure that the big screen has always got the prime game on it and the commercial breaks get scotched. That's a tough job. I mean, he's operating under some serious pressure." It was, of course, John Madden's dictum that when the game on Screen One went to a commercial break, another game would get switched in.

"All he has to do is pay attention and focus. When he doesn't pay attention and focus…I mean, his rule, in all due respect to advertisers, his rule is to never have a commercial up on that main screen."

Playing along, I asked, "When he doesn't pay attention and focus, is there anyone in the big room that calls that to his attention?"

"No one. I mean everyone. I mean, you know, mi casa es su casa, *everyone can relax. No one yells at anyone. Of* course *there's someone that calls it to his attention!"*

I went on to tell our audience about John's seating arrangement and how much I enjoyed getting a chance to sit near him and swap thoughts on the game. He'd often be sending and receiving text messages, connecting with former players, coaches, and broadcasting colleagues. Then I reminded John of the time our KCBS colleague Holly Quan showed up.

Holly is an Oakland native who grew up watching John coach the Raiders. Her role at KCBS was that of a utility player; she'd often fill in for either Susan Leigh Taylor or me when we had time off. I think we all knew that Coach adored Holly because he seldom failed to pull her into the conversation on the days she was filling in.

"Remember the day Holly came over and brought her sister?" I asked.

"She brought more than her sister. I think she brought her whole family, like a contingent."

It had been Holly's first Madden football viewing experience. As we walked out of the facility that afternoon, she leaned toward me and asked, "Is John always that intense when he's watching football?" I related that story to Coach, and all he could do was laugh. The answer was pretty obvious.

As I mentioned earlier, my dad and *his* dad were football coaches, so I learned a fair amount about the game from them. Watching a game with John Madden took it all to another level. I can recall times when, early in the first quarter, he'd point out what he considered to be a mismatch and sure enough, eventually, it would be exploited, often for a touchdown.

An indelible memory was watching the Kansas City Chiefs beat the San Francisco 49ers in Super Bowl LIV. That 2020 game gave Coach's friend Andy Reid his first Super Bowl victory. As we watched that day, Coach anticipated plays, dissected complex formations, and, like any fan, griped about penalty calls. It was like a graduate-level course, and I felt blessed to be enrolled.

Coach and I had thousands of public conversations on the radio. Each year, we'd perform together in front of a live audience exactly once, at the annual KCBS barbecue.

The barbecue began as a way to bring together the radio station's advertisers, our sales team, and the morning show crew for a chance to mingle with John and his family. Oh, and do some eating. A *lot* of eating.

The on-air lead-up to the barbecue would go on for weeks. Coach would make a pilgrimage to California's Central Valley farm country where a pig would be selected to be the "guest of honor." Most years, the pig would somehow acquire a name as it was fattened up for the slaughter. There was Pippy the Pig, Big Red, and a host of others.

One year, the porker remained anonymous until the morning of the barbecue.

"The pig is about done. You know, we put it on yesterday afternoon, and it was the biggest one we've ever had. He weighed 400 pounds on the hoof, and then on the roasting bar, he was 260. I was looking at him. And you know how some people look like a name? He looks like Herman. If he were to have a name, it would be Herman."

There was also the Year of the Goat, where my co-anchor Susan Leigh Taylor decided the vibe would be improved if a live goat could be spared so it could attend and be her companion. A couple of days before the big bash, we asked Coach how the preparations were going.

"The first update I have to give, Susan, is about the goat that's going to be there as your companion."

"That would be Andre Agassi, the goat," Susan responded. She's a big tennis fan and had decided that Agassi was the GOAT (Greatest Of All Time), thus, in her way of thinking, a goat named Andre Agassi.

"That's the news that I have to give you right now. The goat's a she."

Susan didn't miss a beat, simply switching from the men's draw to the women's side of the tournament, saying, "Martina Navratilova, the goat." She wanted to know what sorts of arrangements were being made for her guest.

"Well, he who says he wants a companion and will take care of that companion has to make those arrangements. In this case, she. You have to host the goat. You wanted the goat. I mean, I'm the host to you. And then you have to host the goat. You wanted the goat. Even my mother, I saw my mom the other day. The first thing when I walked in, she says, 'Save the goat.' I mean, if you're getting all this credit for saving this goat, then you have to take care of it."

Susan lived up to her responsibilities, making plans to show up for the barbecue with a pile of alfalfa hay and a collar for what turned out to be a young kid, just a few months old.

"This isn't a big old goat. You can't bring a big, old goat and then carry it around all day. I mean, this is something you can handle."

Susan brightened. "Oh, so I can maybe tuck her under my arm and just walk around?"

"Well, no, I don't think you'll do that either. I think we're somewhere between tuckable and runnable."

The agenda for the barbecue was pretty straightforward: show up hungry and leave a few hours later stuffed to the gills. It helped if you were a carnivore. There'd be smoked bacon-wrapped beef tri-tip, grilled goat, lamb stew, the whole spit-roasted pig, deep-fried turkey, sausages, barbecued chicken, and a whole lot more. And that was just the "standing-around" food.

Rookies at the event would fill up outdoors before being ushered into the big soundstage where banquet tables had been set up. There'd be a full buffet with even more food, topped off by Virginia Madden's chocolate cake for dessert. When I say, "Virginia Madden's chocolate cake," I don't mean "cake made with Virginia's recipe." She baked them herself, cranking out enough cakes for a crowd of over a hundred people.

We almost went without cake one year. Unbeknownst to us, the Maddens had just lost one of their beloved Newfoundlands and Virginia was not in a great mood. The morning of the barbecue, the KCBS crew was happily anticipating the feast, each of us expounding on our favorite food. Susan brought up Virginia's cake. There was a long pause.

"Uh, there's not going to be any chocolate cake, Susan."

John's response caught us off guard and there was no further explanation, so we let it drop. That's why we were surprised to arrive at the event and see the usual scrumptious cakes arrayed on the dessert table. It was only later that we learned that Virginia had heard the on-air exchange and rushed out to get the ingredients, then fired up the oven to get the cakes back on the menu.

While the guests worked their way through the sit-down portion of the feeding, Coach and I would grab a couple of wireless microphones and stand up to say a few words. For me, the first few years of this were a bit intimidating. It was one thing to goof off on the radio with John Madden. It was quite another to stand next to the big guy in front of a live audience. As time went on, I came to truly enjoy the role, handing over the event to its host and sitting back to watch his ability to connect with people.

A few years after launching the event, we began to get inquiries from listeners, wanting to know how they could attend. I also recall being badgered by a guy who wrote a blog about Bay Area media, insisting that I could get him into the barbecue if I really wanted to. Well, I *didn't* want to; the barbecue was like a family gathering. No room for outsiders.

Eventually, someone came up with an idea: we'd auction off a few passes to the barbecue, donating the money to the Maddens' favorite charities. That's how longtime listener George Barron wound up there with his 96-year-old mother. He introduced Martha Barron to Coach upon their arrival, and was amazed to hear John tell the audience three hours later that we had quite an age span there that day, from John's two-year-old granddaughter Makenna to Mrs. Barron. He'd heard her name once, remembered it, and given her a shout-out neither she nor her son would forget.

One year, prompted by one of our guests, we got into a discussion about something we'd covered on the radio a few days before the barbecue. John had told our listeners a memorable story about the long-outlawed "head slap," a tactic defensive linemen would use to stun the guys trying to block them.

"It was Bob 'Boomer' Brown when he was playing with the Rams. It was Deacon Jones who did the head slap. So Bob Brown was an offensive tackle and he was practicing against Deacon Jones, and in practice, Deacon Jones would always head slap him. So Bob Brown said, 'Hey, don't head slap me. You know, we don't have to head slap in practice.' And Deacon wouldn't stop it."

John Madden, Master Storyteller, was off and running, talking about two of the greatest linemen in NFL history. Both were inducted into the Pro Football Hall of Fame before John.

"But now Bob Brown went in and took the facemask, up there at the end where your eye kind of meets the mask, he put a screw in there and he filed the screw to make it like an ice pick and he left it to hang out there. So now Deacon Jones goes 'BOOM,' to head slap him, and he nails his hand right to Bob Brown's helmet. Now the hand is stuck on the helmet. Bob Brown is moving his head up and down. He said, 'I told you not to do that.' And Deacon said, 'I won't do it anymore.' If you ever saw Deacon Jones, I swear this is true, because he'd always show it to you, right in the middle of his hand. He had a scar where that thing went in. That was the end of the practice head slap."

Now we're at the barbecue, and Coach decides to use our little two-man show as an opportunity to provide some visuals to go with that story. I took off my eyeglasses and prepared to play the role of an NFL offensive lineman getting smacked in the head. We told our listeners about it a few days later.

"John dragged me up as, what would you call me? A punching bag?" I said.

"A demonstrator. You were the offensive tackle. I was Deacon Jones and you were Bob Brown."

Susan, who'd watched this all play out from her table at the barbecue, broke into laughter. "I think John mostly wanted to tell that story so he could keep smacking you in the head," she said.

I admitted, "I was a little nervous. I'm thinking, 'John is very demonstrative. He's into this. I'm thinking any moment there's going to be a 'BOOM!'"

"Well, there was a 'BOOM,' but I have control of my 'BOOMS.'"

That he did, and full control of the room, too. The party would always break up with a line of guests waiting to have a snapshot taken with Coach. At first, good old Polaroid photos were handed out. As time went on, the photos were shot in front of a green backdrop, background images were edited in, and the resulting picture printed on the spot. Everyone headed home with proof that they'd spent a moment beside John Madden—to go along with a very full stomach.

Coach told us one morning that he had an engagement later that day. He'd be heading over to a barbecue at television partner Al Michaels' place after a day of meetings heading into the NFL season. "No offense to Al Michaels," Susan said, "but I'm willing to bet money that an Al Michaels barbecue does not quite stand up to the John Madden barbecue."

"Not. Even. Close. But I'll say this for Al, he does it himself. He does it all by himself with no help. He does this annually. I was impressed the first year because I thought he'd have a crew of guys helping him or something. And yet no one; he just does it himself."

So let's give Al Michaels the trophy for Single-Handed Barbecues that met John Madden's muster. The team award stays with Coach.

For me, the day of the KCBS/Madden Barbecue itself was like Christmas Day in a family that opened its packages on Christmas Eve. The Night Before the Barbecue was circled on my calendar every year.

It was a chance to just hang out with Coach, Virginia, and a crew of real people who put the thing together. John's buddy Dominic Mercurio from Café Fina in Monterey was the maestro, overseeing the guys from the farming town of Los Banos who raised the meat and cooked it. They were aided and abetted by friends and family.

I'll forget a few names, but I'll never forget hanging out with solid, no B.S. people like Danny Fialho, Kevin Gill, Jose Hernandez, Ron Lemos, Carmelo D'Angelo, Rudy Labrado, George Leonard, David Sagouspe, Roger Pruitt, Anthony Pereira, John Muller, Pat Gallichio, and Rocco DiMaggio. Oh yeah: Vance Wolfsen, straight outta Gustine, CA, with his sausages, too. Glad I could name-check you in the book, guys. You earned it.

They'd arrive at midday the day before the barbecue. It was like a military field kitchen operation (even though the Madden production facility had its own full commercial kitchen); they'd bring grills and roasters and more, including a giant vat in which to cook lamb stew that would be stirred with a shovel.

There was also a huge fire pit equipped with a sturdy spit on which the whole pig would slowly spin as it roasted. By late afternoon, the coals would be hot, the pig would be starting its voyage to succulence, and the stories would be flowing.

Not unlike the "family meal" served to the staff before a restaurant opens, the crew would dig into a spread that was not on the next day's menu. I can recall quite a variety over the years, including grilled sardines, calamari, sliced tomatoes, grilled quail, frog's legs, a tray of pasta with spareribs deep inside, and the fried Italian donuts called *sfingi*.

"The guys started talking about, 'Let's make sfingi,' these Italian donuts. And to be honest, I love the guys like brothers, but none of them knew how to really make them. They didn't know the recipe, so they had to call their mothers. Then they made enough so that they could have coffee and more sfingi in the morning. You can't beat a good sfingi."

There was even some dumpster diving. One year, I spotted a cluster of guys standing around a big trash can. Next thing I knew, we were *eating* out of the can.

"We wrap bacon around stuff. We put it in a smoker, so they must have taken something out of the smoker that was wrapped in bacon. Was that what it was?"

It sure was. Coach had been around the corner and had missed the bacon-feeding frenzy, but he wasn't judging.

"Oh yeah, that's something I would do."

And then there was Virginia's bread pudding.

"That's just for the night before. That's become a tradition now, that the night before it's a bread pudding, and the day of, it's a chocolate cake."

She'd make two kinds, one with dried fruit and one without. I would stand there salivating, telling her how good it was, and in her deadpan way, she'd just say, "It's easy. Anyone can make bread pudding." Ultimately, my on-air raving about the bread pudding forced Virginia to crank out enough for the barbecue crowd too.

The barbecue itself was like any good party: a lot of energy, some great food and conversation, but honestly, a bit exhausting. The Night Before was a relaxed hangout, a chance to really get to know the Maddens and the folks who'd been invited into their world.

There would always be some nice wine and the conversation would flow as the smoke from the roasting pig drifted past. Coach would sit in the middle of it all, a man truly in his element.

CHAPTER 22

The Fourth Quarter

JOHN MADDEN WAS 85 YEARS OLD WHEN HE PASSED AWAY. HE WAS 64 WHEN I started chatting with him every weekday morning. That last quarter of his life brought many changes: retirement from his highly visible career on television, the arrival and growth of his grandchildren, some significant health issues, and more. All of these life changes played out before the KCBS radio audience.

It almost feels voyeuristic to write about some of these moments. But on second thought, I'm happy to be able to share them with you because there's a lot of wisdom and joy locked up in these episodes that slid by so quickly in the rush of our day-to-day relationship on the air.

When I replaced Al Hart at KCBS in the summer of 2000, John was at the peak of his fame and fortune. His face and voice penetrated tens of millions of American homes during NFL broadcasts. He still had his apartment at the legendary Dakota building in New York City. Heck, he'd just made a cameo appearance in U2's "Stuck in a Moment You Can't Get Out Of" music video!

Less than a year into our on-air relationship, John was marking a milestone. He and Virginia were grandparents for the first time. Sam Madden was born on his grandpa's 65th birthday. A day later, it was all soaking in.

"You know what I'm thinking about now, seriously, on this grandfather deal. You know how all your life you've said, 'Someday I'm going to be sitting around and I'm going to tell my grandkids about this.' Now I have to remember all those things that happened to me in my life. But see, he's not ready yet to hear them. I think you start telling them those things when they're 10, 12, 14, 16 years old. My whole life, I thought, 'Someday, I'll be sitting around and I'm going to tell my grandkids a story.' And now you're a grandfather and you say, 'Holy moly, I'm going to have to start thinking of all those things that I said all those years and I was going to tell my grandkids.'"

At that point in our lives, my colleague Steve Bitker and I each have two teenaged children and we can see that maybe, just maybe, we'll be in John's place someday. Steve says, "John, we've got a lot of those stories on tape. Most of them are embarrassing, but we can help you out."

I follow Steve's lead. "Let's dig into the archives. You know, like the bird that pooped on you at Pebble Beach." This brings one of those patented John Madden guffaws, and a reply.

"So a lot of love, huh? Like ripping my pants and putting duct tape on them." This actually happened.

I add, "Yeah, that's the trouble with living a public life, big fella. Ya got a track record."

And Kim Wonderley, our traffic anchor who's known John since his KNBR days 25 years earlier, pops in to wrap things up. She says, "By the time you're old enough to tell the stories, you're so old you can't remember the stories."

A week later, Coach was still bubbling about his new role and the newest member of the family.

"Little Sam's doing well. Those are two things that are hard to remember, that you are being called 'grandfather,' and that there is a little Sam Madden around. He's doing fine. In fact, he was out yesterday. Sam will be working in another week or two. He came over to the office yesterday to see what was going on. And I mean, he's not really talking or walking yet but I think he's ready to go to work in a couple of weeks."

So many stories. A lifetime *living* a story that even now has Hollywood wanting to tell it, because it's so remarkable, so American, so relatable.

I'm not sure if the arrival of grandchildren started John thinking about stepping away from the grind of the NFL schedule. After all, he had a very specific view of what it meant to consider retirement.

"I've always said that in life, in any job, once you say you're going to retire, you've already retired. If you say you're done, you're already done. And then I don't know how they say, 'One more year.' To me, you can either play or you can't. You're either finished or you're going to play. And then if you're going to play, you can say, 'I'll take it one year at a time.' But I don't know how you can say, 'I'm going to play for one more year and then retire,' because doing this takes competitiveness at its highest level."

That particular morning, he was talking about a famous athlete's announcement that he'd be taking a "farewell tour," playing a final season before hanging them up. As I often did, I tried to make light of one of John's heavy thoughts, saying, "So for example, if Steve was to say to you, 'I'm going to go around the block one more time with this bocce, and then that's it,' you wouldn't be okay with that?"

"He's already quit in his mind. If he says, 'I'm going to give it one more try,' then he's already quit."

In the same way some people save voicemails after loved ones die, I've kept my text message string with Coach. I just looked back at the message I sent him two months before my own planned retirement date, letting him know of my plans. His reply, verbatim: "When you say you are going to retire, you have." He also mentioned a story in that day's *Wall Street Journal* about how people handled retirement. It was typical Coach: on top of it, aware, still coaching.

The transition from road-tripping broadcaster to stay-at-home grandfather didn't happen right away; there were five grandkids by the time John closed out his TV career. First-born Sam was eight by then.

John didn't jump immediately into the deep end of the grandparenting pool, but for a guy who acknowledged he'd missed a lot of his own two sons' upbringing, these were new experiences.

My predecessor Al Hart was one of those old-school gentlemen, the kind of guy who sent birthday and anniversary cards to everyone he knew. He'd even make sure that kids got a card on their first birthday. Coach had his own way of referring to someone who hadn't yet celebrated a birthday.

"Jesse was none years old until Saturday, and then he got to be one. And lo and behold, he got a card in the mail, and it was from Al Hart."

Al was still joining us every Wednesday morning to join the Madden conversation when Coach called him on a goof a year later: Al had sent the wrong birthday card to young Jesse Madden.

"I mean, he just turned two and you send him that 'Happy Birthday Six Year Old' card. And Jesse's really confused. He thinks he's six and he ought to be in school but he's only in preschool. I mean, he still has that deal where he eats his dinner while sitting on his lunch. We got to get that one straightened out."

It took a moment for us all to absorb what Coach meant about kids in diapers. While we were still laughing, he carried on.

"I had to babysit for Jesse the other night. I was on the four to midnight shift. And I've never changed a diaper in my life. I told the other babysitter who I was relieving, 'Change his diaper and put him in his pajamas.' And I told Jesse, I said, 'Jesse, from now until midnight, whatever you do in those, you're going to live in them until you go to bed and then you go to sleep.'"

We're laughing even harder now. I asked, "And how did that work out for you and Jesse?"

"I don't know if he understood what the heck I said, but that was the deal. I put him to bed. There was no way…I mean, not only did I not check him, I didn't even give him the stink test. I said, 'To heck with it, man. I mean, that's the deal.'"

Coach loved holidays. It didn't always mean he was actually home for them, but he could live vicariously.

"Halloween is big at my house. You got to carve the pumpkins and you got to get all the stuff ready."

By "you," he meant "Virginia," who had a habit of putting up elaborate decorations and handing out the full-sized candy bars, drawing crowds that John typically missed because he was on the road.

"With Virginia, everything is big on Halloween. And I think she had a lot of trick-or-treaters last year, well over 500. The police were out there directing traffic."

A traditional Madden family Thanksgiving? Not so much.

"I've really never had many Thanksgivings in my life. When I was in high school at Jefferson High School in Daly City, we used to play on Thanksgiving Day. We played South City [South San Francisco High School]. So Thanksgiving in high school was a football game. And then in college I was always away. And then pro football, again, it's a Thursday before a game, so it's a regular Thursday at work. And then I got into broadcasting and for years and years I always did a game on Thanksgiving, either in Detroit or Dallas."

After his retirement, John would recall those Thanksgiving Day games on the road as among his favorite times in broadcasting, celebrating the holiday with the rest of his TV "family," the production crew.

He might have found joy in a Thanksgiving feast surrounded by the folks he worked with, but the end-of-the-year holidays were a different deal.

"This is always a tough time because in television or even when I was coaching, you always want to be in the playoffs. You always want to be part of the playoffs. And if you are part of the playoffs, that means the holidays of Christmas and New Year's, you're away from home, which I am. And then you add that in between Christmas and New Year's, I also have an anniversary. So every year I tend to hit a trifecta, or more literally, I tend to miss a trifecta."

The realities of a 24/7, all-news radio format also meant somebody had to be on the air every day of the year at KCBS. The full complement of five Madden grandchildren was on my colleague Susan Leigh Taylor's mind one Christmas Eve. She'd drawn the holiday short straw and was holding down the fort while I enjoyed the day with my wife and kids. She asked, "John, are you on special assignment today? I mean, since you're out there on the road in your bus, if Santa needs some help, are you going to be his assistant?"

"We talk constantly. We talk about the weather and the roads and the geography. You know, what Santa Claus does is he starts east and then goes east to west, kind of the way we're going, because there's a three-hour time difference.

For example, it's 11:15 AM here in the east right now. Some people think that he kind of starts out there in California, but actually he starts back here on the East Coast and works from north to south and then from east to west. So that's the way we're going too; we went from north to south and then we're going from east to west now. And so we've been talking to the North Pole, to Santa Claus, and to some of his people and we're kind of telling him about weather conditions and all those things. So we stay in touch."

Susan chipped in, "So this is good information for Sam and Jack and Aiden and Jesse and Makenna to know that since Grandpa can't be with them for Christmas, that at least he'll be on hand to help out Santa in case he needs a little extra help there along the way."

"And I'll direct Santa to their houses because you never know. Sometimes he forgets and sometimes he isn't sure. And he's not sure if they were good or bad so I talked to him about that too."

As Coach passed his 70th birthday, he remained at the top of his profession and was still fully engaged in his other ventures, including the video game and yes, those daily conversations with his hometown radio station. It was in April 2009, a few weeks after calling an exciting Super Bowl between the Steelers and the Cardinals (a game that produced the largest single audience in American television history to that time) that John Madden downshifted.

His most extensive comments about his decision came on our broadcast, so I'm happy to present them in their entirety.

"I decided to retire. Heck, I can't even say it, but I decided to retire. And, you know, it's tough because…not because I'm not sure it's the right time. I mean, I really feel strongly that this is the right time, but I'm just going to miss everything about it because I enjoyed it so much. It was one of those things, when you get around 70, you have to start thinking, 'You know, at some point it's going to be over.' But I was one that always believed that you never say you're going to retire before you do, because once you say it, then you've already done it in your mind and you've already quit.

So the last three or four years, I would do this every year: in my mind, take two months, which I think you have to do, and think about it. And that's what I did. We did the Super Bowl and I thought about it the last two months and I vacillated. I mean, sometimes, I felt like I'm going to keep doing it, and then there'd be days I'd say, 'I'm going to retire.' And then finally I was up against it. The two months were up, the NFL schedule was coming out. And I said, 'You know, this is what I'm going to do.'

So I called Dick Ebersol [Chairman of NBC Universal Sports & Olympics] about a week ago and told him, and then he came out yesterday and we talked about it and we talked about some other possibilities. And I said, 'No, you know, I'm ready to do this.' One of the points I made is that now my grandkids are old enough that they know when I'm gone and when I'm not. When they were younger, they weren't always sure. And this year is my 50th wedding anniversary; that comes in December, and I have to be there. And anyway, you just add up everything and it's just the right time.

It's kind of on my terms. There's nothing wrong. You know, everyone's going to say 'Madden retires. What's wrong?' There's nothing. There's nothing wrong with me. There's nothing I have. You know, I'm in the middle of a contract. I have three more years on my contract at NBC. So it's not that. It's not that I'm tired of traveling on the bus, but you just get to the point that, at some point, you have to do this. And I got to that point. And the thing that made it hard is not because I'm second-guessing, 'Is it the right decision?' but I enjoyed it so damn much. I enjoyed the games and the players and the coaches and the film and the travel and everything. So that's why it took me so long because…I know I'm rambling here, but what the heck?

You know that if you hated part of it or if there was something wrong, it would be easy. Like, 'I'm tired of travel' or 'I'm tired of football.' But I'm not tired of anything. But I am going away. That's what makes it hard.

It's the second time I've done it. When I coached the Raiders, I kind of did it that way. I didn't say, 'This is going to be my last year.' I took some time off and felt that I didn't want to go through it again, and then that was it. I still loved pro football. So I retired from coaching and then I came into television broadcasting and it was the same way. It wouldn't have been me to say, the week of the Super Bowl, 'This is my last game.' That's not me. I don't do that. And I wouldn't do that. And I don't believe in it.

You know, I'm a grinder and you just grind and you go through it, and then when it's all over, you think about it and you don't rush into any decisions because, as you know, we've talked about this with coaches and athletes. At the end of the season, you're tired and you know it and it kind of drains you. A lot of people think of quitting or retiring so they do it. Then they start to feel better. Then they want back. So I had to guard against that. I didn't want one of those things that, you know, right after the Super Bowl, I would retire and then two weeks later say, 'Hey, I was just kidding, I want back.' So I had to make sure that that wasn't going to happen. I had to make sure that, when I did this, that I was sure about it. Like I said, Dick Ebersol and Sandy Montag [John's agent] came out yesterday and we talked all about it. We talked about other possibilities and other things that I could do. No. I just wanted, 'whoosh,' and he's gone.

I didn't say, 'I want to do the Super Bowl and go out.' This is my third year at NBC. I enjoy the heck out of it. Al Michaels, and before that Pat Summerall, I mean, I was lucky. I just had great broadcast partners and then the last game I did was a Super Bowl, which, you know, is pretty good. But again, that wasn't planned. I didn't say, 'I want to go out on a high note. I want to go out on a Super Bowl.' That wasn't part of it. It just boils down to: at the end, it is just time. I strongly believe that this is the right time. This is the right thing. And you just do it. Now, is it easy? No, I love it too much for it to be easy.

I'm still going to travel. I'm not going to stay put because I can't do that. I'm still going to have the bus. I'll be going to the Hall of Fame in August. There's always going to be something coming up. So it's not like I'm going to stop traveling or stop doing stuff. I'm still going to be doing things. I'm just not going to be doing pro football on television anymore."

There was obvious emotion in John's voice as he closed that long and successful chapter in his life. Steve Bitker responded, "The most poignant thing that you've said to me is the fact that your grandkids are at an age now where they know when you're not home. And most importantly, I think, how long you're away. The kids grow up so fast."

"Well, yeah. And I kind of missed a lot of that with my own sons. Earlier, when they were babies, they really didn't know when you were there and when you weren't. But Sam was just eight last week and he's the oldest one. They're eight, seven, six, five, four, three. So now they know. I mean, they know when I'm here and they know when I'm gone."

With five grandkids, there were plenty of Proud Grandpa moments.

"The big news: I had my first grandson that wore eyeblack. Yeah, that is a milestone. You know, you think of milestones in your life; you have grandkids and you can't wait till they do this or they do that or they do the next thing. So here we have eyeblack for the first time with six-year-old catcher Jesse Madden."

As Coach played out his final years, he had more time to look back at his legacy. We've talked about his family life and his dedication to the NFL. As for his broadcasting work, all anyone had to do was turn on a television to see and hear sports analysts who'd built their careers on the back of John's pioneering approach. He won the last of his 16 Emmy Awards the year before he retired from NBC Sports.

And then there was the video game. One Sunday, I showed up to watch football with Coach on his big video wall. Several other guests turned out to be key members of the *Madden NFL* team from video game publisher EA Sports. I asked John if he was sometimes a bit overwhelmed by where the video game had gone.

"Yeah, I am. When I have these meetings with those guys, I'm just…I mean, it's unbelievable where we were when we started and how far it's come and where they're going. This meeting yesterday was about what the game is going to be next year. They're so far ahead and just doing so many things. It's just mind-boggling."

I'd been amazed to learn from the EA Sports guys about the existence of websites dedicated to analyzing the play-calling tendencies of people competing at Madden NFL.

"I know. I mean, they study. They study everything. And everything that is in the game that's new and technical, they have it and they use it and pretty soon, you know, we get to the point where the dish just runs away with the spoon."

When Ray Guy, the peerless Raiders punter, finally reached the Pro Football Hall of Fame in 2014, John traveled to Canton to present him, then later that year stood in a driving Oakland rainstorm as Guy received the Hall of Fame Ring of Excellence. Each of these late-life ceremonies gave Coach a chance to summon up memories.

"I remember Ray's first training camp. We put in the defense and he runs out with the defense, at safety. And I told him, 'Get the heck out of there.' And so he walks off the field. So as we're leaving practice, he said, 'But I want to play defense.' I said, 'No, you'll never play any defense. We've got safety covered. We don't need you at safety. We need you as a punter.' And he said, 'Well, [Raiders director of player personnel] Ron Wolf told me I could play defense, too.' And I said, 'Ron Wolf lied.' The conversation never came up again."

Coach was nearing his 80th birthday when Father Time caught up with him. He'd been hobbling on bad hips and knees for years, but what happened in November 2015 was a bigger deal. He developed breathing problems the day before Thanksgiving, was taken by ambulance to a medical facility near his home, and underwent multiple-bypass heart surgery at the UCSF Medical Center in San Francisco a few days later.

None of us saw it coming, though when I listen back now to the last broadcast he did with us before the surgery, two weeks before that ambulance ride, I hear a pronounced weakness in his voice. Our conversation that morning focused on the death of Scotty Stirling, a sports executive with whom John had worked during his years with the Raiders.

Coach reviewed the highlights of Stirling's remarkable career but mostly wanted our listeners to remember the person behind the career.

"He was really a good guy. I mean, every time you'd see Scotty, you just put a smile on your face because he always had a quip or a joke. He was a friend for a long time and a really, really, really good guy."

The conversation went on that morning to cover ambidexterity in athletes before Coach veered off course.

"Just reading something in the paper about quilting. I just thought that's a good word to throw out sometimes, you know? 'What are you doing?' 'Well, I'm getting ready to go quilting.'"

Just another slightly off-kilter observation, but none of us realized it would be his last for many months. In fact, it would be nearly two years before Coach returned to regular appearances on the radio with us.

John's friend and occasional target for on-air jibes, Jim Ghielmetti, was among Coach's first post-surgical visitors. Jim told me in an email, "As you know, John was very careful about using profanity [note that Jim's not saying John *didn't* use profanity, only that he was careful about when and where he swore]. Right after his open-heart surgery, I went to visit him in rehab. My opening question to him was, 'How are you feeling?' to which he ripped open his robe to expose where they cut him open and replied, 'How the f— do you think I feel?' Classic John."

There was quite a bit of consternation among management when it became clear John was not returning to the airwaves anytime soon, and maybe not ever. On an emergency basis, Coach's buddy Steve Mariucci, by then working as an analyst for the NFL Network, sat in for the 8:15 AM segment several times. So did Garry St. Jean, the former coach of the NBA's Golden State Warriors and Sacramento Kings (and general manager of the Warriors). Both are great guys, terrific broadcasters, and fit in nicely. Either would have made for a wonderful morning radio teammate. But neither is named John Madden.

I can recall several meetings at which names were tossed around. I championed Ted Robinson, who'd joined KCBS as a young sports reporter in 1982 before moving on to a long career in play-by-play, most notably working marquee events like the Olympics, Wimbledon, and the French Open for NBC Sports. The management response was lukewarm.

Some other well-known names were floated. But mercifully, KCBS never got around to hiring "the next John Madden." We soldiered on, keenly aware of his absence, until I got a text message and email one day in early June 2017. It was Coach's longtime agent, Sandy Montag, reaching out.

"Ready for a surprise guest at 9:15 AM tomorrow?" Sandy wrote. Yeah, I think we could make that work!

It was a cameo appearance; Coach was excited to indulge in some brief trash talk promoting that day's annual Madden-Mariucci charity bocce tournament. Sadly, this broadcast vanished into the ether, another victim of the haphazard archive system at KCBS. But Coach, having regained his health after the open-heart surgery and a hip replacement, was apparently ready to fall back into his radio gig.

By the time the 2017 NFL season kicked off, Coach had agreed to a less-hectic schedule: instead of appearing every day, he'd join us just on Mondays and Fridays. I could barely contain myself when I introduced him that Friday morning in September 2017.

"We're fired up," I said. "John Madden, are you fired up?"

"I stayed fired up. I've been fired up the whole time. I just haven't had any place to put it. It's great to be back. It really is. I just want to say that right off the bat."

"Well, it's terrific," I responded. "The love that's been shown since we announced it yesterday, people are going nuts over it. Two years is a long time to stay fired up with no place to put it, though."

"Well, that's right. I mean, it was hard to do, but sometimes you just have to push through. You get through it and keep fired up."

Steve Bitker jumped in, speaking for all of us, "You sound six or eight years younger." Steve was absolutely right; it was a bit startling to hear the vigor in Coach's voice.

"I know. I'm feeling great. I really am. I mean, a lot of that stuff's behind me now."

I took a pass on asking him for the details, happy just to have him back where he belonged. "You're sure Virginia didn't slip a little something special in the orange juice this morning or anything like that?" I quipped.

"Oh, no, no, nothing like that. You know, we had a double dip there. After I had my hip surgery and other surgeries, then Virginia fell and broke her hip and she had surgery. We had two of us limping around here."

And from there, we moved on to talk about the previous night's NFL game, an NFL quarterback controversy, and a bunch of other stuff before I wrapped up his return appearance by asking, "Did you enjoy this? Should we do it again Monday?"

"Yeah. Yeah. Let's try it again so we can get it right."

John's last lap on KCBS had the sweet feeling of a second chance, without the melancholy nature of a last lap. After all, this was a guy who'd always sworn that saying you were *going* to retire meant you already *had* retired.

We carried on with our Monday and Friday "Mornings with Madden" (at 9:15 rather than 8:15 so Coach could sleep in a bit) until I got another text message from agent Sandy Montag. It was short, to the point, and jarring. "Just wanted to let you know that tomorrow will be John's last regular show. Decided he doesn't want to do anything regular this season," Sandy wrote on August 16, 2018.

"I don't know any other way to do this," I began as I introduced Coach the next day, "but just to get right to it. And that's for us to let our audience know that we're giving you a new title. John's new gig is 'Senior Investigative At-Large Correspondent.'" I actually got the company to print up a box of business cards bearing the title; he got a kick out of it when I delivered them to him a few weeks later.

Traffic reporter Kim Wonderley slipped in, "Now when you say 'at-large,' that means 'not regular' to me." Coach was waiting.

"No, that means 'large guy.' 'Senior' means 'old.' You know, 'big, old fat guy.'"

I didn't have a script for this. I just wanted Coach to be able to tell the listeners who loved him that this was his decision, not ours. We'd have kept him forever.

"Well, you know, the thing is, and this is probably silly, but unless you under-stand me a little bit, there's this: Monday and Friday at 9:00 are the last scheduled

things that I have. I mean, I don't have any other schedule. And so there's only two things every week that I have to do. And I thought 'Jeez, if I could just get rid of those things, I wouldn't have to do anything!' You know, I'm at a point in my life where I can do that. I'm not going anywhere. I'm not leaving. Any time you want me or I have something that I think I could say, I'll try to get on. But I just don't want the schedule of Monday and Friday. And now I'm going to have a clear, open schedule. Really, I really will. Everyone gets to that point sometime in life. That's what I'm thinking. You know, 'If you have to get there sometime in life, what the heck are you waiting for?'"

We joshed around a bit more, a group of old friends realizing this really and truly was our last get-together. Eventually, it was time to give Coach his final say.

"I enjoy every part of it and I enjoy everything you guys do. And I thank you for everything."

Back at ya, Coach.

CHAPTER 23

Farewell

THE PROCESS OF GATHERING, ARRANGING, TRANSCRIBING, AND RESEARCHING
John Madden's appearances on KCBS was complex, arduous, and frustrating.
At times it seemed impossible, stretching, as it did, all the way back to the
days of analog recording tape. Episodes existed in some form or another on
cassette, CD, and digital file. Some episodes were lost. Some were partially
recorded over. Some were recorded onto CDs which were now unreadable.
And somewhere along the way, a network crash left an untold number of files
corrupted. Attempting to play them back would produce two or three seconds
of good-quality audio, a blast of digital static, another few seconds of intelligi-
ble sound, more noise, and so on.

A special thanks needs to be made to Jennifer Seelig, who became the
news director at KCBS in the final few years of my career. She found a
couple of digital stashes of Madden files. One was on a portable hard drive
left in her office by a predecessor, the other was tucked away on the network
and included "clean" copies of many of the files corrupted in the network
crash.

I downloaded everything I could from the network and hauled home
boxes of two dozen cassette tapes and more than 80 CDs.

It was overwhelming.

And yet, I wish I'd had access to all of this in 2020 and 2021. I was in my final year before retirement, and one thing I wanted to make sure I got finished before I signed off for the last time was a radio obituary for John Madden.

For those unfamiliar with the news business, the long, detailed obituaries you read immediately after the passing of a famous person don't get pounded out on deadline. News organizations put considerable effort into researching, writing, and producing these pieces so they'll be ready when the news breaks.

In Coach's case, I had no special knowledge that he was nearing the end. But I did know that my own career was winding down, and if I didn't produce the Madden farewell my own way, the job would fall to someone else who wouldn't know the whole story.

Finding the bits and pieces of audio to help tell the "radio years" part of John's life story proved difficult, even though I was working from inside the very radio station where he'd spent the bulk of his Bay Area radio career. Among the segments I simply couldn't find was his 2018 radio farewell (though it did surface later, in time for inclusion in this book).

I would work on the Madden obit in fits and starts, often using time spent waiting for my morning show colleague and carpool partner Steve Bitker to finish up so we could head home together. When the COVID-19 pandemic emptied the radio station in March 2020, I was one of a very small number of people to actually come back to the facility every day. (I tried doing the morning broadcast from home, but the effort was a spectacular failure.)

As I neared the finish line, that obit remained unfinished. I kept trying to find that elusive Madden farewell broadcast. Eventually, concluding it wasn't going to turn up, I finished the job, recording my voice track at home and editing the piece together on my home computer.

Here's what that farewell script looked like on paper:

Stan: *For a kid from Daly City, it was always a magic carpet ride for John Madden.*

John: *I have never worked a day in my life. I went from player to coach to a broadcaster, and I am the luckiest guy in the world.*

Stan: *His 2006 speech at his Pro Football Hall of Fame induction, of course, downplayed the reality. John Madden was one smart cookie who knew how to work hard but who never forgot where he came from.*

John: *I've always felt that I'm the luckiest guy in the world. It's not something that was planned when I went into the Hall of Fame. And John Robinson was there, just two doofuses from Daly City hanging out at the Relish Bakery at the Top of the Hill and you end up in the Hall of Fame?*

Stan: *John Madden's career arc might have been different had the young Philadelphia Eagles draftee out of Cal Poly not suffered a knee injury. What he learned by watching the game led him into coaching at a young age, and at 32, he was the head coach of the Raiders. Ten years, more than 100 wins, including a Super Bowl and many memorable moments.*

Raiders radio announcer Bill King, describing the 1978 "Holy Roller" play: *Madden is on the field. He wants to know if it's real. They said, 'Yes. Get your big butt out of here.' He does.*

Stan: *And then he walked away. He'd had enough and years later would often speak of the harsh reality of the business.*

John: *Coaching is so tough today that the only way that anyone should do it is if they can't live without it. And if you can live without it, then you shouldn't do it because there's no way you can just stick your toe in the water in this deal.*

Stan: *A retiree in his early forties with a wife and two sons, and it didn't exactly play out the way he drew it up in his mind.*

John: *I'd say, 'Yeah, I'm home now, with my wife and the kids,' and they're gone. They've got stuff to do. They're here. They're there. And there was me and the dog.*

Stan: *But what happened next sort of came from nowhere. Big John Madden was suddenly everywhere selling stuff on TV.*

John (montage of his TV commercials): *Excuse me. I'm not the same crazy coach who used to storm around the sidelines yelling at the officials. I've learned to relax. And I drink Lite Beer from Miller. You know that Lite's got a third less calories than a regular beer. And listen to this. Lite doesn't fill me up....*

Hey, you get a tough case of athlete's foot, the itching, cracking, the burning. You want a medicine that acts tough. Boom! Tough actin' Tinactin.

Stan: *And launching a 30-year run on NFL broadcasts where nobody had ever heard anything like him before.*

John (montage of TV analysis): *And then the minute it's over, you got to pull the pants up. You always block, block, block. Then you pull up your pants.... Big, old big cat. You got all this stuff going. You go whop, whop, whop, whop. That's more than encroachment.*

Stan: *And if that wasn't enough, Madden's idea that maybe computers could be used to teach football led to the* Madden NFL *video game, now a cultural phenomenon in its own right. And somewhere in there, radio came calling, at first just a fill-in gig.*

John: *They wanted someone temporary to fill in until they hired the sports guy. And then when they hired the sports guy, I figured, 'Boom, I'm done.' That's it. No more radio. And they said, 'Oh, no, no, no. You're still on.'*

Stan: *Soon, John Madden was a Bay Area radio fixture, what broadcasters like to call 'appointment listening.' After working with Bay Area radio legends Gene Nelson, Frank Dill and Mike Cleary, Madden switched to KCBS in the summer of 1997. A big, successful man unafraid to poke fun at himself. A winning formula.*

John (montage from KCBS Radio segments): *But if I don't have something down in front of me in my shirt by noon? Something's wrong.... Dead last. Not the second to last. Not third to last. Not fourth to last. Didn't win. Didn't come in second. Didn't come in third. Didn't come in fourth. Dead last.*

Stan: *John was a busy man, traveling the country by bus to get to his network TV assignments and calling in from who-knows-where.*

John (montage from KCBS Radio segments): *I'm doing fine. I'm down in Florida already.... I just left Santa Rosa, New Mexico. We're just like maybe 10, 15 miles outside of Santa Rosa.... We're right there, we're right by the Salt Flats. And we're right there where they pull the salt out of the Salt Lake. And then they just have like big mountains of salt here.... When you get down here in*

Georgia and Florida, there's more stuff creeping and jumping and crawling around on the ground than you've ever seen in your life.

Stan: *Part of the Madden Magic was a keen eye for the human condition. For example, sneaking a partly eaten candy back into the box.*

John: *People that tell you that their kids don't do that, then they're not watching their kids. I mean, you know, they'll take a bite, you know, because they don't know. They'll take a bite. And if it's one they don't like, then they'll just put it back and then go get another one.*

Stan: *Those thousands of "Madden Segments" generated millions of memories. We shared his life with him, the dogs, his long-suffering wife, Virginia, the kids and grandkids, the friends who themselves became familiar names and the big moments like when John retired from TV in 2009.*

John: *It's tough, because…not because I'm not sure it's the right time. I mean, I really feel strongly that this is the right time, but I'm just going to miss everything about it because, you know, I enjoyed it so much.*

Stan: *And then finally, after battling a few health issues, it would be time to truly relax. Our morning conversations came to an end. Any of us, all of us who came into John Madden's orbit were the better for it. A big man and an even bigger presence.*

Once it was all edited together, I passed it along to KCBS news managers, telling them to be damned sure the audio file didn't mistakenly get aired while Coach was still alive.

The news came on December 28, 2021. I'd been out in the yard pulling weeds and came in to find my cell phone full of text messages and voicemails. A producer asked if I'd go on the air to talk about the late John Madden; it's what all-news radio stations do at a time like this.

I don't recall exactly what I said. I do recall telling our listeners about my last text-message exchange with Coach. He'd reached out to me two days before his death to ask what I thought of the Fox Sports broadcast *All Madden*. I told him I'd loved it.

And then I told him I'd been working on digitally restoring a family heirloom: a 100-year-old photo of my grandfather as a University of California football player, posing in front of the seven-man blocking sled Coach loved so much.

I sent him the photo. It was our last communication, until now. Consider this book my real farewell to Coach Madden.

Acknowledgments

WHEN I FIRST STARTED MUMBLING OUT LOUD ABOUT THIS PROJECT, I GOT A great deal of exuberant encouragement from people who'd never written a book and a more measured level of enthusiasm from those who'd seen first-hand what it takes. I'm grateful to them all, idealists and realists alike. It's been a remarkable journey. I'm glad I took it.

The book is merely the culmination of a voyage that began when I wandered out of San Francisco State University with a degree in Broadcast Communication Arts, a fiancée, and a hazy idea that I could make a living as a radio news broadcaster. I remain indebted to my alma mater and the remarkable faculty whose lessons remain with me beyond my working days.

More about that fiancée later, but there are three other SF State classmates who put up with my mediocre golf game in recent years, while providing encouragement as well as specific guidance on this project. Thanks, Jeffrey Green, Jim Draper, and Fred Greene (whose own John Madden connections were noted in Chapter 2), and I'm happy to tee it up with you guys anytime.

Another SF State connection of note is Don McPhail. The two-time All-Conference quarterback of some very good SF State teams in the 1960s might never have played for his hometown college if he hadn't gotten stuck on the depth chart at the Naval Academy behind a guy named Staubach. Don's a novelist and a source of positivity who offered frequent support.

Novelist and longtime friend Amy Peele gave me some straight advice about the book business. In typical Amy style, she didn't sand off any of the edges.

Judy Bowman, a hardcore Cubs fan like Amy, ought to be writing books. Sharp of wit and warm of spirit, I'm happy she's my friend and thankful for her feedback.

Thanks to Noah Amstadter, Bill Ames, Jesse Jordan, and the whole team at Triumph Books for taking a flyer on a first-time author and providing a warm, comfortable experience throughout. Anything wrong with the book you're reading is on me, not them.

My introduction to Triumph Books was through two longtime fixtures on the Bay Area sports scene, Andy Dolich and Dave Newhouse. I'm pleased that both saw fit to offer help and support on this project. They say you stand on the shoulders of giants, and these fellows lifted me up.

More Bay Area guys: Oakland A's announcer and onetime KCBS colleague Ken Korach blessed me with his wisdom at a crucial point in the process. Bruce Jenkins and Dan Fost share my love of the San Francisco Giants and both offered advice that mattered.

The Saturday Morning Strada Grupetto is my cycling bunch. Some of us go back more than 30 years together. That's a lot of miles and plenty of coffee and conversation. Many of those chats revolved around this project. Dr. Don Curtis requires a special salute for his relentless insistence that I had a book to write and it was high time to get after it.

A fair share of this book was written at my second home in Menton, France. It's a lovely city populated by a fascinating mix of people, one of whom happens to be my downstairs neighbor. I was privileged to read the manuscript of Alex Wade's *A Season on the Med*, an account of what Britons like him call "football" as played on the sunny shores of the Mediterranean Sea. Alex's prose, professionalism, and wit set a bar for me to attempt to clear; his friendship is deeply treasured and his advice has been invaluable.

Vaud Massarsky is an American in Menton who graciously agreed to read my manuscript and offer advice. His wise counsel helped sharpen some edges and round off some corners. Whatever mistakes and crappy prose remain are not Vaud's fault.

KCBS Radio was my professional home for more than 30 years. I am forever indebted to Ed Cavagnaro, whose willingness to bring me back to the station after a hiatus allowed my "Mornings with Madden" to happen. As noted in the book, Ed also played an instrumental role in securing John Madden's services for KCBS.

There aren't enough words to adequately thank my "radio wife," Susan Leigh Taylor. We spent 20 years caged in the glass box known as Studio A, sometimes fighting like siblings but always working to honor the great legacy of KCBS. Susan's professionalism, intelligence, and instincts combined with her spectacular radio voice to create a world-class performer.

Steve Bitker had the unenviable task of trying to dig some sports content out of the daily Madden conversation. Often, under my unsteady hand, the dish would run away with the spoon (to use a favorite phrase of Coach's). Thanks for being there, Steve, and for all those hours and miles in our carpool. I'd still let those bananas ripen one more day, though.

Kevin Radich and Kim Wonderley are husband and wife, two terrific KCBS colleagues and even better human beings. Their extended history with John Madden helped me flesh out the part of his Bay Area radio story that played out before I came on the scene.

Two others whose days with Coach predated mine are living legends: Frank Dill and Mike Cleary. I still pinch myself sometimes when I'm hanging out with these guys. They're throwbacks in the best sense of the term and their Madden memories were invaluable.

I will forget some names, so I beg the indulgence of my former KCBS colleagues in calling out a few who connected with Coach, either on the air or in the thankless but crucial roles of producers and editors. Super-utility player Holly Quan, Hal Ramey, Frni Beyer, Nic Palmer, Jeff Bell, and Ted Goldberg are all on the roster.

The current director of news and programming at KCBS, Jennifer Seelig, played an important role in helping me gather the most complete possible version of the KCBS/John Madden recordings. As noted in the book, it's not a perfect archive, but without Jennifer's assistance, I'd have had even less with which to work.

My longtime KCBS colleagues and fellow members of the Eyewitness Blues Band, Doug Sovern and Mike Sugerman, are part of my creative DNA. Glad we got to cook those brats at Lambeau, boys.

The late Al Hart was my friend and hero. I know he held a special place in Coach's heart, too. Their interactions set the tone for what would happen during my years with John.

Countless friends and neighbors suggested "Maddenisms" and favorite episodes, many of which made it into the book. Specific thanks to listener George Barron, who truly went above and beyond in helping me pinpoint some memorable material. I'm still amazed at the clear recollections held by listeners of conversations that aired nearly 30 years ago.

Lesley Visser is one of the great ones, and the short conversation I had with her at Coach's public memorial service helped me understand that this book should be more than just a transcript of John Madden's radio bits.

David Jackson dug deep into his vast knowledge of Bay Area radio history to clarify the complicated series of transactions that shifted Gene Nelson and John Madden from KYA to KSFO and then back to KSFO and KYA together, which is probably a topic for another book.

Cynthia Edwards is another Bay Area radio history buff whose collection of memorabilia and "can-do" attitude helped verify some facts.

Special shout-out to the folks who built the cloud-based transcription service Trint. Without it, I'd never have been able to wade through the thousands of recordings.

Bob Cullinan and Ed Jay are superb photographers whose presence at numerous John Madden events produced many of the images you've enjoyed. An extra dose of thanks to Bob for reading the draft manuscript and offering valuable suggestions.

John Madden's longtime agent, Sandy Montag, as well as his friends, Jim Ghielmetti and Dominic Mercurio, played crucial roles in recalling details and, in Sandy's case, clarifying legal issues surrounding the use of the KCBS/John Madden archive.

Without the enthusiastic support and endorsement of John's sons, Mike and Joe Madden, I'd never have tackled this project. I am indebted to those men on many levels. If this book helps round out the reader's understanding of their father's accomplishments and what he brought to his devoted listeners, I'll be very proud.

Virginia Madden: there ought to be a whole book about her. Though her voice was never heard on KCBS, she was definitely a member of our team. They only made one Virginia Madden and while she may not know it, her spirit guided this whole enterprise.

John spoke often about his family, a source of support and stability in the fast-paced world of sports that was his life. I have been equally blessed. My late mother, Madeleine (Keller) Bunger, should have been on the KCBS payroll, so devoted was her boosterism of her son's work. My father, Jim Bunger, is still a great source of support and inspiration at age 95. My two children, Brenley and Geoff, had to put up with the regimented life of a morning radio guy and all my rules about proper speech. I'm proud to say we're all still on speaking terms.

And then there's that fiancée I mentioned earlier. I met Tharon Flocker in the dormitories at SF State when we were both 19 years old and she has been my main source of support and encouragement ever since. Don't misunderstand me here: she's an ass-kicker when she needs to be. I'm glad she's on my coaching staff.